(continued from front flap)

The Crying of Lot 49. Essays on Pynchon's later work include studies by Richard Poirier, Paul Fussell, and—from the pages of *Scientific American*—Philip Morrison.

Offering numerous insights into Pynchon's most celebrated novel, *Gravity's Rainbow*, this collection of writings shows how Pynchon's fiction, in its range and profundity, occupies a prominent position among the literary achievements of our time.

PYNCHON

PYNCHON

A COLLECTION OF CRITICAL ESSAYS

Edited by
Edward Mendelson

Prentice-Hall, Inc. *Englewood Cliffs, N.J.*

A SPECTRUM BOOK

Library of Congress Cataloging in Publication Data
Main entry under title:

Pynchon: a collection of critical essays.

    (Twentieth century views) (A Spectrum Book)
    Bibliography: p.
    1. Pynchon, Thomas—Criticism and interpretation.
I. Mendelson, Edward.
PS3566.Y55Z8   813'.5'4   77-12699
ISBN 0-13-744714-0
ISBN 0-13-744706-X pbk.

The editor wishes to thank Candida Donadio, literary agent for Thomas Pynchon, for permission to quote from the stories and novels of Thomas Pynchon. Copyright in all passages quoted from Thomas Pynchon's work is the property of the author.

10 9 8 7 6 5 4 3 2 1

PRENTICE-HALL INTERNATIONAL, INC., *London*
PRENTICE-HALL OF AUSTRALIA PTY. LIMITED, *Sydney*
PRENTICE-HALL OF CANADA, LTD., *Toronto*
PRENTICE-HALL OF INDIA PRIVATE LIMITED, *New Delhi*
PRENTICE-HALL OF JAPAN, INC., *Tokyo*
PRENTICE-HALL OF SOUTHEAST ASIA PTE. LTD., *Singapore*
WHITEHALL BOOKS LIMITED, *Wellington, New Zealand*

PYNCHON

Introduction

by Edward Mendelson

A writer's name, in this and recent centuries, stands for both his work and his person. "Byron" refers to a row of books as well as to a life and the myths which cluster around it. "James" means both a collected edition and an articulate presence at dinner parties. In the past few decades there have even been writers who have tried to gain through their persons a fame their books alone could never achieve. Their authorship dissipates into press interviews, entries on the police-blotter, advertisements for themselves, vivid self-destructions. And even those writers who prefer craft to display still find it hard to resist the attentions of television cameras. Almost alone among his contemporaries, Pynchon has refused to let "Pynchon" stand for anything but his books.

This is not mere eccentricity. Pynchon's anonymity—like his books—calls into question the familiar modes of modern writing and the styles of modern authorship. Just as his books take little interest in the interior psychological labyrinths and the narrow domestic landscapes which are the fields of this century's fiction, so his minimal personal presence in the literary world, the vacancy he offers to the eye of the camera and the interviewer, deliberately rejects all the varieties of artistic heroism which the romantic and modernist traditions have created. Pynchon's books try to be seriously *there*; while he himself is somewhere else entirely.

The aggrandizement of the self-conscious artist, the conflation (as in Joyce) of his person into his work—or, conversely, the cultivation (as in Beckett) of a detachment so complete and serene that it lifts the artist entirely away from the world of his subjects— are both consequences of the change in sensibility which marked the end of the eighteenth century, whose effects are still with us. That change established self-consciousness (or its corollary, the self's consciousness of a world important only to the extent that it is perceived) as the central fact of human existence and as the central subject of art. It transferred the significant aspects of history from the stable generalities of the human race to the dynamic particularity of individual nations and individual minds. The romantic era hardly invented self-consciousness, but until then it had been a *problem* only for the exceptional—only for the rare Oedipus or Hamlet whose self-conscious isolation could be watched with pity and fear by audiences who were secure in the knowledge that they would never share it. But the psychological conditions that one era thinks exceptional and horrifying are those that a later era will accept unquestionably as a universal norm. In the romantic age, as in the later age of psychoanalytic interpretation of human motive and detached scientific interpretation of the social and physical world, self-consciousness has become a universal problem rather than an exceptional one (much as sexuality seems to have become a universal problem only after the cult of romantic love took root during the twelfth century).

But the assumptions of the romantic and modernist era seem to have begun to exhaust themselves. Pynchon is one of a few, as yet a very few, major writers for whom self-consciousness is a central problem only in their early work, a problem they eventually manage to put aside. In these writers' maturity, self-consciousness becomes only one of many possible channels of perception, and not the most important one. (Brecht is another such writer; Auden is a third.) To the methods of reading and criticism which the past two centuries have developed in order to domesticate romantic and modernist literature, the work of these writers is almost opaque and impermeable. But those methods of reading have reached the point of diminishing returns. Pynchon suggests this in *Gravity's Rainbow*. The one character whom the book presents through the techniques of self-conscious modernism ends in disintegration and dissolution. He literally falls apart, diffuses. This character is Tyrone Slothrop, the reflexive, isolated, mysteriously inspired charismatic who attempts a quest for an understanding of his own uniqueness. His literary modes of being, the means through which he exists on the printed page, are private perspective and interior monologue—the central literary modes of the great Moderns. Slothrop's failure and disappearance dramatize Pynchon's conviction that these modes are no longer sufficient to the tasks of literature. The work of self-discovery which they were designed to perform has now been done. For Pynchon there are other tasks, and other methods, and most of them need not be invented from nothing, but need only be rediscovered from the past.

"As things developed, she was to have all manner of revelations. Hardly about Pierce Inverarity, or herself." This is Pynchon's introduction to the education of Oedipa Maas in *The Crying of Lot 49*. What she will learn will not be about herself (and, outside the wastes of science fiction, one searches in vain for another recent novel where this is the case), "but about what remained yet had somehow, before this, stayed away." Like all literary innovations, Pynchon's novelty, in comparison with those of his immediate predecessors, is in part a recovery of a literary past that had "remained yet had somehow, before this, stayed away." Readers who celebrate Pynchon's literary sophistication are often embarrassed by his willingness to put aside the rigors of modernist technique, and by the enthusiasm with which he adopts a repertory of older techniques that had long been pronounced obsolete. Pynchon uses omniscient narrators, direct addresses to the audience, characters capable of heightened speech (in the form of a song), authorial judgments on character and situation, verse epigraphs—all the paraphernalia of the loose baggy monsters of an earlier age of fiction.

If Pynchon embarrasses the literary avant-garde which wants to think him a doctrinaire member of its own party, he also embarrasses that part of his audience which might be thought of as an ethical avant-garde. He furnishes some of his most sympathetic characters with unfashionably conventional morality: distaste for both abortion and marijuana (Rachel Owlglass in *V.*), impatience with ethical relativism (Oedipa Maas), the decent loyalty of monogamous love (Roger Mexico in *Gravity's Rainbow*). If Pynchon were merely a modernist, these attitudes would be nothing more than the corollaries of the literary styles in which their associated characters are presented: that is, characters who are delineated according to the conventions of character in bourgeois novels would, through the logic of reflexive form, display the bourgeois virtues. But Pynchon is less programmatic than this, and more serious.

His seriousness, that is, his responsible attention to the world outside his books, is not always evident on first reading. Pynchon always refuses to take himself seriously—a refusal that, to readers accustomed to claims of high seriousness, seems an offense. But it

is an offense only in terms of a decorum that gives the greatest
honor to the artistic creations of a centripetal self. Pynchon insists instead that the issues he writes about and the problems his
literary manner brings to light are more important than anything
he, as a writer, can ever say about them.

But this offense becomes benign when it is removed from the
contexts of the romantic tradition and its successor, modernism.
Both these traditions find the greatest seriousness in the act of imagination. They therefore can have little tolerance for comedy, as
they can never admit the possibility of a contradiction that is
without pain. *Any* contradiction is ultimately tragic in the romantic and modernist world, for the only contradiction that world
can recognize is one that divides the world perceived and ordered by the artist's imagination, and so divides and destroys
the artist's imagination itself. The closest approach these traditions can make to comedy are the Olympian smile over human
futility (the expression on the face of Joyce), or the slap-
stick grimace of despair (on the face of Beckett). Both are
tragic masks deformed. Comedy flourishes only in a tradition
that is able to accept contradiction and celebrate its resolution (as at the end of a marriage-comedy). Such a tradition
never elevates art or the imagination to a status from which it
will eventually topple in disillusionment; instead, a comic tradition accepts the division between art and the world, and never
attempts vainly to overcome it. Pynchon's comedy, his jokes at
the expense of his own verbal contraptions, his violations of literary decorum, his low puns and choral celebrations, are ironic
signals of his seriousness of purpose. He is always pointing towards the real conditions of a world more serious than the world
in his imagination: *pointing towards*, not embodying, not
displacing.

There is another apparent offense in Pynchon's work, one
which the modernist tradition finds even harder to accept than
his comedy, which is his refusal to dwell on psychological drama
or domestic detail. From the perspective of modernism, this refusal looks to be a deliberate narrowing of focus. But Pynchon
is actually opening his fiction to fields that the novel has in
recent years discreetly ignored. In its attention to the interior
landscape, recent fiction has forgotten the density of the exterior
one. Modernism prefers to speak of the world of politics and ethics

in personal and aesthetic terms. Pynchon does the opposite. In his books, character is less important than the network of relations existing either between characters, or between characters and social and historical patterns of meaning. Pynchon also tries to attend to the force with which history, politics, economics, and the necessities of science and language shape personal choices and are in turn shaped by those choices. To see in this a deliberate turning away from novelistic realism, as some readers have done, is to confuse certain mediating literary conventions with un-mediated reality. For most of this century, fiction has located the origins of human action in the depths of personal psychology. Pynchon comes up for air and looks elsewhere. What he finds seems cold and abstract only to the extent that it remains un-familiar in literature and art (if nowhere else).

Pynchon's realism, in short, is built on an attention to real-ities ignored by the fiction that we have come to accept as "real-istic." That is, Pynchon has begun to develop or revive a repertory of conventions that can render aspects of non-literary experience that Modernist conventions are unable to compre-hend. To choose a small but significant example: the characters in *Gravity's Rainbow* are among the very few fictional characters whose thoughts and actions are affected by the work they do. In the world outside fiction, anyone can recognize that there is a con-nection between one's work and one's idea of the world, but Mod-ernism never found — and necessarily could never have found — a way of making use of this recognition. In part, this is because Modernism itself had no work to do, no *use* or *occasion* that de-manded its existence, no function in the world beyond its self-declared claims to significance.

In *Gravity's Rainbow* Pynchon begins to find work for his fic-tion. He tries to respond to an occasion created for his book by the conditions of recent history; that is, he recognizes the changes in modern culture that have created, as other changes have done in the past, a felt need for an encyclopedic fictional survey of the new conditions. Pynchon's book tries to fulfill a public function. From the perspective of *Gravity's Rainbow*, his earlier books, *V.* and *The Crying of Lot 49,* have the appearance of pre-paratory exercises for this public work; but they have their own importance as well. *V.* served in part as a preliminary essay in organizing vast quantities of data into a coherent literary form.

As a piece of apprentice-work it is already mature in technique, but it also has clear signs of the later depths and range. *The Crying of Lot 49*, Pynchon's most attractive and accessible book, was his first effort, in a narrow field, at detailing the kinds of relationships and responsibilities he would explore massively in his third book.

V. is often mechanical and programmatic, in comparison with the later work. Its faults are, however, the faults of *Ulysses*. Both are overgrown elaborations of a simple idea. In *Ulysses* the idea is paternity; in *V.* the decline of the animate into the inanimate. Both books are enormous puzzles, exercises in teasing out of their dense texture the single thread that runs through every individual detail. The thread in *V.* is the idea of decadence or decline, and everything in the book is an analogue of the induration or hardening of the woman V. This applies to its most comic details as well as to its most solemn ones. The opening pages include a brief history of Seaman Ploy, whose teeth have been replaced by false ones which he has filed down to dangerous points. It takes a second reading to find in this bit of sailor's wit a prefiguring of V.'s own replacement of parts of her body with dead substitutes—or to find a prefiguring of the "psychodontia" of a later chapter (in the forbidding range of pointed V's which Ploy's filed down false teeth display to the bar at the Sailor's Grave). V. herself embodies nothing less than an historical process of induration infecting a whole century. The manikin SHROUD, a dead replica of a human form, tells Benny Profane that it, SHROUD, is "what you and everybody will be someday." There is much more than a *memento mori* in this: SHROUD speaks of an ethical death *in* life, not after it, of passivity rather than mere death.

The historical process that Pynchon proposes in *V.* is, however, mostly a sterile fantasy, although its intellectual origins lie in the more substantial fin-de-siècle theorizing of Henry Adams and in the classic science of the second law of thermodynamics. At its worst, Pynchon's vision (in *V.*) is an arbitrary connective among bits of miscellaneous knowledge. At best, it serves as an implicit— but usually only implicit—metaphor of an ethical problem which takes explicit shape only later in Pynchon's work. But Pynchon includes characters in his book who manage to act outside its generalized historical process, characters who learn to take responsibility and become consciously active once again. One character counsels simply—too simply, perhaps—"Keep cool, but care." Another writes in his diary of a day that was "like a resurgence of humanity in the automaton, health in the decadent." The choices made by these characters assert that the process of decline is not inescapable, but that it is ultimately the consequence of a deliberate refusal of responsibility on the part of almost everyone in the book's world. Yet in *V.*, Pynchon finally seems unable to decide whether he is (to use Blake's distinction) a Seer or an Arbitrary Dictator, whether he is describing an inevitable historical process whose existence he has decreed through his authority as an artist-hero, or whether he is warning of the consequences of actions that we have chosen to make—and we were free to choose otherwise. That is, to continue in Blake's words, he cannot decide whether he wants to say, "If you go on So the result is So," or, instead, "Such a thing shall happen, let you do what you will."

If Pynchon seems undecided in *V.* about his relation to his audience, that indecision disappears in his later work. Paradoxically enough, he decides to take a stand which leaves the important decisions with his readers. The problem of responsibility, which arises mostly by indirection in *V.*, makes a direct appearance in *The Crying of Lot 49.* This may be why the second book, although much shorter than the first, is far more substantial. Unlike *V.*, *Lot 49* never evades the question of its own problematic status. *Lot 49* is informed by an historical process, as is *V.*, but instead of making the world rocklike and moribund, the process in *Lot 49* potentially restores the world to vitality and freedom. There is generally no doubt, in the world of *V.*, that a process of decline is universal, but it is the reader—and not any of the characters—who is in the privileged position of having no doubt about the matter. In *The Crying of Lot 49*, the status of reader and character is altered. Again there is a universal historical process, but now the reader and the book's central character, Oedipa Maas, have equal knowledge of it—and not only equal knowledge, but equal doubt, and comparable responsibility for its existence or non-existence. There is no certainty in *Lot 49* (as there is in *V.*) that the book's historical process is "really" (by which, in speaking of fiction, I mean "virtually") there: the book ends with both the reader and Oedipa in doubt. The reader is left not with a puzzle to be solved, as in *V.* or *Ulysses*, but with a radical and insoluble problem of interpretation. *V.* leaves its reader secure in his superiority, once he has found the key to all its mysteries of detail.

Lot 49 leaves its reader caught in an irreconcilable ambiguity, one which takes on a disturbing moral weight. The book ends with Oedipa left alone to decide whether the events she has witnessed do in fact cluster together to point to a "reason that mattered to the world" or whether they simply amount to a chaos which her own paranoia has set into a spurious, projected order. The book offers an analogue of this choice to its reader as well: Is the book in part an ethically disturbing parable of the choices he must make in interpreting the world, or is it merely an aesthetic structure? The book challenges its readers to choose their relation to experience. Either, like the romantics and Modernists, they will project their private aesthetic order onto what they perceive as the malleable or ultimately inaccessible objects of the world, or else they will accept responsibility for and to the order which exists already in the world of which they are an active part. This choice is one that everyone confronts at every moment; but great works of art, those works which both rebuke and console, can make the issues vivid and memorable.

By the time Pynchon wrote *Gravity's Rainbow*, there was no longer any doubt about the difficulty of this choice. Responsibility was now real. Everyone in the book is inextricably implicated in complex patterns of meaning, in large historical processes which at once limit freedom and are themselves established by individual acquiescence and choice. In direct addresses to his readers, Pynchon tries to implicate them also in the choices the book itself includes — either passive acceptance and impersonal detachment, or ethical resistance and personal love. *Gravity's Rainbow* is in part a second-person novel which periodically addresses "you." When a question of interpretation — and its ethical consequences — arises, like the question Oedipa must face at the end of *Lot 49,* Pynchon poses the alternative responses and asks, "Which do you want it to be?"

This is more than a rhetorical stance, more than an artist's self-important pose. Pynchon's questions and challenges to his readers have force — in part because in *Gravity's Rainbow* he himself has changed his literary status from *author* to *institution.* Few authors ever undergo this transition; only one or two who achieve it have ever desired it; and some have endured it who wished it had never happened. But when an author becomes a monument in his own lifetime, the history of his work becomes entangled with the history of his readers and his culture. *Gravity's Rainbow* is in part *about* the kinds of institutions which have sprung up in response to its existence. Just as the book traces the proliferation of self-sustaining bureaucracies out of the transience of charismatic heroes and charismatic moments (the terms are from Weber, whom Pynchon quotes), so the book itself has already generated institutions that seem entirely innocent of any sense that the book they honor criticizes precisely the kind of honor they offer. Professional critics will find an object lesson in this, but so will all students of literature. The Modern Language Association has received petitions urging the maintenance of a continuing seminar on Pynchon; Pynchon Reading and Study Groups meet regularly in New York and elsewhere; indexers, bibliographers, allusion- and lexica-compilers are all hard at work on their bureaucratically defined tasks. Collective enterprises have built themselves up around Pynchon's work—and this book is one of them. But I hope this book is one which is at least aware of its paradoxical dilemma in offering Pynchon an honor which he implicitly condemns.

Critical industries tend to organize themselves around a special variety of book (or author) which is encountered only rarely in literary history. A useful term for such a book is *encyclopedic narrative*; and one can speak also of an *encyclopedic author*. Not all books that establish industries are authentic narratives of this kind (Pound's *Cantos* demonstrates that critics can be found who will accept almost any spurious claim to coherence as genuine); but all encyclopedic narratives are eventually recognized not only as books which have industries attached to them, but also as *national* books that stand as written signs of the culture of which they are a part. The industries devoted to Dante, Shakespeare, Cervantes, and Goethe are not restricted to the academy; they are national industries as well.

All encyclopedic narratives (in the case of Shakespeare the corpus of plays and poems takes the place of a single narrative, although *The Canterbury Tales* are an earlier attempt at an English encyclopedia) are metonymic compendia of the *data,* both scientific and aesthetic, valued by their culture. They attempt to incorporate representative elements of all the varieties of knowledge their societies put to use. (The absence of all intelligent science in *The Cantos* is one of the factors limiting its status to an aca-

demic cult-book; likewise, the primitive sentimental politics of
Ulysses limits Joyce's industry to academic culture and makes that
industry unsuited to the larger culture's continuing effort at self-
comprehension.) All encyclopedic narratives contain, *inter alia*,
theoretical accounts of statecraft, histories of language, and images of their own enormous scale in the form of giants or gigantism.
They are generally set a decade or two before publication, so that
they can include prophecies of events that actually occurred in
history. All are polyglot books, and all are so determined to achieve encyclopedic range that they exclude from their plots the single centripetal emotional focus that develops when a narrative
records a completed relation of sexual love. These books usually
appear at the moment when a national culture begins to recognize
its uniqueness—at that cusp (to use a word from Pynchon) divid-
ing the pre-history of a national culture from its history, its potential from its actual achievements and failures. At least six such
books are familiar to literary history: Dante's *Commedia*, Rabelais' five books of Gargantua and Pantagruel, Cervantes' *Don
Quixote,* Goethe's *Faust,* Melville's *Moby-Dick,* and (a special
case) Joyce's *Ulysses.* Shakespeare's plays, as I said, hold a comparable place in English culture, as do Pushkin's works in Russia.
(If I knew enough about Portugal, I would propose Camões' *Os
Lusiadas* as another encyclopedic narrative; and, to complete
the catalogue, one should mention comparable books that were
put together by Scandinavian and Eastern European patriots in
the nineteenth century who tried to answer their countries' felt
need for encyclopedic narratives of their own. That such a need
should be felt at all is in part a consequence of romantic nation-
alism—but that is a subject which deserves extended treatment
elsewhere.)

The genre of national encyclopedic narrative is severely exclusive in its numbers but massively inclusive in the contents of
its individual members. *Gravity's Rainbow* offers itself as the lat-
est member of the genre. The book proposes itself as the encyclopedia of a new international culture of electronic communication and multi-national cartels. Whether or not Pynchon's historical conceptions will eventually correspond to our culture's
perception of itself, at least those conceptions have an urgent
plausibility. *Gravity's Rainbow* is a book which hopes to be active
in the world, not a detached observer of it. It warns and exhorts in
matters ranging from the ways in which the book itself will be

read, to the way in which its whole surrounding culture operates.

With some exceptions, critics seem uncomfortable with *Gravity's Rainbow's* efforts at *agency*. Like generals who are ready to fight the last war but not the next one, critics who dislike *Gravity's Rainbow* try to read it as if it were another *Ulysses*. But to read it this way is to mistake its purpose and its role. The genius of *Ulysses* lies in its conjunction of plausible observed detail with grossly implausible principles of organization. In its factuality, especially in the early chapters, and in its vision of the details of the ordinary, *Ulysses* has no rival. But as it proceeds, it becomes increasingly a book concerned with itself, not with its Dubliners. Its later chapters are almost exclusively about its earlier chapters. And Joyce's organizing ideas derive, especially towards the end of the book, not from systems of ethics or politics or psychology, as observed and derived from the world outside literature, but from the fantasies of historical amateurs or the claptrap of religious frauds. Joyce, that is, uses for the structure of his mock-encyclopedia of the modern world a set of ideas derived from the crackpot theosophy of Mme. Blavatsky or the speculations on the *Odyssey* proposed by Victor Bérard. Even when Joyce plunders Vico, he chooses Vico's least plausible and most erratic ideas (and those who know Vico through Joyce have a very lopsided idea of what Vico actually wrote). The deeper one goes into *Ulysses*, the sillier it becomes. Joyce knew this, and his own ambivalence towards his book was among the consequences of that knowledge. When he described his ideal reader—an isomniac who does nothing but read Joyce—he acknowledged that his book focuses on its own structure, and that an understanding of the world outside *Ulysses* is of little use in understanding the world within it. No other major work of art is at the same time so extreme in its factuality and yet so tenous in its relation to its historical setting.

The inward turn of *Ulysses,* the circularity of its narrative, is among the late consequences of the romantic and modernist sensibility whose triumphant achievement is a literature which exists finally only for itself. Such literature may claim a public function or an unacknowledged legislative role, but these are claims best honored when left untested. A distinguished critic, writing within the tradition he describes, can write of literature in the early romantic period as "separated from imposed religious or communal ends." (This happens to be by Geoffrey Hartman, but the idea is common to all critics whose assumptions are derived from romanticism.) The unexamined emotive word here is *imposed*. It suggests that the earlier social purposes and occasions of literature and art amounted to a straitjacket restraining aesthetic impulses that were in themselves essentially free and untrammelled—as if literature had been a type of Rousseauistic man, born free and everywhere in chains. But this kind of understanding of literature can only emerge from a non-historical interpretation, a projection of present conditions onto the past. And it is precisely in order to justify this kind of understanding that historical interpretation has, during recent decades, been placed under attack. Critics in the romantic and Modernist line often refuse to acknowledge that their concepts of literature may be local rather than universal; and so they attack the historical evidence that would introduce an intolerable contradiction into their concept of the world. (Such a contradiction would, as I argued earlier, have intolerable tragic force if it were to be admitted into the romantic tradition; but in the alternative tradition it is the saving reminder of a critic's or reader's limitations and responsibility.) It would make far more sense, in both detail and larger pattern, to say that romantic literature did not lose its *imposed* tasks, but instead lost the *occasions* that had, for most earlier literature, provided it with reasons to exist in the first place. It lost too its well-defined *audiences* and gained instead only a vague *public*. This is a loss which may be observed in the history of English poetry around the end of the eighteenth century, and in the novel at the end of the nineteenth.

One reliable indicator of this loss of occasion is a radical shift in the idea of the journey or quest. Until the shift occurred that I have been describing, a quest was invariably an allegory of *purpose*. One went on a journey not because the journey in itself was felt as a necessity, but because one had an urgent and obligatory goal. The arrival, not the journey, mattered. But in the romantic quest (as in its comic prefigurings like *Don Quixote*, where the purposeless quest is insane, not, as it later would be, sublime) the goal has disappeared or has become shadowy and terrifying. The voyager now does not know why he seeks a goal at all. Byron's Childe Harold is such a goalless voyager; so are Browning's Child Roland and the hunter of the Snark—and, later—Jude the Obscure and Leopold Bloom. (The belated recognition of *Moby-Dick* may have resulted in part from the prematurity, in the history of the novel, of Ishmael's apparently goalless voyage.) The romantic quester thinks himself—in Kierkegaard's phrase—out over seventy thousand fathoms, journeying in a direction he does not know, for a goal he may not recognize even if he finds it. In short, the romantic quest is the image of romantic literature's own condition: purposeless, aspiring to a goal it can never achieve or define. And in *Ulysses*, the circular journey of Bloom, turning in an endless and purposeless repetition, is the culminating disillusioned image of that same condition.

It is different in Pynchon. There is a quest-without-object in *Gravity's Rainbow*—the journey of Tyrone Slothrop—but Pynchon knows that it must lead only to disintegration and dissociation. Pynchon faces, possibly for the first time, the consequences of the romantic quest. Outside the disintegrating Slothrop, the book insists on calling attention to real tasks and purposive choices that cannot be evaded. In *Ulysses,* all ends in resigned forgiveness; from its vast final perspectives, no single event in human history matters very much. But as *Gravity's Rainbow* nears its end, Roger Mexico finds himself approaching a dilemma which he must somehow resolve, a decision from which he cannot turn aside, one which will have irreversible consequences. "It is not a question he has ever imagined himself asking seriously," Pynchon writes. "It has come by surprise, but there's no sending it away now, he really does have to decide, and soon enough. ...He has to choose between his life and his death. Letting it sit for a while is no compromise." And in raising problems like this one, Pynchon never suggests any comforting possibility that the solutions can be simple or painless.

The ethical problems in *Gravity's Rainbow* have analogues in the linguistic and interpretive problems it raises as well. Language for Pynchon is not a system complete in itself but an ethically and socially performative (his word is "operative") system, one which can be altered by deliberate acts. The model of language in *Ulysses*, on the other hand, is characteristically self-enclosed. For Joyce, the history of language is, in effect, an embroyological history (in the chapter known as "Oxen of the Sun"), a version of an unconscious cycle unaffected by personal or social choice. *Gravity's Rainbow's* history of language (in the episode set in the Kirghiz) is instead political, "less unaware of itself," determined by conscious decisions. Consistently, *Gravity's Rainbow* refers outside itself to the cluster of problems raised by political and ethical conditions, and insists that "letting it sit for a while is no compromise."

In Pynchon, unlike Joyce, the surface details are often incredible and baroque, while the underlying organization is all too plausible and disquieting. Beneath the fantasies and the paranoia, Pynchon organizes his book according to historical and scientific theory—according, that is, to an order independent of *literary* imagination, an order derived more from the realms of politics and physics than from the self-conscious Modernist reflexivities of language and literature. *Gravity's Rainbow's* large vision of political connectedness has domestic analogues in its vision of sexuality perverted by local varieties of compulsion and control. And, similarly, the book's vision of Slothrop's personal *discon*nectedness (what the book calls "anti-paranoia") has its correspondences in the political chaos of the post-war German Zone—a chaos that is about to be ordered once again into bureaucracies, just as the vacancy left by Slothrop's disintegration will be filled with comforting explanations and organized memorialists.

Serene in its vision of unalterable cycles, *Ulysses* ends just before its beginnings, and closes with its tail in its mouth. *Gravity's Rainbow* devotes its final hundred pages not to a return on itself, but to an effort at finding ultimate beginnings and endings. *Ulysses* ends in an eternal return, *Gravity's Rainbow* in the dangerous facts of a moment of crisis—which is, always, our present moment.

Pynchon himself is one of the dangerous facts of the present moment in literary history, one of the crossroads his book persistently evokes. Pynchon's enlarging critical industry, like all literary enterprises, depends for its survival on economic and political conditions, which, in order to maintain itself, it must wish to preserve. (There is nothing craven or contemptible in this—especially when one considers some of the alternatives offered in societies where the critical enterprise does not exist at all.) But the special challenge that Pynchon offers to critics and readers is the challenge to become aware—and publicly aware—of their motives and, in the political sense, of their *interests*. This challenge is never made by modernist literature, which, like romanticism, imagines that it establishes its own value, and uses only its own terms to question itself. Joyce actively encouraged—surreptitiously and openly—scriptural readings of his books, and by doing so helped to establish the bureaucracy of expositors which all scripture requires. Pynchon does nothing of the sort; in fact, he does the opposite. His contract with his publishers reportedly forbids them to print anything about him. *Gravity's Rainbow*, when intelligently read, gives little comfort to the interpretive legions who would rationalize and restrain. And the book has no tolerance for their unacknowledged social motives. The "Counterforce," which tries to save Slothrop from the vast anonymous "They" who search for him, ends by saying—as they give an interview to *The Wall Street Journal*, solicitously careful to tell its editors only what they will want to hear—that they were not concerned, really, with "Slothrop *qua* Slothrop."

It would be satisfying if one could report that Pynchon's challenge has been met by his critics, but for the most part this has not been the case. There is, of course, nothing that requires a critic to think as his author does—literary history would be in chaos if there were—but when an author questions the basis of a critic's enterprise, then that critic ought at least to acknowledge that the question has been raised. Pynchon's challenge to confront the motives of criticism, his insistence that readers consider the *effects* of interpretation in the world of ethics, is precisely the challenge that criticism must face if it is to escape at last from the centripetal, reflexive momentum of romantic and Modernist writing and of the literary theory that such writing has engendered. Recent critical theory, especially in its philosophical branches, merely extends the hermetic self-referentiality that has already brought literary Modernism to its unmourned dead end.

Pynchon's challenge to literary studies offers one means of turning away from this dead end—there are other means available as well, of course—and to turn instead to methods of reading that have (as Oedipa Maas imagines in a similar context) "a reason that mattered to the world." As with criticism, so with the act of reading itself: Pynchon challenges his readers to participate, not merely in the linguistic and philosophical puzzles of his books' interpretation, but in the choices that those books make plain. It is a challenge with special urgency, for it is offered by a writer who—in the judgment of this reader, and of many others—is the greatest living writer in the English-speaking world.

V. and V-2

by Tony Tanner

I. *Caries and Cabals*

> Cavities in the teeth occur for good reason, Eigenvalue
> reflected. But even if there are several per tooth, there's
> no conscious organization there against the life of the pulp,
> no conspiracy. Yet we have men like Stencil, who must go
> about grouping the world's random caries into cabals.
>
> v.

> *"Shall I project a world?"*   THE CRYING OF LOT 49

Thomas Pynchon made his intentions clear from the outset.
The title of his first important short story is "Entropy" and it contains specific references to Henry Adams. Whereas some novelists
would prefer to cover the philosophic tracks which gave them decisive shaping hints for their novels, Pynchon puts those tracks
on the surface of his writing. Indeed his work is about those tracks
and, more largely, the whole human instinct and need to make
tracks. Adams wanted a theory which would act as a "trail" in "the
thickset forests of history" and even if we change that metaphor of
the forest to that of the urban wasteland, thick with the rubble
and dead of our century of total wars, the need for a trail or a track
may still remain. A philosophy, a theory of history, a law of thermodynamics—any one of these may be a "trail" and their significance may reside not so much in their verifiable applicability
as in the human compulsion to formulate them. Pynchon sees all
this quite clearly, and while his work is certainly about a world

"V. and V-2." Part I, "Caries and Cabals," from *City of Words: American Fiction, 1950-1970*, by Tony Tanner (London: Jonathan Cape; New York: Harper
and Row, 1971), pp. 153-80. Copyright © 1971 by Tony Tanner; reprinted by
permission of the author and publishers. Part II, "V. & V-2," from *London
Magazine*, 13 (February-March 1974), 80-88. Reprinted by permission of the
author.

succumbing to entropy, it is also about the subtler human phenomena—the need to see patterns which may easily turn into the
tendency to suspect plots.

The situation in "Entropy" is simply and deliberately sche-
matic. There is a downstairs and an upstairs apartment. Downstairs,
Meatball Mulligan is holding a lease-breaking party which tends
increasingly towards destructive chaos and ensuing torpor. This
is a recurrent motif in all Pynchon's work, no doubt exemplifying
the entropic process (the party is a relatively closed system of people, no one seems able to leave, and the only terminating point is
sleep). The entropic process applies to the decline of information
as well: two people discuss communication theory and how noise
messes up significant signals. Upstairs, an intellectual called Callisto is trying to warm a freezing bird back to life. In his room he
maintains a little hothouse jungle, specifically referred to as a
"Rousseau-like fantasy." "Hermetically sealed, it was a tiny en-
clave of regularity in the city's chaos, alien to the vagaries of the
weather, national politics, of any civil disorder." His room is his
fantasy, a dream of order in which he has "perfected its ecological
balance." But the story follows the Adams formulation, "Chaos
was the law of nature; Order was the dream of man." Callisto and
his girl have effectively sealed themselves up in the room, never
going out, living a life like a perfectly executed piece of music.
Downstairs the jazz gets ever more raucous and the party noises
constantly reach up into the "music" of Callisto's domain.

The house, then, is some sort of paradigm for modern consciousness; the lower part immersed in the noise of modern distractions
and sensing the failing of significant communication, while the
upper part strives to remain at the level of music, yet feels the
gathering strain as dream is encroached on by life. Life, in this
context, is not only the party downstairs, but the weather. Callisto
finds that the temperature has remained at 37 degrees Fahrenheit
for a number of days, and he is by nature quick to detect omens of
apocalypse. "Henry Adams, three generations before his own,
had stared aghast at Power; Callisto found himself in much the
same state over Thermodynamics, the inner life of that power."
What Pynchon puts before us is the effort of the man in his upstairs sanctuary, with life-destroying weather outside, and sense-
destroying noise downstairs, to articulate his theory of what is
going on. Callisto finds Adams's ideas relevant to his idea of the

situation. At one point he starts to dictate to his girl, using—
like Adams in *Education*—the third person.

> As a young man at Princeton...Callisto had learned a mnemonic
> device for remembering the Laws of Thermodynamics: you can't
> win, things are going to get worse before they get better, who says
> they're going to get better...he found in entropy or the measure
> of disorganization for a closed system an adequate metaphor to apply
> to certain phenomena in his own world...in American "consum-
> erism" discovered a similar tendency from the least to the most
> probable, from differentiation to sameness, from ordered individ-
> uality to a kind of chaos. He found himself, in short, restating Gibbs'
> prediction in social terms, and envisioned a heat-death for his cul-
> ture in which ideas, like heat-energy, would no longer be transfer-
> red, since each point in it would ultimately have the same quantity
> of energy; and intellectual motion would, accordingly, cease.

This is a man drawing on various ideas or laws which he has
learned, to project adequate analogies for the cosmic processes
in which man is so helplessly caught up. It is an attempt to make
some intellectual music; a music to harmonize the increasing
noise.

The story has in effect two different endings: downstairs Meatball is feeling the temptation to crawl off to sleep somewhere.
But he resolves to do what he can to keep the party from "deterio-
rating into total chaos." He acts; he starts to tidy up, gets people
calmed down, gets things mended. Upstairs however, Callisto is
"helpless in the past," and the bird he had been trying to save dies
in his hands. His girl realizes that his obsession with that constant
37 degrees has brought him to a state of paralysed terror. Her act
is a symbolic one—she smashes the window of their hermetically-
sealed retreat with her own bare hands. It is tantamount to the
breaking of the shell round their whole fantasy life of perfect har-
monies and maintained ecological balances.

In that composite image of the pragmatic man actively doing
what he can with the specific scene, and the theorizing man passively attempting to formulate the cosmic process, Pynchon offers
us a shorthand picture of the human alternatives of working inside the noisy chaos to mitigate it or standing outside, constructing patterns to account for it. Man is just such a two-storied house
of consciousness, and in the configuration of that shattered window and Callisto's paralysis, Pynchon suggests the potential peril

of all pattern-making, or plot-detecting. Callisto cannot save the bird — he cannot transfer his heat energy to it, presaging the time when there is no more energy available to be transformed into work. But where Callisto is in the grip of the hothouse of the past, Meatball is engulfed in the riotous present. Pynchon would return to these two figures in the characters of Stencil and Benny Profane in *V.* (1963).

Norbert Wiener said that it is always likely to be a problem whether we interpret whatever it is that makes for disorganization in nature as merely a neutral absence of order (the Augustinian view, he calls this), or as a positively malign force dedicated to the annihilation of order. He adds, "The Augustinian position has always been difficult to maintain. It tends under the slightest perturbation to break down into a covert Manichaeanism." This is crucial for an understanding of many contemporary American writers who are either sufficiently perturbed themselves, or are aware of the perturbations in the characters they write about, to have made the tendency to begin to see the world in Manichaean terms a recurrent motif in recent novels, Pynchon's above all. The temptation to regard all signs of entropy in the world as the work of hostile agents is like the demonism in the work of William Burroughs. Both represent attempts to "give destruction a name or face" (to take a phrase from Pynchon's short story "Mercy and Mortality in Venice"), and both those reactions to the world reveal themselves in the individual as a continous leaning towards paranoia.

One aspect of paranoia is the tendency to imagine plots around you; this is also the novelist's occupation and there is clearly a relationship between making fictions and imagining conspiracies. The difference is between consciousness in control of its own inventions, and consciousness succumbing to its inventions until they present themselves as perceptions. But the line between these two states of mind is inevitably a narrow one and a great deal of oscillation and overlap is common. Adopting Wiener's terms we can say that for a novelist looking back over the first half of the twentieth century the "Augustinian" vision of a world deprived of order in some parts more than in others could easily shade into the "Manichaean" vision of something demonically at work to annihilate all order, with phenomena such as Hitler and the atom bomb only among its more obvious agents.

Pynchon, I think, understands this very well and, while his novel

V. contains a variety of plot-makers, he is in no sense committed to
the plots they might make. It would be too glib to say that his is an
"Augustinian" novel about "Manichaean" people; it would also be
misleading, since the novelist is clearly inwardly affected by the
Manichaeanism of his characters, just as he is by the pessimistic
theories of Henry Adams. But he manages to preserve his distance,
particularly by locating the main plotting instinct in one character,
Stencil. He is the man who is trying to make the connections and
links, and put together the story which might well have been Pynchon's novel. By standing back from this dedicated pursuer and
collector of notes towards a supreme fiction, Pynchon is able to
explore the plot-making instinct itself. To this end his own novel
has to appear to be relatively unplotted—leaving chunks of data
around, as it were, for Stencil to try to interrelate. Inevitably
this is only an illusion and we need not belabour the point that when
a strange bit of Maltese history turns up, Pynchon put it there, and
when Stencil finds a clue it is only because his author laid it for
him. The point is that by taking bits of history from different countries at different times during this century and putting them in the
novel with no linear or causal relationship, Pynchon is able to explore the possibility that the plots men see may be their own inventions. The further implication of this—that such things as the
concentration camps may be simply meaningless accidents—is
responsible for the sudden depths of horror in the book.

The narrative material consists of episodes from history since
1899, and episodes in the lives of various people living in contemporary America called, as a group, the Whole Sick Crew. Just as
the historical episodes tend to focus on various sieges, and chaotic
violent events preceding or involved in the two world wars, so
the episodes connected with modern America tend to focus on
wild parties sinking into chaos and exhaustion which seem to reveal morphological similarities with the historical events not
otherwise directly related to them. The character most concerned
with the historical dimension is Stencil, while the character who
experiences most of the modern extension is Benny Profane. The
two characters come together and finally travel to Malta at the
time of the Suez crisis. Chronological linking is avoided. Of the
sixteen chapters, ten are about Profane and the Whole Sick Crew.
Five interpolate accounts gathered from various sources or documents of historical episodes, starting with some espionage con-

nected with the Fashoda incident, going on to disturbances in
Florence connected with a Venezuelan rebellion and more international plotting and spying, then to a native uprising in German
South-West Africa in 1922 which results in a long siege-party, then
to an account of the siege of Malta during the Second World War,
then back to Paris in 1913 on the brink of the outbreak of the First.
The last chapter brings past and present together on Malta, while
an Epilogue goes back to 1919 when there were riots on the island.
The presence of these apparently random episodes from twentieth-
century history is largely due to the research work of Stencil. His
father was a British agent who died off the coast of Malta in 1919;
he was in some way involved with a woman referred to as V. and
in pursuing this figure through her various incarnations, or differing roles and disguises, Stencil finds that he is astray in the
history of our century, as Benny, looking for no one, wanders up
and down the streets of the present.

We may start by noting that while the endlessly ramifying and
superimposed plots of the book defy summary, the general theme
of the operation of entropy on every level serves to relate the disparate temporal and geographic material the book contains. Every
situation reveals some new aspect of decay and decline, some
move further into chaos or nearer death. The book is full of dead
landscapes of every kind — from the garbage heaps of the modern
world to the lunar barrenness of the actual desert. On every side
there is evidence of the "assertion of the Inanimate." Renaissance
cities seem to lose their glow and become leaden; great buildings
progress towards dust; a man's car is disintegrating under tons of
garage rubble. Benny Profane's late feeling that "things never
should have come this far" is appropriately ominous if you allow
the first word sufficient emphasis. For the proliferation of inert
things is another way of hastening the entropic process. On all
sides the environment is full of hints of exhaustion, extinction,
dehumanization; and *V.* is a very American novel in as much as
one feels that instead of the characters living *in* their environment,
environment lives *through* the characters, who thereby tend to
become figures illustrating a process. At one point Benny Profane
is having an imaginary conversation with an automaton named
SHROUD (synthetic human, radiation output determined). Such
automata, composed entirely of inanimate materials, not only
offer a worrying parody of human identity, but seem to embody a

prophecy that they represent the condition to which human identity is moving in this century. Benny tells SHROUD that he ought to be junked like an old car. SHROUD willingly concedes that such will be his graveyard, but counters with reference to the pictures of the corpses stacked like junk that came out of the German concentration camps. Benny objects that Hitler was crazy. SHROUD asks, "'Has it occurred to you there may be no more standards for crazy or sane, now that it's started?'" And Benny answers. "'What, for Christ's sake?'" What the "it" is that has started (if there is an "it"), what common process links remote imperialist incidents with contemporary automation, tourism, Hitler, and the Whole Sick Crew (if there is any linking common process)—this is what the whole book is about.

One common background is the accelerating release of power which Adams spoke of and foresaw. Man's ingenuity in this respect is kept in view by references to trains, planes, ships, all kinds of mechanical appliances and weapons of war. At the same time all these inventions are often more productive of destruction than anything else. At one point Pynchon simply lists the disasters recorded for a short period of time in an almanac, prefacing it with the generalization that at this time "the world started to run more and more afoul of the inanimate." This points to perhaps the most inclusive theme of the book: not that man returns to the inanimate, since that is the oldest of truths, but that twentieth-century man seems to be dedicating himself to the annihilation of all animateness on a quite unprecedented scale, and with quite unanticipated inventiveness. If the "it" is anything, it is entropy turned Manichaean and working through a whole spectrum of agents; most spectacularly through figures like Hitler who turned millions of people into junk, but also through many minor figures, such as a doctor who favours the introduction of inert substances into the living face.

But Pynchon would scarcely have needed to write so intricate a novel if his only intention was to show a graph of increasing destructiveness manifest in recent history. As he indicates, you can cull that from an almanac. What he shows—and here the juxtaposition of the historical and the personal dimensions is vital—is a growing tendency, discernible on all levels and in the most out-of-the-way pockets of modern history, for people to regard or use other people as objects, and, perhaps even more worryingly, for people to regard themselves as objects. There is in evidence a systematic and assiduously cultivated dehumanization of the human *by* the human. Just as the tourists in the book cut themselves off from the reality of the lands they pass through by burying themselves in Baedeker versions, so do most of the characters avoid confronting the human reality of other people, and of themselves, by all manner of depersonalizing strategies. If one theme of the book is the acceleration of entropy, another is the avoidance of human relationships based on reciprocal recognition of the reality of the partner. Instead of the recognitions of love, there are only the projected fantasies of lust. These two phenomena—entropy and the dread of love—may well be linked in some way, for they show a parallel movement towards the state of lasting inanimateness, and share an aspiration to eradicate consciousness and revert to thing-status.

One agent in the book is killed because of a fatal lapse into humanity, an act of recognition. The description of his death points to a threshold which is a crucial one for the figures in the book. "Vision must be the last to go. There must be a nearly imperceptible line between an eye that reflects and an eye that receives." Death is the moment when that line is irrevocably crossed, but the book shows innumerable ways in which that line is crossed while the body is still technically alive, thus producing a mobile object which reflects but does not receive. That this is related to the narcissistic habit of turning people into reflectors of one's own fantasies and obsessions is alluded to by a series of references to mirrors, culminating in the episode called "V. in love" which describes a Lesbian affair conducted entirely by mirrors. What unspeakable cruelties are made possible when that line is crossed and both self and others are experienced as inanimate objects, the various unpleasant scenes of sadism and sadomasochism, which recur throughout the book, serve to dramatize. The general falling away from the human which is under way is underlined by the transformations in the lady V. In her appearances she becomes gradually less human and more composed of dead matter. When she is finally dismantled, it is suggested that she was found to be composed of entirely artificial objects. Imagining V. as she might be at the present moment, Stencil envisages a completely plastic figure, triggered into action by miracles of technology. This is in line with the more general tendency towards fetishism and away from humanity detectable throughout.

The way in which people avoid their own reality (or are refused it) is paralleled in the book by the way in which events are
experienced as staged episodes in a meaninglessly repetitious
masquerade. On the political, as on the personal, level, role-
playing has pre-empted the possibility of real experience, leaving
only symbols and games. History is as "stencillized" as the people
who compose it, and the result is the theatricalization of reality
on a massive scale. Thus history becomes a scenario which the
participants are unable to rewrite or avoid. Once again, we find
a vision of people being trapped inside an unreality which seems
to be the result of some nameless conspiratorial fabrication; humans are akin to props in a cruel and dehumanizing play by
author or authors unknown. (Of course Pynchon is aware of the
additional irony that these characters are also caught up in a play
arranged by *him* — the affliction of his characters is the condition
of his form.)

In this world there is very little chance of any genuine communication. Language has suffered an inevitable decline in the
mouths of these stencillized and objectified figures. Rachel Owlglass, the figure who more than any other seems to harbour a
genuine capacity for love, is reduced to speaking to her car in
"MG words"; while Benny Profane, who seems to want to love,
feels his vocabulary is made up of nothing but wrong words. A
foreign girl called Paola is presented as a person who has retained
her capacity for direct emotion, and she seems to speak "Nothing
but proper nouns. The girl lived proper nouns. Persons, places.
No things. Had anyone told her about things?" In a world in which
the human is rapidly being replaced by things, this quaint linguistic limitation offers the possibility of an enviable immunity
from the tendency towards a reification of people which is inherent in the prevailing language. At the same time, this kind of
restricted language may be put to a very different purpose, as the
Whole Sick Crew reveals. They play at verbalizing endless possible versions of things. They use mainly proper nouns, literary
allusions, philosophical abstractions, and they put them together
like building-blocks. "This sort of arranging and rearranging
was Decadence, but the exhaustion of all possible permutations
was death." There is an heretical sect in a Borges story which
seeks to hasten the advent of God's rule on earth by trying to exhaust all the possible permutations of sins; there are similar attempts to cover all permutations in the lexical sphere, in his

Library at Babel. Just so, the Whole Sick Crew seems to be hastening the entropic decline of language as a vehicle for the transmission of significant information, by playing with all its permutations irrespective of what reference any of the permutations may or may not have to reality. One result of this decline in language is that people scarcely manage to converse in this book, and if they do they fail to establish any real contact.

But if the characters in the book seldom truly talk to each other, they often look at each other. As might be expected, various forms of voyeurism are part of the normal behaviour patterns of a world where any attempt at human inter-subjectivity has been replaced by the disposition to regard people as objects—inside the field of vision but outside the range of sympathy, if indeed any such range exists. Eyes, straining or blank and dead, are emphasized throughout. The sailor whose main joy is to photograph his friends while they are having sexual intercourse is only one of many whose most intense relationships to reality are detached and impotent stares. Another reason why so many characters live in, and by, mirrors, and indeed at one point are said to be living in "mirror time," is that they experience life only as spectacle. Voyeurism is another way of evading true selfhood and denying or avoiding the possibility of love. Most of the characters "retreat" from the threat of love when it presents itself, and even the sympathetic Benny wastes himself in avoiding dependencies, and disengaging himself from any field of gathering emotional force. It might be added that Pynchon finds it difficult to suggest what genuine love would be like in this world. Some characters from older civilizations and cultures seem to have retained an ability to love. But the guarded maxim of the black jazz musician, McClintic Sphere, "Keep cool, but care," is about as much genuine emotion as the book seems to allow. As such it is unconvincing. This may be part of the vision of the book: in this world people have lost contact with the forms and modes of loving. At the same time it is in part a result of Pynchon's stylistic and formal decisions. You cannot render great emotions in a comic-strip, and "Keep cool, but care," is just such bubble talk or the sort of slogan-jargon mongered by advertisements. In proximity to the multiple parodic references which the book contains, any potentially serious emotion is bound to turn into its own caricature and join the masquerade as a costumed sentimentality.

Moreover, in the main, people seek to avoid caring. One girl specifically yearns to become like a rock, and a state of emotional impermeability is sought by many others. Just as the main characters move towards the rock of Malta, so more generally the human race seems to be hastening to return to "rockhood." Indeed in Malta we read that manhood is increasingly defined in terms of rockhood. It is part of the basic ambiguity of Malta as described in this book that while on the one level it is an image of an island of life under siege, attacked by the levelling bombs of the Germans, and constantly eroded by the sea, on another level it is an image of a central point of inanimate rock and death drawing people back to that inert state. The Epilogue describes how the ship carrying Stencil's father was suddenly sucked under by a freak waterspout just off Malta, leaving a dead level sea which gave no sign of what now lies beneath the flat surface—this concludes the book.

One way and another, then, everything is sinking. Mehemet, a sage friend of Stencil's father, points out cheerfully, "'The only change is towards death...Early and late we are in decay.'" To Stencil's suggestion that the world recently contracted a fatal disease leading to the First World War, Mehemet replies with more Oriental largeness of perspective, "'Is old age a disease... The body slows down, machines wear out, planets falter and loop, sun and stars gutter and smoke. Why say a disease? Only to bring it down to a size you can look at and feel comfortable.'" We are always in decay: the question is, is there a plot in the universal rot? Stencil, son of Stencil, is, like his father, inclined to detect plots. A dentist in the book named Eigenvalue regards Stencil's belief in a plot as being like an amalgam to fill "a breach in the protective enamel." He reflects that teeth do indeed decay, but that is no reason to conceive of some conscious organization conspiring against the life of the pulp. "Yet we have men like Stencil, who must go about grouping the world's random caries into cabals." It is precisely Stencil's compulsion to group caries into cabals which makes him one of the central figures in the book, and we should now consider his dominant obsession.

This obsession is the quest for V. V. is an elusive female spy/anarchist who appears in one of her multiple identities in all these episodes; she once seduced Stencil's father, thus becoming, it seems, Stencil's mother. Her names have varied—Virginia, Victoria, Veronica Manganese, Vera Meroving—and at the end

Stencil leaves for Sweden to follow up a remote clue connected with one Mme. Viola. Stencil's quest is thus linear through time; but as the book shows—and indeed as Stencil realizes as he turns this way and that, following up peripheral clues—there are innumerable Vs, a point made on the first page of the book which shows a V-shaped cluster of innumerable smaller Vs. There is the jazz club called the V-note, patronized by the Whole Sick Crew; Veronica the sewer rat, so named by Father Fairing during his efforts to convert the rats of New York to Roman Catholicism, and chosen by him as his first saint and mistress; Queen Victoria, Venezuela, Valetta, the strange land of Vheissu and volcanoes like Vesuvius; it is the shape of spread thighs, the initial of Venus but also the initial for Vergeltungswaffe (retaliation weapons).[1] So from one point of view Stencil has far too much to go on, since he is bound to find clues everywhere—a fact he recognizes, near the end: "V. by this time was a remarkably scattered concept." Indeed, as this "concept" expands to include ever more manifestations of V., and as opposites such as love and death, the political right and left, start to converge in this inclusiveness, it points to that ultimate disappearance of differences and loss of distinctions which is the terminal state of the entropic process. If V. can mean everything it means nothing.

On the other hand Stencil really has very little to go on. Most of what he has is inference. "He doesn't know who she is, nor what she is." Near the end the suspicion is strengthened that all it adds up to is "the recurrence of an initial and a few dead objects." Stencil himself is aware that although he pursues V. as a libertine pursues spread thighs (the comparison is explicit), his quest may all be "an adventure of the mind, in the tradition of *The Golden Bough,* or *The White Goddess.*" Stencil's father had strange fever dreams of exploring for something in his own brain. Stencil is the copy of his father; the quest is his legacy. The historical melodrama of international interconnections which he puts together may be only the map of his own obsessions. At the same time, the

[1]As Dan Hausdorff suggests in his helpful article "Thomas Pynchon's Multiple Absurdities"(*Wisconsin Studies in Contemporary Literature,* vii, 1966), Pynchon's V. undoubtedly owes something to Henry Adams's interest in the Virgin-Venus symbols, just as his using the name of Yoyodyne for the company run by Bloody Chiclitz is probably an intentional echo of Adams's use of the dynamo to symbolize the amoral power being released in the modern world.

sieges and wars were real enough, with or without mysterious links, and Stencil is representative enough to be called "the century's child."

He is also representative of many American heroes in as much as he was powerfully attracted to sleep and inertia, wandering around in a slothful directionlessness, before he came across references to V. in his father's papers. In the suggestiveness of this entirely documentary stimulus, Stencil finds his motive for motion. Out of a few cryptic clues he maps the quest he needs to keep him awake; his terror is that the quest may succeed, returning him again to "half-consciousness." "Funking out, finding V., he didn't know which he was most afraid of, V. or sleep. Or whether they were two versions of the same thing." The point at which all versions merge into the same thing signifies the final entropic stillness: Stencil's strategy is, "Approach and avoid." He suspects that he needs "a mystery, any sense of pursuit to keep active a borderline metabolism," but such self-knowledge does not obviate the need to pursue the phantom he has at least half-created. The book recognizes that such fantasies may be necessary to maintaining consciousness and purposive motion; yet it reveals the solipsism that is implicit in them as well, for one of the subjects of Pynchon's book is the inability of people to love anyone outside their own fantasy projections.

Stencil is the key figure — one can hardly speak of characters — in the book. The O.E.D. defines a stencil as "a hole in a card which when washed over with colour leaves a figure"; "stencilling" is defined as "a process by which you can produce patterns and designs." Like the lady V. who shows inexhaustible dexterity in handling her different appearances, Stencil is pluralistic in his projection of himself. He also goes in for disguises, finding some relief from the pain of his dilemma in "impersonation." Like children and like Henry Adams in the *Education* (Pynchon again makes the comparison explicit) Stencil always refers to himself in the third person. This helps "Stencil" appear as only one among a repertoire of identities, thus he turns himself into an object, possibly out of some regressive instinct, a dread of taking on full self-hood. He thinks of himself as "quite purely He who looks for V. (and whatever impersonations that might involve)." This definition may mean that he is in fact a vacancy, filled in with the colours of his obsession, not a self, but in truth a stencil. And all his techniques of self-duplication and self-extension may be construed as protective screens for avoiding direct engagement with reality.

Stencil's obsession is with a structure of inferences based on an old dossier, cold clues, scraps and fragments from history's littoral which he has transformed into the strange flowers of his fantasy. One character believes, "that V. was an obsession after all, and that such an obsession is a hothouse: constant temperature, windless, too crowded with particoloured sports, unnatural blooms." Like Callisto in "Entropy," Stencil lives in a hothouse of hermetically-sealed fantasy where the past is arrested, as in a museum, immobilized in memory pictures to create an inner climate impervious to the inclemency of outer weather. Paradoxically, those objects which fed Stencil's obsession and gave him an illusory sense of vitality sealed him off as well, turning him into a stencil with a hothouse mind. Like a stencil, he will admit no configurations of experience that cannot be shaped into the pattern of his fantasy. Like a hothouse, his identity is a protected enclosure, given definition by the exotic growths artificially fostered within it.

If Stencil is trapped in the hothouse of the past, Benny Profane is astray in the streets of the present. The book opens with him walking down a street and we last see him running down a street in Malta. The street is his natural domain, for he is a rootless wanderer, as unaware of clues and indifferent to patterns as Stencil is obsessed by them. He says expressly that he has learned nothing from his peregrinations up and down the streets of the world, except perhaps to fear them. They fuse into a "single abstracted streed" which causes him nightmares without yielding him insights. The only job he can do—and that not well—is street repair work. Devoid of all sense of positive direction, he reacts passively to any puff of momentum that happens to touch him; by himself he cannot initiate or construct anything—no projects, no relationships, no dreams. His movement is a long flight from nowhere in particular to nowhere in particular.

Himself rather a faded copy of the traditional *picaro* and *schlemiel* figures combined, he is almost a cartoon reduction of another of the century's children, for if Stencil is he who searches

for V., Profane is he who experiences the street: "The street of
the 20th Century, at whose far end or turning—we hope—is some
sense of home or safety. But no guarantees…But a street we must
walk." Benny seems at the start to be a lonely seeker, hungering
for some human authenticity in an inanimate world; he emerges,
however, as a participator in the very process he seemed to oppose. He belongs with the Whole Sick Crew, and, despite his
schlemiel status, his Buster Keaton-like inability to avoid running
foul of a world full of things, he can scarcely be considered a
victim. If anything, he simply is, as Dickens said of one of his
characters, "of the street, streety."

It is in the street that the various destructive energies involved
in the history of this century erupt—from riots in Florence or
Malta to a gang fight in contemporary New York. Throughout
the various street episodes, historical and contemporary, there is
the sustained feeling that the walls, buildings and shopfronts are
an insubstantial façade, that the street itself and all man-made
structures are temporary illusions. ("The city is only the desert
in disguise," thinks one character in Cairo. "Nothing was coming.
Nothing was already here.") The last account of violent mob
action in the book is situated in Strada Reale, but the idea of a
royal street is a very ironic one by this time.

The fact that it is in the street that revolutionary mobs pursue
their demands for change prompts Stencil's father to write in his
journal: "we carry on the business of this century with an intolerable double vision. Right and Left; the hothouse and the street.
The Right can only live and work hermetically, in the hothouse
of the past, while outside the Left prosecute their affairs in the
streets by manipulated mob violence. And cannot live but in the
dreamscape of the future." The implication of this is that all
political thinking—and by extension all man's mental projections
—is either a dream of the past or a dream of the future. By this
account, man himself can never properly occupy present time.
The street and the hothouse are the dreams by which man avoids
confronting that nothingness which is the shapeless truth behind
the structured fantasy of human history. As with so many apparent opposites, the street and the hothouse meet and merge in
V. She is equally at home in both of them. And almost her last
reported words are: "'How pleasant to watch Nothing.'"

An important part of the intricate spatial geography of the book is that area which lies under the street—the sewers in which Benny Profane hunts alligators under New York, in which Father Fairing converts and seduces his rats. References to channels and tunnels occur in the description of the strange land of Vheissu and the subway travel in modern New York. Hints at the possible existence of an inherited reservoir of primordial knowledge suggests that a deliberate Jungian dimension has been added. The notion that the unconscious nourishes art, even if the unconscious is comparable to a sort of primeval sewer, and that there is much to be gained by descending into our dreams, is so customary by now that one can see that Pynchon has gone some way to turning it into dark farce—Benny and the alligators. At the same time he seems to want to preserve the notion that somehow it is more "real" under the street than in it. When Benny finally has to end his job we read: "What peace there had been was over. He had to come back to the surface, the dream-street."

The far-ranging geography of the book provides a composite image of the various areas of human consciousness. The street is the zone of the waking, planning consciousness which, unable to endure the meaninglessness of the absolute present, projects plans into the future or finds plans in the past. The hothouse is the realm of memory where the mind is sealed up in the secretions of its reveries over the past. The sewer or under-the-street (also compared to under the sea) is that area of dream, the unconscious, perhaps the ancestral memory, in which one may find a temporary peace or oblivion, and into which the artist must descend, but where fantasy can run so rampant that you may start seeing rats as saints and lovers if you remain down there too long. Indeed all three areas suggest the human compulsion or need to construct fantasies, as though each level of consciousness was another form of dreaming.

The modes of motion which prevail in the street are yo-yoing (in the present) and tourism (in the past). The historical episodes are full of references to people living in a "Baedeker world." Tourists are "the Street's own." The north European tourists who create a *bierhalle* in Egypt "in their own image" which results in "a parody of home," are only revealing the tourists' flight from reality even while in the act of travelling; they too live among illusions, inhabitants of their own stencillings, or the stencillings put out by Baedeker. The particular futility of that sort of "touring" movement is echoed in the activity of yo-yoing practised by various members of the Whole Sick Crew, and particularly by Benny Profane. It consists of shuttling back and forth on the subway for long periods, the ultimate expression of movement without destination—a parody of purpose, we might say. Less literally, it covers all the meaningless movements of their parties and hectic, reversible driftings. (More cosmically, the planets are said to yo-yo around the sun.) When Stencil (super-tourist) and Profane (super yo-yo) converge on Malta without quite understanding their motives for doing so, we read: "Malta alone drew them, a clenched fist around a yo-yo string." The illusory purposiveness of Stencil's travels, and the manifest purposelessness of Profane's meanderings, both serve to illuminate the condition of movement bereft of all significance except the elemental one of postponing inanimateness. Both modes of motion, in fact, accelerate entrophy, just as they both serve to bring Stencil and Benny Profane to the rock of Malta.

As well as writing about a quester and a drifter, Pynchon writes about all kinds of spies and agents. Their epistemological stance —looking for possible clues to possible plots—is only a projection of that of the novelist himself. Perhaps, indeed, they create the patterns of hostility they set out to trace; perhaps, too, does the novelist. Stencil's ingenious linked detections spread back in time and across space. Is this creative vision which sees a truth beneath the drifting contingencies of life; or is it a paranoid fantasy, an obsession akin to an oblivion? If the latter, then is Benny Profane's unco-ordinated empiricism of the eye, which looks out and sees no plots and learns nothing, true vision? We can hardly expect to adjudicate finally between them.

The preoccupation with signs, codes, signals, patterns, plots, etc., permeates the book so thoroughly that it—the preoccupation, not just the signals and patterns themselves—could be said to be the subject of the book, tying up with the central question, is entropy neutral or malign? From the opening scene in the bar when drunken feet move about in the damp sawdust "scribbling it into alien hieroglyphics" to the final barely uttered question as to whether there is a "third force" manipulating V. and her opponents alike, we are never far away from the feeling that there is something afoot, something going on "beneath," a code or clue to be deciphered, a plot or portent to be dreaded. Maps abound, whether of the New York sewers or Florence and the Uffizi, or German South-West Africa, and mapping is of course only another form of plotting. It is suggested that for a brief space of time when two of the characters are young and in love "they seemed to give up external plans, theories and codes...to indulge in being simply and purely young," but this idyll of unpatterned emotional directness is momentary, and most of the people at one time or another are involved rather in constructing a plot or a myth.

The various agents and plotters in the historical episodes, while planning their own cabals, are always worried that they may in fact be taking part in a larger cabal of which they have no knowledge. Stencil always finds some form of V. connected with some kind of conspiracy, if not a plotter then the cause of plots. Whatever V. might be, Stencil affirms "that his quarry fitted in with The Big One, the century's master cabal." Stencil's father had found that if people cannot find some sort of explanation for "this abstract entity The Situation" they "simply run amok." He is implying that for most people, worse than the idea of a master cabal is the notion of no plots at all. One character writes that life really has only one single lesson to teach: "that there is more accident to it than a man can ever admit to in a lifetime and stay sane." That is why Stencil sees planned cabals in random caries — paradoxically it might be his paranoia that keeps him sane. It is suitable that the last clue he picks up, which will keep him moving on (approaching and avoiding), this time to Stockholm, is about a certain Mme. Viola, who is an "oneiromancer and hypnotist." She will not only be able to divine his dreams, but also induce and prolong them.

In one of the incidents set in South-West Africa there is a character named Mondaugen who has the job of studying "sferic" signals. At first they come through as mere noise, but then he thinks he detects a regularity of patterning which might be "a kind of code." Out of some instinctive wariness he holds back from trying to break the code, but someone else works out a solution. Extracting certain signals from the overall noise, he demonstrates that they add up to Mondaugen's own name, plus the statement DIE WELT IST ALLES DAS DER FALL IST. This of course is the opening proposition in Wittgenstein's *Tractatus* (a proposition, incidentally, which seems to haunt contemporary American writers). As a coded message it would be the supreme irony, like discovering that the secret is that there is no secret. The assertion that the world is everything that is the case repudiates the very notion of plots, and arguably leaves things and events standing in precisely describable inexplicability. As the book shows, human instinct pulls in the other direction: towards cabalism, or demonism, or projected fantasies, and away from the rarified objective clarities attainable through linguistic analysis. People would rather detect an "ominous logic" in things than no omens at all. In this book, even the most jumbled atmospheric noises must contain some kind of signal, even if it is only your own name and a bleak tautology. What kind of world it might be to live in if we could love other people instead of our own fantasies, the book does not pretend to say.

The question of whether or not there are meaningful shapes to be detected is also raised by a number of references to geometric shapes and calculations. In a Robbe-Grillet type of episode, a barmaid named Hanne is uncertain whether or not there is a triangular stain on the plate she is washing. She is experiencing as a temporary puzzle what for Stencil is a lifelong dilemma. According to how she focuses her eyes or tilts the plate, the stain changes its shape—crescent, trapezoid—and sometimes fades away altogether. "Was the stain real? She didn't like its color. The color of her headache...." The problem of the book is here in miniature. Perhaps the changing shapes we see on the external blankness are the shifting projections of our own "headaches" or subjective pressures; on the other hand there might actually be a stain on the plate. The description of the shape in geometric terms is of course deliberate; throughout the book we constantly come across specific angles, intersections, details of linear arrangements and numerically charted positions. It is one of the most enduring of all human dreams (or needs) to feel that we live among geometry. Rather than confront shapeless space, we introduce lines and angles into it. Surrounded by the desert, man builds a pyramid. That would be another way of saying what *V.* is all about.

Related to references to geometry (and chess) are numerous references to the aesthetic patternings of music and painting. The notion of painting being a compensatory activity for the general decline of things is taken up overtly when Mehemet tells a rather unlikely tale of coming across a strange sight in the middle of the sea—a man "alone on the sea at nightfall, painting the side of a sinking ship." The implication is made explicit. We do cover the blank surfaces of our sinking world, and then live within our paintings; as D. H. Lawrence said, we live in the paintings we put on the underside of our umbrellas. For Lawrence this was a suffocation, a deprivation, and he considered it the artist's job to come along and slash a gap in the protective umbrella and let in reality. But in Pynchon's world there is a more ominous feeling that if you did cut through the painting a something or a nothing more frightening might be revealed. In one of the historical episodes there is a plot to steal Botticelli's "Birth of Venus." The thief is entranced by the "gorgeous surface" of the painting, but as he starts to cut it out of the frame a great horror grows in him and he abandons the project. This horror at stripping away the coloured surface is connected with something that a character named Hugh Godolphin told him about the strange land of Vheissu, and we should now consider that unmapped country.

Hugh Godolphin found Vheissu on one of his surveying trips for the British Army; his description of the journey and the land itself reads like a mixture of Borges and Conrad. There are no maps to Vheissu, but it is the country which is really at the heart of the book. As Godolphin describes it to Victoria, it might seem like any other remote region except for the changing colours which are "'its raiment, perhaps its skin.'" When Victoria asks what is beneath, he admits that he wondered whether the place had a soul. What this meant for Hugh Godolphin apparently was a determination somehow to return to Vheissu and find "'what was beneath her skin.'" Making his way to the pole, he digs for his answer, and when he does penetrate the surface what he finds is—"'Nothing...It was Nothing I saw.'" He continues his account: "'If Eden was the creation of God, God only knows what evil created Vheissu. The skin which had wrinkled through my nightmares was all there had ever been. Vheissu itself, a gaudy dream. Of what the Antarctic in this world is closest to: a dream of annihilation.'" That last definition is suitably vague as to whether the whole place is Godolphin's dream, or whether in itself it is a dream of annihilation. What we are given is a notional place with a dazzlingly coloured surface covering Nothing, or perhaps worse, a void of icy negation. The status of Vheissu as a sort of dream is underlined when Godolphin later on in the century complains that Vheissu is gone and impossible to bring back. He means his own particular kind of Vheissu, his private dream: "'our Vheissus are no longer our own, or even confined to a circle of friends; they're public property.'" It is part of the intention of the book to suggest that the world may now be engaged in making actual a mass dream of annihilation, submitting reality to a nihilistic fantasy.

In Malta, in a final talk with Goldolphin, V. reveals her similarity to Vheissu further; for, having expressed her delight at watching Nothing, she goes on to say how much she would like to have a whole wardrobe of different shaped feet in a rainbow range of colours. V. *is* all those constantly changing coloured shapes which make up the dazzling and enchanting surface of Vheissu. She is also the void beneath the decoration, the Nothing at the heart of the dream. We need all those coloured dreams to get us along the street—which may also be a dream. At the start we see Benny walking down East Main Street, underneath a row of lamps "receding in an asymmetric V to the east where it's dark and there are no more bars." We last see Benny apparently making a bid to leave the street for the last time, this time in Malta. "Presently, sudden and in silence, all illumination in Valletta, houselight and streetlight, was extinguished. Profane and Brenda continued to run through the abruptly absolute night, momentum alone carrying them towards the edge of Malta, and the Mediterranean beyond." V. is whatever lights you *to* the end of the street: she is also the dark annihilation waiting *at* the end of the street.

What Pynchon manages to suggest is that the fantasies we build to help us to live represent, in fact, an infiltration of that death we think we are so eager to postpone. They represent an avoidance of reality, by substituting for it a fetishistic construction. One man in the book has a private planetarium which is a highly complex mechanism of moons and planets, pulleys and chains, and yet which is, after all, "a parody of space." If our constructed fantasies are effectively parodies of reality, then this has certain implications for the self-conscious author of the overall fiction of the book. For a particular literary style is a construction analogous to that private planetarium, a personal way of organizing things in space, and thus to some extent a parody of it. Of course there need not be any deliberate attempt to burlesque and ridicule reality present in the construction, and one does not readily think of Tolstoy or George Eliot as "parodying" reality. The matter of attitude comes up here, and it is a distinctive trait of many contemporary American writers that they are very quick to be suspicious of any one stylistic version of reality and regard it as inescapably parodic.

In this connection we should note Pynchon's systematic stylistic evocation (often parodic) of previous writers as he deals with different episodes in different times and places. Conrad, Evelyn Waugh and Lawrence Durrell are in evidence in many of the historical and colonial episodes; Melville, Henry Adams, Nathanael West, Djuna Barnes, Faulkner and Dashiell Hammett are among the American writers whose work is in some way detectable; Joyce and Nabokov are clearly present in the way the book is organized; and there is one of Borges's mysterious kingdoms at the heart of the book. This is not to suggest that the book is merely a pastiche, a collage of scrambled sources. Pynchon's point seems to be to remind the reader that there is no one writable "truth" about history and experience, only a series of versions: it always comes to us "stencillized." In such a way he can indicate that he is well aware of the ambiguities of his own position, constructing another fiction and at the same time underlining the fallacies involved in all formal plottings and organizations of space.

In addition I think it is part of Pynchon's intention to demonstrate that the various styles of writers of this century who, in a sense, have imposed their private dreams on us are like those iridescent surfaces with which we adorn the walls of our galleries and cover the countries of our dreams. The attendant implication is that under all this decorative sheen there lies the cold truth of the void. One result of this is, I think, that Pynchon himself has written, no doubt deliberately, what amounts to a "hollow" book. He brilliantly shows how man produces the painting on the side of the sinking ship; at the same time the detectable element of near-compulsive parody serves to call into question the value and validity of any one style—indeed of style itself. What is felt to be true is the emptiness under the coloured surface, the ice at the pole, the rock to which we all return, the final stillness of the level sea. The book itself is a "dream of annihilation": it is Pynchon's Vheissu.

This rather ambiguous relationship to the multiple styles made available to the modern artist seems to be a very American preoccupation. As I have tried to suggest, the American writer at times seems to want to shed a style even while he is using it; this is perhaps indicative of a suspicious unwillingness to get too involved in anyone else's particular dream of reality. There is a

passage in Nathanael West's *The Day of the Locust* which is in-
structive here. Tod Hackett is an artist working in Hollywood.
The following is a meditation he has when he looks out at the great
dumping ground for old sets and props from finished films.

> This was the final dumping ground. He thought of Janvier's "Sar-
> gasso Sea." Just as that imaginary body of water was a history of
> civilization in the form of a marine junkyard, the studio lot was
> one in the form of a dream dump. A Sargasso of the imagination!
> And the dump grew continually, for there wasn't a dream afloat
> somewhere which wouldn't sooner or later turn up on it, having
> first been made photographic by plaster, canvas, lath and paint.
> Many boats sink and never reach Sargasso, but no dream ever en-
> tirely disappears. Somewhere it troubles some unfortunate person
> and some day, when that person has been sufficiently troubled, it
> will be reproduced on the lot.

Hollywood as the American dream factory is of course a well-
known image by now; but this image of a great vista of discarded
fantasies—a dream dump—seems to have a more than usual
relevance and vividness for the American artist, particularly one
like Pynchon who writes both to demonstrate the need for fictions
and to impugn or revoke their validity. This attitude he mimes
out in the process of writing his book, for, apparently at home in
many styles, he finally trusts none. From one point of view, both
in content and form, his book is a dream dump too.

It is worth pointing out here the connection between problems
of narration and problems of identity in the contemporary American novel. In *V.* there is a character called Fausto, a man of letters who indeed writes his own book within the book. It is a sort
of apologia, and he says this about his activity: "We can justify
any apologia simply by calling life a successive rejection of per-
sonalities." Where Fausto divides himself up into "successive
identities" which he has taken on and then rejected, Pynchon
takes on and rejects successive styles in his book. For both, this is a
way of seeing past all the fictions which fix the world and the word
in particular patterns and styles, and as such it is an activity very
common among contemporary American writers. But whether
man can live beyond all fictions, whether, even when faced by
the pathos and mockery of the dream dump, it would be desir-
able, let alone possible, to put an end to man's addiction to fantasy, is not explored. Perhaps the advice of Mark Twain's Satan

to mankind is the relevant consideration here—"'Dream other dreams, and better!'"

> Americans start with the assumption that they are working with a *synthesized* system. We are driven by our own way of looking at things to synthesize almost everything.
>
> *The Silent Language,* Edward T. Hall

The synthesizing instinct that Hall refers to in these words is obviously not limited to America. But in stressing what he sees as a peculiarly American compulsion to synthesize environmental data into a system—a need perhaps related to the fact that in America the many patterns, visible and invisible, which constitute the determinants of a culture, are less familiar and less established and articulated than elsewhere—Hall provides a good point of departure for a consideration of Pynchon's second novel, *The Crying of Lot 49* (1965). It is a short, curiously lyrical novel which forms what amounts to an addendum to *V.* Oedipa Maas is a girl like Rachel Owlglass, willing to try to sustain at least the illusion of love, but finding herself in a world where people will not share in this attempt. Indeed they evade it in a variety of ways. At the same time she is involved in a quest like Stencil's, a compulsive and widening effort of "synthesizing" which may be hallucination and may be discovery. The novel starts when she learns that she has been named as an executrix of the will of an old lover, Pierce Inverarity, a tycoon whose holdings and enterprises in California turn out to be almost limitless. Before he died he had the habit of calling her up from unknown distances and places and speaking to her in a range of assumed and bewilderingly differing voices—from comic tones to simulated Fascistic threats. His will, as it transpires, "speaks" in comparably multiple ambiguities, and as Oedipa tries to discover the meaning of the will, in a sense her inheritance, she enacts, by analogy, a quest into the meaning of that larger heritage called America.

The strangeness of the will leads her to become a cryptologist, in an unending effort to discover whether the will itself contains a code which she has to interpret; or whether in fact the will has been tampered with and a false code inserted in order to distract her from discovering the revelations of the will and the truth

about Inverarity Holdings. What she discovers, or seems to discover, is an elaborate series of scattered clues which when "synthesized" all point to the existence of a strange secret system called
The Tristero. This she traces back to sixteenth-century Europe
when it started as a rival group to the Thurn and Taxis Postal
System, later coming over to America at the time of the Civil War
and ever since then working secretly against the public communications system through an organization called W.A.S.T.E. (We
Await Silent Tristero's Empire). She discovers a great deal of
evidence, but it is possible that it has all been planted for her to
discover. Her quest involves the scrutiny of many documents,
including editions, revisions, variants, textual corruptions and
obvious counterfeits; but she cannot, and at one point will not,
attempt to verify the status and source of the documents, for they
too may have been put in her way through bookshops and university people all somehow connected to Inverarity Holdings.

It is clear that Oedipa has something of the instinct to discern,
or suspect, the presence of patterns of revelation in the local
landscape before she comes into contact with the estate and The
Tristero clues. Driving into San Narciso, the layout of streets
and houses reminds her of a radio circuit—"there were to both
outward patterns a hieroglyphic sense of concealed meaning, of
an intent to communicate." Similarly a map of one of Inverarity's
housing developments flashed on to the TV screen seems to contain "some promise of hierophany." San Narciso is where the
whole possibility of The Tristero System begins to confront her,
and bearing in mind that the good duke in a Jacobean play she
sees, called *The Courier's Tragedy,* meets his death by kissing the
feet of an image of Saint Narcissus which have been secretly poi-
soned, we may be alerted to the possible presence of a deathly
narcissism such as we encountered in *V.*

One form of narcissism is to regard one's particular fantasy of
the world as the definitive reality, and it is part of Oedipa's growing agony that she cannot be sure to what extent she herself is
guilty of this. In the past she had, we gather, seen herself rather
in the role of the maiden imprisoned in the tower, waiting for the
knight who would invite her to let down her hair and so deliver
her. She had let down her hair for Pierce "but all that had then
gone on between them had really never escaped the confinement
of that tower." Then follows a long and crucial passage based,
once again, on a painting. The painting was entitled "Borando el

Manto Terrestre" and showed a number of girls imprisoned in a tower where they were working on an endless tapestry which they allowed to flow out of the windows, "seeking hopelessly to fill the void." In the painting "the tapestry was the world": it contained all you could see outside the tower. The picture makes Oedipa cry. It makes her feel that although she may travel to Mexico she will never really escape from the tower of her lonely self.

The implications of this are worth pondering. The painting of the "Embroiderers of the Terrestial Blanket" (no doubt owing something to Homer's Penelope, the Three Fates, and perhaps to Tennyson's Lady of Shalott) is of course a lyrical reflection of Oedipa's own embroidery work, those self-spun versions of reality with which she tries to fill the void. The fact that other creatures accept the embroidery as reality is an indication that many people live unquestioningly inside other people's versions or pictures. The sadness that overcomes Oedipa seems to stem from the sudden recognition that she will never escape from her own tapestries. We may take it as a psychological truth that perhaps the only way to escape from one's "tower" is through the act of love. But then the passage goes on to describe Oedipa's recognition that the tower is incidental and that what keeps her where she is is "formless magic, anonymous and malignant." Here again we encounter that suspicion of a demonized reality, with evil as an inexplicable and anonymous force beaming in on people for no discoverable reason. Oedipa's need (and compulsion) is to give a face and a form to the power which she suspects is at work. But she has to work alone; there is no knight of deliverance in her story. She finds no love, or willingness to be loved.

The theme is picked up when we are given at least the suggestion that one object behind her discovery of what she comes to call The Tristero System was "to bring to an end her encapsulation in her tower." She comes to be haunted by "the way it fitted, logically, together. As if...there were revelation in progress all around her." We learn that a lot of the revelation comes from Pierce's stamp collection which was often his substitute for her — "thousands of little coloured windows into deep vistas of space and time." This stamp collection is one of the central objects in the novel. It is this collection which is to be sold at the auction which ends the book, as Lot 49. As a "lot" it is related to the used car lots which are an important part of the background of the book;

as representing postage, and the whole idea of communication and information, the stamps are related to The Tristero System. As forming a series of little coloured windows on to exotic landscapes and designs which Pierce used as a substitute for his relationship with Oedipa, they are samples of all those dreams and substitute objects by which people avoid love and human relationships. The connection between rubbish and fantasy is close in this book, as the code cryptogram W.A.S.T.E. indicates.

What the book raises as the central and insoluble problem is whether Oedipa has discovered or hallucinated her synthesization which adds up to The Tristero System. Twice she goes into a ladies' toilet: once there is a mysterious message and sign on the wall, which adds fuel to her sensitized, inquiring mind; the second time there is a totally blank wall and she is somewhat unsettled at the absence of any calligraphy or drawing. Both the presence and the absence of signs is disturbing: which is almost the epistemological or metaphysical verdict of the book. As Oedipa gets deeper into her quest (which is, to repeat it, an attempt to find the real meaning of the estate) she finds she is losing all the men who might have loved or helped her—one to suicide, one to LSD, one to a depraved nymphet (three ways of evading reality, however one wants to appraise them). At the same time, the stimulus to fantasy, or synthesizing perception, grows in the form of proliferating clues.

At this point we should consider the nature of The Tristero System—whether it is real, or a staged hoax, or a private hallucination. It may be a genuine conspiracy, a second and hidden America; it may be a simulated conspiracy made up of genuinely perceptible clues and put on by real plotters for the bewilderment of Oedipa; or it may be a conspiracy of the imagination, which cannot stand too much nothingness or loneliness. When Oedipa first goes to see Genghis Cohen, the eminent philatelist who helps to extract a lot of suggestive hints from the stamp collection, she sees him framed in a long succession of doorways, at the end of a seemingly endless series of receding rooms. It is an appropriate spatial metaphor for the way the Tristero plot looms at the terminal point of endlessly receding possible interpretations. Something of its ambiguity is suggested by its different spellings—Trystero/ Tristero. But whatever its ultimate source and status, as a plot with its sources deep in history (real or imagined), it has certain recognizable features (or attributes ascribed to it).

It had its beginning in an attempt to rival the official mail which became a conspiracy to subvert the public systems of communication flow. According to clues and inferences provided by various characters, it was often connected with rebellions and wars—perhaps responsible for the French Revolution, perhaps linked in some way to Nazism, perhaps, coming nearer home, perpetuated through some of the extreme right-wing secret societies of California. One scholar tells Oedipa about a seventeenth-century sect called the Scurvhamites who held somewhat Manichaean beliefs. They became too fascinated with the negative forces of death working against God's creation: "the glamorous prospect of annihilation coaxed them over." The scholar suggests that this sect felt that Tristero could well symbolize "the Other." The secrecy and subversive acts of The Tristero System may have led people to regard it as representing some "blind, automatic anti-God." There is a strong suggestion that The Tristero System represents the process of entropy-turned-Manichaean, stealthily at work bringing disorder and death to the human community. (D.E.A.T.H. is another cryptogram discovered by Oedipa on her night wanderings—Don't Ever Antagonize The Horn.)

However, it is one of the ambiguities of the book which a reader may find as worrying and confusing as Oedipa, that The Tristero System might represent some secret, second America, which in many ways may be preferable or more genuine than the surface society. It is at night and away from the main highways that Oedipa really discovers the Tristero sign everywhere, "Decorating each alienation, each species of withdrawal." The Tristero System in its present-day manifestation is that underground America made up of all the "disinherited"—racial minorities, homosexuals, the poor, the mad, the lonely and the frightened. It also contains revolutionaries from both extremes of the political spectrum who are crazily dedicated to the overthrow of the present society. These inhabitants of the night are both pathetic and frightening; as the concealed pun in Tristero suggests—it represents both the sadness and the terror of America.

But, as Oedipa comes to put it to herself, since the surface society and official communications system are so spiritually impoverished and dedicated to lies, since indeed so much of the visible America seems given over to denying human variety and turning people into objects, perhaps The Tristero is a network by which an unknown number of Americans are truly communicating, perhaps it represents a "real alternative." Walking along some rail tracks laid over a cinderbed, as she has throughout looked to find and follow lines and connections in the wasted landscapes of her surroundings, Oedipa meditates on the possibility that "it was all true." She imagines all the disinherited squatters by the rail lines, and wonders if perhaps they keep in touch with each other through Tristero. She starts to think of all those others who make up a different America, *in* the great industrial superstructure erected by Inverarity and his kind, but not *of* it: like the squatters who dare to sleep up a telegraph pole in the lineman's tent—"swung among a web of telephone wires, living in the very copper rigging and secular miracle of communication, untroubled by the dumb voltages flickering their miles." Here indeed is the nub of the book. Is there another America; can entirely different universes co-habit?

If Tristero is indeed a world of waiting outcasts, keeping themselves aloof from contemporary society, then Oedipa feels she may be drawn to join it. Particularly if they are waiting for "another set of possibilities" or at least for the current rigid "symmetry of choices to break down": for Oedipa too, like so many American protagonists, feels that something has gone wrong with the choices offered by America, a country in which the chances were "once so good for diversity." Her meditations bring her to the point of envisaging extreme alternatives. "Behind the hieroglyphic streets there would either be a transcendent meaning, or only the earth...Another mode of meaning behind the obvious, or none. Either Oedipa in the orbiting ecstasy of a true paranoia, or a real Tristero." The possible existence of The Tristero is now associated with the possible existence of "transcendent" meaning, almost equivalent to a redemptive vision of another America behind the material concretions of the land. The Tristero is also associated with that yearning for diversity, a world of unprogrammed possibilities, so persistent in American literature.

The "silence" of The Tristero has hitherto been dedicated to disrupting the customary flow of information. As such it was on the side of entropy, making for loss of order, increase of waste, and death. However, in contemporary America when the public world seems to be on the side of entropy, the silence of The Tristero starts to appear as something positive, a pregnant withdrawal and waiting which may yet hold hopes of another America, another legacy. The confusion for Oedipa, and perhaps to some

extent for Pynchon, is that the hidden plot seems to range from
that dream of annihilation familiar from V. and Vheissu, to those
for Transcendence, a better America one day to be made manifest, which have formed the optimistic (and, arguably, counter-
entropic) side of American thought at least since Emerson. If The
Tristero does exist, who can be sure, from this range of possibilities, what the true legacy of America will finally turn out to be?
If it does not exist, then the only legacy of America is a paranoid
fantasy. If this seems like a confused and ultimately pessimistic
range of alternatives, then one can only say that at the time of
writing they exactly catch the mood of contemporary America,
for which Oedipa's baffled attempts at deciphering, synthesizing
and prognosis are an accurate paradigm.

What makes this deceptively slight book finally so moving is
the aching sense of loss and waste which pervades the failing human relationships and the declining landscape alike. There is,
for instance, a very poignant meditation on an old car lot which
itemizes, in a Whitmanesque way, all the wretched detritus gathering there, and goes on to ponder how saturated the old cars and
wrecks must be with human feelings of all kinds. It is as though
man is putting his passions into his objects as never before:
"things" have come this far, and we have come this far into things.
Or again, Oedipa engages in a related meditation on the old mattress of a down-and-out, drunk sailor. She conceives of the mattress
as a "stuffed memory" and imagines how one day it will inevitably
go up in flames as the dozing sailor drops his cigarette on it. It
is a vision of what entropy really means. "She stared at it in wonder. It was as if she had just discovered the irreversible process.
It astonished her to think that so much could be lost, even the
quality of hallucination belonging just to the sailor that the world
would bear no further trace of."

This sense of whole constructed mental worlds of dream and
memory—she groups those of the saint, the clairvoyant, the paranoid, and she could have added the artist—vanishing irreversibly
away, just as the mattress we lie on will rot or burn or somehow
decay, is another linking of rubbish and fantasies suggested by
the sign W.A.S.T.E. Do we live in fantasy because things have
usurped too much of the human domain; or is the visible accumulation of junk around us only the result of our proclivity for
fantasy-life? Either way, the result is an increase in entropy,
though the process does not pass unnoticed, for here is Oedipa,

and her author, to witness and lament the great sadness and awe-
some mystery of its unpreventable successes. To this extent, at
least, the book is counter-entropic, yet it also adumbrates the final
entropic victory even in its very structure.

The uncertainties in the structure and overall tone of the book
are radical and distinctive. Just as Oedipa doesn't know whether
she is discovering another America or simply developing the intricacies of a paranoia, so Pynchon himself is ambivalent about
his own fiction-making. The tone of the book oscillates between
crude farce and passages of poignant and serious lyrical lament.
It is as if the book itself does not know whether, of the available
genres, it is trash or tragedy. This is part of that new anxiety in
fiction which reveals itself as a nervous compulsion to under-
mine the fiction in the act of erecting it—the verbal equivalent
of auto-destructive art. Needless to say this can become as much of
a gimmick as any other convention in fiction writing. But in Pynchon it seems to me that the anxiety about the status of *all* plots
is so deeply a part of the subject of the book that the uncertainties
infecting the structure of the book are a genuine part of his whole
vision.

The blank wall and the encoded wall are both finally disturbing;
just so, in the case of a plotted or a plotless universe. By balancing
between the two possibilities, it seems to me that Pynchon does
produce a serious study of the state of consciousness in contemporary America, while a writer like Barth, who opts to emphasize
his mockery of plots at an extreme, excessively plotted length,
seems to me to fall away from seriousness without discovering
any compensating new sources of interest or beguilement. There
comes a point beyond which the mockery of fictions and plots
becomes sterile and boring, whether or not one holds to the view
that we do after all live by fictions. The joy of pure invention is
perhaps the main spur for the writer, but this does not have to be
dissociated from a conviction of relevance which makes some fictions more valuable than others. Pynchon did, after all, have a
story to tell—how Oedipa Maas inherited America and came to
the edge of madness and despair. It is a fiction we learn from by
not disbelieving. We are all of us "synthesizing" one way or another, sensitively or crudely, to our liberation or to our confusion
as the case may be, and Oedipa's plight is only an extension of
our own. If Pynchon's books are confusing, then it is because he is
charting and evoking a state of affairs in which authentic inter-

subjectivity has all but vanished. He communicates an increasing failure in communication, and is the plotter of a growing disarray. If there is tension and uncertainty in his tone it is because his style is taking issue with the entropy to which it knows it must, like all styles, succumb.

II. *V. & V-2*

"A screaming comes across the sky." These are the opening words of Thomas Pynchon's new, enormously long, novel *Gravity's Rainbow*. The screaming in this particular instance is the sound of a V-2 rocket falling on London towards the end of the last war, though, as the V-2 travelled at about a mile per second, the screaming was only heard after the rocket had struck, or, depending on where you happened to be at the time, never heard at all. First the annihilation, then the warning; an eerie reversal. And with nothing audible or visible to indicate its approach, death became permanently, silently imminent. The one you didn't hear could be your own. Even those of us over 35 tend to forget that over one thousand of those V-rockets fell on London between September 1944 and the end of the war. What is interesting to consider is why a post-war American novelist should base such a long novel on that final period of the war, reconstructing in quite amazing detail the whole atmosphere of London at the time, and, in the event, producing a work of genius which establishes Pynchon as one of the few major novelists to have emerged in any country since the war. Perhaps a brief reference to his earlier work may help to establish a context for this extraordinary novel.

Pynchon's first story was entitled "Entropy," a word used in the second law of thermodynamics and in common parlance taken to mean that everything in the universe is running down. The vision of a world in decline, heading irreversibly for the terminal wasteland and scrap heap, permeates Pynchon's work. The theme itself is not new; it is what Pynchon makes of it that reveals, for me, the most original imagination to have appeared in American fiction since the war. His first novel was called simply *V.*, an immensely long and complex book which centres on two figures named Stencil and Benny Profane who in an unusual but brilliantly handled way echo that archetypal fictional pair, Don Quixote and Sancho Panza—the deranged dreamer who is constantly seeking to rearrange reality according to his fantasies and imagination; and the foot-loose empiricist who takes things as they come, or, we might say, allows himself to be taken by things as they beset him. Stencil is on an endless quest for a mysterious woman called simply V, a spy-anarchist who may have been his mother. Clues proliferate as he delves into the past, a Virginia leads to a Veronica, a Vera; then they start spreading out into vaguer fields of reference—Queen Victoria, Venezuela, Vesuvius, and reaching out even to the opposites of love and death, Venus and Vergeltungswaffe, those German V-rockets, or vengeance-seeking weapons, to which Pynchon returns in *Gravity's Rainbow*. The point is that Stencil finally sees evidence of V everywhere; but if V can mean everything, it means nothing. Pynchon is dramatising the dangerous tendency to allow an obsession to take over one's reading of reality, so that one may begin to see plots and connections everywhere, and fantasized inventions present themselves to the mind as interpretative perceptions. One name for this is paranoia and it is a recurring theme in all Pynchon's work. But he also explores the alternative. What is it like to live with a sense that nothing is connected to anything, in a state of volitionless rambling, with no clues to follow, adrift in pure contingency and randomness? Pynchon calls this "anti-paranoia"—"a condition not many of us can bear for long." This is the condition experienced by Benny Profane who is a constant, motiveless wanderer up and down the streen—the generic "street of the 20th Century," going nowhere, seeing only separate objects in a disintegrating world. Is Stencil a lunatic, or a man with creative vision? Is Benny Profane a realist, or a figure of impoverished perception? Between them these two figures point to the question which worries so many of Pynchon's characters. Are we surrounded by plots—social, natural, cosmic—or is there no plot, no hidden configuration of intent, only gratuitous matter and chance? And pain and loneliness, for by either version these are real. This is a crucial part of Pynchon's vision. Not only does he see a world apparently hastening to return to the inanimate state; he sees a world in which many human beings seem willingly to accelerate this process—in particular by avoiding human relationships and treating themselves and other people as objects. One character specifically aspires to "rockhood," and the central characters in *V.* finally converge on the rock of Malta. What is avoided, or found to be impossible, is authentic communication, tender reciprocal contact, and love.

This was the poignant discovery made by the woman Oedipa Maas in Pynchon's second novel, *The Crying of Lot 49,* a deceptively simple book which seems almost to present itself as a kind of comic strip and turns out to be one of the most moving books written about America in recent years. Oedipa discovers that she has been named executrix of a will by a Californian tycoon, who was also an ex-lover. It is a very ambiguous will and as Oedipa tries to discover its meaning, which is the meaning of her inheritance, she is effectively exploring the ambiguous meaning of that larger heritage, America itself. She feels plots starting to take form around her, and she becomes perforce a desperate cryptologist. Is there some strange system at work, an ambiguous conspiracy, a second America hidden but surviving and operating in the interstices of the visible social structure? Or is Oedipa hallucinating, "in the orbiting ecstasy of a true paranoia?" Part of her problem, and her pathos, is her growing isolation. She gradually finds she is losing all the men who might have helped or loved her; in one way or another they are in flight from the burden of human relationships. She had once thought of herself as being the maiden imprisoned in the tower, waiting for the knight who would ask her to let down her hair, but however she had tried, she "had never really escaped the confinement of that tower." There is no knight of deliverance in this story. If she has constructed a fantasy around herself, it may be to compensate for an unbearable solitude and blankness. If the final "truth" about her America is the non-human lapping of the cold Pacific at its edge, then Oedipa may well need to remain astray in her unverifiable fictions. And yet, whether she is a true visionary or a pathetic paranoid, at the end, bereft of love, she comes to the final loneliness of the void when the tower is finally everywhere.

Pynchon's new novel centres on the rocket—phallic and fatal, Eros transformed into Thanatos, invading "Gravity's gray eminence" only to succumb to it, curving through the sky like a lethal rainbow, then crashing to the earth. Does it strike by "chance," or according to some hidden pattern, some "music" of annihilations which we will never hear but is always being played? Around the rocket and its production, Pynchon builds up a version of wartime England and post-war Europe which is equally rich in

authentic detail and dazzling fantasy. And, as there seem to be no
limits to the fecundity of his imagination, the novel reaches back
into colonial and American history, down into the world of molecules, up into the stars, back even to Bethlehem when men saw
another kind of burning light in the sky. In all this, certain abid-
ing preoccupations may be discerned. Patterns, plots and paranoia
abound—these are familiar in Pynchon's world; add to those the
following words—paper, plastics, preterition, and Pavlovian conditioning—and some of the main themes of the book are listed.
But before examining what, in a conventional sense, the book is
"about," I think it's important to consider how to read the book,
for more than anything else this novel provides an experience in
modern reading. Pynchon's characters move in a world of both
too many and too few signs, too much data and too little information, too many texts, but no reliable editions. As you read the
book you seem to pass through a bewildering variety of genres,
activities, types of discourse—at different times the text seems to
partake of such different things as pantomime, burlesque, cinema,
cabaret, card games, songs, comic strips, spy stories, serious history, encyclopaedic information, mystical and visionary meditations, the scrambled imagery of dreams, the cold cause-and-effect talk of the Behaviourists, and all the various ways men try to
control and coerce realities both seen and unseen—from magic
to measurement, from sciences to seances. At one point, one character is reading a Plasticman comic; he is approached by a man of
great erudition who engages him in a conversation about etymo-
logy. Here is a clue for us: we should imagine that we are reading
a comic, but it is partly transparent, and through it we are also
reading an encylcopedia, a film script, a piece of science history,
and so on. There is only one text, but it contains a multiplicity
of surfaces. This is not such a bizarre phenomenon as it sounds.
We can all read and decode the different languages and genres
Pynchon has brought into his book. Modern man is above all an
interpreter of different signs, a reader of differing discourses, a
compelled and often compulsive decipherer. But never before
has there been such an uncertainty about the reliability of the
texts. One character in the novel, making his way across the waste-
lands of post-war Europe, wonders whether it does contain a
"Real Text." He thinks that such a text may be connected with
the secrets of the Rocket: but perhaps the "Real Text" is the

desolate landscape he is traversing; or perhaps he missed the Real
Text somewhere behind him in a ruined city.... Reading Pynchon's novel gives us a renewed sense of how we have to read the
modern world. At times in his book it is not always clear whether
we are in a bombed-out building, or a bombed-out mind, but that
too is quite appropriate. For how many of those rockets that fell
on London fell in the consciousness of the survivors, exploding
in the modern mind? And, looking around and inside us, can we
be sure how much is Real Text, and how much is ruined debris?

I will have to simplify material that Pynchon's genius has made
at once slap-stick and sombre, wildly funny and deeply moving.
Roughly, what emerges from the book is a sense of a force — something, someone, referred to simply as "They" — which is actively
trying to bring everything to zero and beyond, trying to institute
a world of non-being, an operative kingdom of death. They seek
to convert the organic world into an inert world of plastic and
paper. This is a vision of entropy as an extremely powerful worldwide organization. From Their point of view, and in a world of
insidious reversals and inversions, the war was a great creative
act, not the "destruction" but the "reconfiguration" of people
and places. Their great achievement is the establishment of an
area called in the book simply "the Zone," which is a vision of
post-war Europe. In this world of complete displacement, countries
no longer mean anything. There are "no zones but the Zone" says
one character. It is also a world of "the new Uncertainty" — "in
the Zone categories have been blurred badly," and everything
and everyone is adrift. Pynchon is a genuine poet of decay and
decline, of the disinherited and the lost, of lateness and absence,
of a world succumbing to an irreversible twilight of no-love, no
human contact. In situating his novel at this point in time, I
think Pynchon is concentrating on a crucial moment when *They*
seemed to set about imposing a new order on the world, an order
apparently addicted to energy — and the whole novel is very relevant to our ecological concern at how technological man is simply using up his own planet — but an order which is ultimately
addicted to Death. At one point Pynchon describes the movement
of displaced people at the end of the war, "a great frontierless
streaming." The sentences that follow mime out this frontierless
streaming in an extraordinary flow of objects and people, and
concludes — "so the populations move, across the open meadow,

limping, marching, shuffling, carried, hauling along the detritus
of an order, a European and bourgeois order they don't yet know
is destroyed forever." A later passage suggests what is taking the
place of this vanished order. "Oh, a State begins to take form in
the stateless German night, a State that spans oceans and surface
politics, sovereign as the International or the Church of Rome,
and the Rocket is its soul."

They work by all kinds of control—hence the number of references to Pavlovian conditioning and Behaviourist experiments
—and Pynchon is by no means alone among American novelists
in wondering to just what lengths They will take their methods of
control (William Burroughs seems to be an influence here).
Sensitive figures, not yet totally taken over by Their System, react
to their intimations of some global conspiracy with the by now
familiar paranoia which, in the world of this book, may figure in
a parodic comic song or be the subject of a quotation from an essay by Pavlov. In general, paranoia is defined as "nothing less
than the onset, the leading edge, of the discovery that *everything
is connected*...not yet blindingly One, but at least connected."
Of course, everything depends on the nature of the connection,
the intention revealed by the pattern. Everything was connected
in Dante's world too, but *con amore.* Just what connects things in
this world of Pynchon's is what worries a lot of the characters
in the book, the most important one being an American service-
man called Slothrop.

Slothrop's fantastic adventures take him through many countries and also through many genres—or experience areas. As a
child he was experimented on in a Pavlovian laboratory; he is last
seen, if seen at all, on a record cover. In between he is Rocketman
of the comic strip and he plays a variety of roles for English and
American Intelligence, getting involved in the distorted fantasies
and obsessions of dozens of figures in post-war Europe. Slothrop
is related to Benny Profane of *V.,* a lonely wanderer up and down
the streets of the world. He knows he is involved in the evil
games of other people, but he cannot finally get out of these
games. Indeed, leaving all the games is one of the hopes and
dreams of the few people with any human feelings left. But it
remains a dream. Reality has been pre-empted by games; or it
has been replaced by films, so that people can be said to be living
"paracinematic lives." Slothrop, we feel, would be more at home
in a simpler world—a non-manipulative world of love and kind-

ness, a world before the rockets, a pre-plastic world. But that world has gone, and its obliteration and supersession are the central subjects of the book.

Slothrop has a notable oddity about him which draws him to the attention of the intelligence groups. He is apparently irresistible to girls and in his office he keeps a map of his many successful amorous encounters which occur at odd moments all over London. In another bureau, a statistician working for intelligence keeps a map with all the rocket strikes marked on it to see whether there is any emergent pattern. And, yes, it turns out that Slothrop's map of moments of sexual excitement and orgasm coincides exactly with the map of where the rockets strike. It may be connected with the Pavlovian experiment conducted on him when he was a child, so that some implanted conditioned reflex connecting sexual arousal to noise has lingered on. But, and you can see that this would tax the rational mind, not only does the rocket strike before the noise can be heard—Slothrop strikes before the rocket falls. So what kind of weird precognition is going on here, with the response preceding the stimulus? It is indeed a world of odd reversals. I won't attempt any further plot summary, but one of the poignant aspects of Slothrop's "progress" is that as he gets sucked into the loveless spaces of the Zone, he himself suffers a loss of emotion, a "numbness," and a growing sense that he will never "get back." Along with this erosion of the capacity to feel, he begins to "scatter"; his "sense of Now," or "temporal bandwidth," gets narrower and narrower, and there is a feeling that he is so lost and isolated and utterly unconnected that he is vaporizing out of time altogether. Near the end of his travels, Slothrop suddenly sees a rainbow, a real one, and he has a vision of it entering into sexual union with the green unpapered earth; it is the life-giving antithesis to the rocket's annihilating penetration—"and he stands crying, not a thing in his head, just feeling natural. ..." After that, he effectively vanishes. There is a story told about him. He "was sent into the Zone to be present at his own assembly—perhaps heavily paranoid voices have whispered *his time's assembly*—and there ought to be a punch line to it, but there isn't. The plan went wrong. He is being broken down instead, and scattered." The disassembling of Tyrone Slothrop may read like a comic-strip story crossed with a spy-thriller. But it has worrying implications and suggests disturbing parallels. The last comment on the possible whereabouts of Slothrop is this: "we would expect to look among the Humility, among the gray and preterite souls, to look for him adrift in the hostile light of the sky, the darkness of the sea. ..." This idea of the "preterite," as Pynchon uses it, refers to those who have been "passed over," the abandoned, the neglected, the despised and the rejected; those for whom the System has no use, the human junk thrown overboard from the ship of state (a literal ship in this book, incidentally, named *Anubis* after the ancient Egyptian god of the dead).

Set against the Preterite are the Elite, the users and manipulators, those who regard the planet as existing solely for their satisfaction, the nameless and ubiquitous "They" who dominate the world of the book. It is one of the modern malaises which Pynchon has diagnosed that it is possible for a person to feel himself entering into a state of "preterition." But the idea of humanity being divided into a Preterite and an Elite or Elect is of course a basic Puritan belief. In theological terms, the Preterite were precisely those who were not elected by God; and, if I may quote from one of those chilling Puritan pronouncements, "the preterite are damned because they were never meant to be saved." In redeploying these terms, which after all were central to the thinking of the people who founded America, and applying them to a cruel division which is at work throughout the world today, Pynchon shows once again how imaginatively he can bring the past and present together with startling impact.

One of Slothrop's ancestors wrote a book called *On Preterition*, supporting the Preterite as being quite as important as the Elect, and Slothrop himself wonders whether this doesn't point to a fork in the road which America never took and whether there might not be a "way back" even in the ruined spaces of post-war Europe? Is there a way back? Out of the streets "now indifferently gray with commerce"; out of the City of Pain, which Pynchon has taken over from Rilke as a reflection of the world we have made? Is there a way out of the cinemas, the laboratories, the asylums and all our architecture of mentally drugging coercion and disarray? Is there a way back out of a world in which emotions have been transferred from people to things and images supplant realities? Of course the book offers no answers, though it holds out the possibility of a "counterforce." It moves to a climax which is deliberately a sort of terminal fusion of many of the key fantasies and obsessions in the book. The opening page evokes the evacuation of London during the war, with the crucial comment—"but it's all theatre." On the last page we are suddenly back in a theatre. We're waiting for the show to start—as Pynchon comments we've "always been at the movies (haven't we?)." The film has broken down, though on the darkening screen there is something else— "a film we have not learned to see." The audience is invited to sing; while outside a rocket "reaches its last unmeasurable gap over the roof of the old theatre." It is falling in absolute silence and we know that it will demolish the theatre—the old theatre of our civilization. But we don't see it because we are in the theatre trying to read the film behind the film; and we won't hear it because, under the new dispensation, the annihilation arrives first, and only after—"a screaming comes across the sky."

A Matter of Gravity

by F. S. Schwarzbach

Thomas Pynchon's work remains relatively unknown in England, despite his canonisation in America as that country's most important living novelist. The English editions of his first two novels, *V.* and *The Crying of Lot 49,* have usually been out of print. His last book, *Gravity's Rainbow,* was widely reviewed here, but met with a bewildered and generally negative critical reception, and its sales have hardly been exceptional. Whatever reputation Pynchon now has in England seems to have arisen by word of mouth.

In America, by contrast, even in the birthplace of instant fame and the home of the super-superlative, the reception that met *Gravity's Rainbow* must mark it as the most critically acclaimed novel of all time. It was reviewed with reverential deference in hundreds of magazines and newspapers, ranging from *Yale Review* to *Mademoiselle;* it shared the National Book Award for 1973; and was denied a Pulitzer Prize at the last moment on the grounds of "incomprehensibility and obscenity," which must have been received as almost a greater compliment than the prize itself. Despite its length and (then) high cover price, the book became a bestseller, at least by the standards for "serious" fiction.

Pynchon's impressive sales figures are matched by an equally impressive Pynchon industry in the American academic world. The periodical notices were clearly on the right track when they compared him to Melville. Nabokov and Faulkner. One reviewer mentioned *Ulysses* and *Moby Dick,* but thought *GR* better than both. The year before *GR* appeared, a bibliography of Pynchon studies listed no fewer than seventy academic works devoted

"A Matter of Gravity," by F. S. Schwarzbach. From *The New Review,* 3 (June 1976), 39-42. Reprinted with revisions, and a new title, by permission of the author. The reply by Jonathan Rosenbaum, from *The New Review,* 3 (July 1976), 64, is reprinted by permission of the author.

wholly or in part to Pynchon's first two novels, but the work since inspired by *GR* easily dwarfs all that. There are also three Pynchon Ph.D. dissertations in progress, and two full-length books already in print.

Why is it that Pynchon is so highly praised in America but not in England? There are a number of possible explanations. For one thing, national literary pride runs deep here, and it cannot be denied that there is something very definitely and perhaps off-puttingly American about his work. It has a jerky narrative style, colloquial tone and off-key black humour that is first nature to American readers weaned on the work of Heller, Vonnegut, Barth and Science Fiction writers, but is still new to many English readers. Yet, despite indifferent reviews, poor publicity, and initially dismal sales, more English readers are discovering Pynchon—over 15,000 paperbound copies of *Gravity's Rainbow* have been bought in the past year. Clearly he does deserve more public attention than he has received up to now.

Who *is* Thomas Pynchon? Pynchon is a recluse, and a very successful one, who has courted obscurity as assiduously as most authors court the limelight. It is not even possible to describe him—he has not been photographed since the 1950s. It is not even possible to say where he lives....

[Quite early on, around the time of the publication of *V.*,] Thomas Pynchon, private person, disappears from public sight, and except perhaps in disguise he has never appeared in it again. But Thomas Pynchon, great writer, had been born. *V.* won the William Faulkner First Novel Award for 1963; another story, "The Secret Integration," was featured in *The Saturday Evening Post* in 1964; after two chapters had appeared in magazines, *The Crying of Lot 49* was published in early 1966, winning yet another important award from the National Institute of Arts and Letters; and late that summer, Pynchon wrote an article on the black Watts slum district of Los Angeles for *The New York Times Magazine*. This was Pynchon's last appearance in print until the publication of *GR* in 1973.

From his very earliest work, Pynchon's apparently encyclopedic knowledge, verbal ingenuity, and particular obsessions are apparent. Certain themes and subjects recur constantly: song, sexual perversion, suicide, science, slapstick, sewers, shit and Southwest Africa are some of them. Pynchon's fictional people are also distinctive from the very beginning of his career. There seem always to be two basic types of characters, those questing after some profound mystery, and those poor suckers who unwittingly are caught up in someone else's mad quest. Isolation and ignorance are the ground rules of the human condition in a bleak and unpredictable world. There is Pynchon's humour too, and Pynchon is a master of every variety from slapstick to parody, all of it based on the theory that no laugh, no matter how cheap, is ever worth passing by.

Pynchon's early stories are competent, workmanlike efforts, formally more conventional than one might expect. They are flawed by an overload of literary allusions, with those to T. S. Eliot, Conrad, Henry Adams and Shakespeare the most frequent. They suffer, too, from being a little too neat, with every strand so carefully tied that the stories exhaust themselves in their unfolding. What they do reveal is Pynchon even at the start of his career employing his most characteristic technique, the use of material from disciplines other than literature as fictional metaphor. In "Mortality and Mercy in Vienna" (the title is a quotation from *Measure for Measure*), Pynchon chooses an obscure bit of knowledge about a North American Indian tribe and tries hard to make it serve as a metaphor to describe our destructive culture. "Entropy," a more successful story, adapts the concept of entropy from thermodynamics. It is a corollary of the law of the conservation of energy which has been used to predict the eventual heat-death of the universe. He plays with the idea of a kind of societal heat-death, predicting the exhaustion of the interchange of human energy, seeing the world as being already in the throes of final collapse. This world in which communication and movement are almost impossible forms the background of Pynchon's early fiction.

Pynchon has continued to use cognitive models from discourses other than literature, like ethnology or sociology, but especially science, as fictional metaphors. *V.*, for example, carries on Pynchon's extension of the notion of entropy, but it contains a great deal more besides. In fact, like most first novels, it deals with far too much. It is several novels under one roof: a New York novel (obligatory for American authors), a Navy novel, an undergraduate novel, a war novel and an historical novel. Through all the overwriting, however, Pynchon's considerable talent is clearly visible. His creation of V, a magnificently decadent woman who moves in and out of the major events of recent European history (and who may be Henry Adams's "Virgin"), is a really traditional novelistic symbol which Pynchon uses to organize the book's loose structure. As V grows older, she replaces more and more of her body with prosthetic devices, until she is almost entirely a mechanical thing, perhaps like modern European society itself. Chiefly through her experiences, Pynchon explores the idea that modern culture is obsessed by the sexual love of death. (This idea, inadequately but tantalisingly adumbrated in *V.*, and several of its characters, will reappear in *GR.*)

The Crying of Lot 49, Pynchon's second novel, surprised his growing cult audience by being as tight and restrained as *V.* is diffuse and self-indulgent. Even so, it manages to include, among other diversions, a running parody of Jacobean tragedy that must be one of the funniest pastiches ever written. The novel's theme is paranoia, and it narrates the discovery by the heroine, Oedipa Maas, of a plot to take over the world existing not only in the present, but throughout the historical past as far back as the Renaissance. Pynchon was on to something: long before Watergate was even a twinkle in CREEP's eye, he had tagged paranoia as the American national disease. *Lot 49* is also a book about the way American society has become an information machine, in which communications are manufactured and propagated faster than they can be absorbed. Under this incessant pressure, the brain reels, circuits overload, and we become oblivious to *all* communication. Communication, in fact, ceases. In this situation, paranoia is not a disease but the only sane response possible. Paranoids sift the endless number of signs bombarding us, and use them to create structures of meaning. They re-interpret empty data into complete, coherent systems. Paranoids are therefore not only creative, they are the true heroes of our time. We abdicate in the face of overwhelming odds—they fight back.

Lot 49 ends—or rather doesn't end—leaving us stranded, coyly refusing to say if there is or isn't a worldwide Plot behind the novel's plot. There is no such ambiguity in *GR*. The hero, American Lt. Tyrone Slothrop, is unabashedly paranoid, and with good reason. An unknown "They" seems to have programmed Slothrop's life. As an infant, he was the subject of a mysterious behavioural psychology experiment run by a Laszlo Jamf, which sensitised his penis to some unknown stimulus. When the novel opens in London during the rocket blitz of Autumn 1944, British Intelligence has discovered an amazing fact about Slothrop: the man is something of a Don Juan and keeps a map of London pinpointing his scores, and believe it or not his scores match V-2 rocket hits. It seems Slothrop is using his penis as a dowsing rod for rockets, but locates them *before* the event. Oddly enough, this parallels the fact that rocket explosions also come *before* the noise of the explosions—if you can hear them, you're still alive.

Is there a connection? "They" decide to find out, and let Slothrop run loose in Europe, first in Southern France, and then, after VE Day, in Occupied Germany, in the hopes he will lead them to some important rocket secret. But, we learn, the rocket secret is a secret rocket, bearing the S-Gerät, a V-2 with the serial number 00000 that the British, the Americans, the Russians, and the Schwarzkommando (a shadowy group of black African rocket troops) are all after. Slothrop, in the course of his mock heroic quest for the modern San' Grail, begins to figure out that somebody somewhere is watching him, not only watching, but organizing events, meetings, messages, all for his benefit. And at every stage of the search, up pops the name of Laszlo Jamf, who, it appears, was an organic chemist in Germany before the war, and invented the world's first erectile plastic, Impolex-G, which was part of the S-Gerät; which plastic was manufactured by I. G. Farben, part of a fledgling multinational corporation which like ITT was building weapons systems simultaneously in all belligerent countries during the war. Perhaps "They" even staged the whole war just for Slothrop....

Well, as even this rather cursory summary of the plot of *GR* shows, the labyrinthine complications of the story are virtually impossible to understand, often even to follow. *V.* was considered absurdly complex, but compared to *GR* (which might well be called "V-2") it is crystalline in its clarity. Sooner or later, one must ask what the point of all this nonsense is.

Of course, it is possible to take it at face value, as I'm sure it has been taken by many: there is a "They" out there, running everything, Pynchon has done us all a service in exposing it. There is a Plot, and we can take even scraps of garbage, like Slothrop does, and "make it all fit," into some great pattern of meaning. Paranoia *is* infectious, and as the novel wears on, even the supercilious detachment of the narrator begins to falter, and he too becomes seduced by the idea of a System which explains everything. The strangest things begin to communicate toward the end of the novel: one character can actually "read" shivers. A talking light bulb gets in on the act as well, Byron the megalomaniac light bulb who has a plot of his own to defeat the international electric power company conspiracy and take over the world. His history is, in fact, a running parody of Slothrop's adventures.

"The Story of Byron the Bulb" makes it virtually impossible to believe that Pynchon intends us to see paranoia as panacea. It is certainly heroic to be paranoid, to face the world of senseless chaos and attempt to impose order and meaning on it. By that definition, all novelists are paranoids, too, and that may explain Pynchon's sympathy for paranoids. But they are doomed to fail. Slothrop, paranoid *extraordinaire,* achieves nothing in his quest. The point is, by paying attention only to details we lose sight of the forces behind them. Cause and effect is not an inherent quality of events, but rather something we invent. There is no "They" behind everything, simply "Us": the cultural forces that determine our lives have been programmed into us just as effectively as Slothrop had been programmed as an infant. And what is worse is that the driving cultural force that has been programmed into us by our culture is that same old lust for death—we have been trained to love destroying ourselves.

Pynchon's belief is that the explanation for this mass death wish is essentially historical, and much of the novel is an effort of historical analysis, finding the roots of the malaise in our distant past. (It is in large part the historical nature of its subject-matter which makes *GR* such a difficult book to read.) He writes about the death instinct:

> It was something we had to work on, historically and personally. To build from scratch up to its present status as reaction, nearly as strong as life. ...

It should be said that this is hardly an original insight, and that Freud and Norman O. Brown, both of whose work Pynchon knows well, have said much the same thing long ago. Pynchon's originality is to be found rather in the way he shows this instinct in operation, and in the way he postulates it came into being. And, paradoxically, he locates the original evil in that most understandable and most noble of human urges, the desire to make sense of the world around us.

There is a vision in the novel of what Europe had been like before the dawn of modern history, as it had appeared to the invading Vikings. It was an open, fertile and virgin wilderness, but one which was apprehended then (and in all subsequent history) as threatening chaos and disorder, rather than as peaceful tranquillity. This awe-inspiring and unstructured void is something man cannot bear, and so he attempts to rationalise it, to remake the outside world in the image of the inside, mental world.

Throughout later history, Pynchon identifies prime villains who have played key roles in this process of rationalising the world: the Calvinists are Pynchon's chief bad guys, because they developed the capitalist ethic, the urge to transform the world physically, as well as imaginatively. It was Slothrop's Calvinist Puritan ancestors who confronted the virgin wilderness of America, and remade it in their absolutist image. This transition, to use Weber's terminology, from *Gemeinschaft* to *Gesellschaft*, happens throughout modern history, and becomes truly global as Europeans colonize the entire world. An Argentine refugee muses about his country, aptly summing up the process:

> We are obsessed with building labyrinths, where before there was open plain and sky—we cannot abide that openness: it is terror to us.

But once created, those labyrinths tend to take on lives of their own, and our tools begin to use us. Many characters in the novel demonstrate this on a personal level, like the Pavlovian Pointsman, who manipulates Slothrop, or the SS Captain, Blicero, who launches the S-Gerät. Both initiate schemes they believe will allow them to control their own and others' destinies, but they lose control and, like Frankenstein, are left at the mercy of their monsters. Perhaps, Pynchon intimates, the cultural forces which we have ourselves set in motion may now also be out of control, irreversible like the descent of a rocket: once launched, it cannot be prevented. Furthermore, this process of rationalisation is seen as a movement toward death because its ultimate goal is the reification of humankind: the only permanent way to ensure the perfect order this impulse demands is to make men into things, inanimate dead objects.

Unconsciously we sense this, and find it too terrifying, so we respond with secret dreams of escape, constructing utopias in which we can transcend inevitable death. Dozens of characters in the novel have such fantasies of personal or collective escape; indeed, there are few characters who do not. The leader of the Schwarzkommando, Enzian, plans a utopian future for his people:

> What Enzian wants to create will have no history. It will never
> need a design change. Time, as time is known to the other nations,
> will wither away inside this new one. ... The people will find the
> centre again, the centre without time, the journey...where every
> departure is a return to the same old place, the only place. ...

This is typical of all these dreams, in that it expresses a desire for
absolute stillness and timelessness. "To perfect methods of immobility is every paranoid's wish," Pynchon writes. Life moves,
and in our world it moves only toward death. Stillness is the only
way to prevent it.

What this is, in fact, is a recreation of the original condition
of the world, the void before the imposition of order. It is a myth
of prelapsarian innocence. The irony, and it is truly a cosmic
one, is that stasis is also death, merely in another form. Life is
process—only a corpse, the body reduced to a thing, can be still.
So even our innermost fantasies of transcendence have also been
programmed to impel us toward self-destruction.

Yet, being human, we go on trying to find a way out. Captain
Blicero (who appears as Lt. Weissman in *V.*) is the most adven-
turous of *GR*'s questors after transcendence: "I want to break out,"
he says, "to leave this cycle of infection and death." For this reason, he assembles and launches the rocket with the S-Gerät. The
rocket, possessor of Weberian charisma, is really the perfect
symbol to organize these many themes: it is, first of all, a force
that can at least for a time overcome gravity, the "law" which has
always dragged men down to earth from their visions of escape.
It also breaks the barrier of sound, cracking not only through the
apparent ultimate limit of speed, but also through the interface
between cause and effect—you hear it only after it has been. It
also achieves perfect stasis, for at its apogee it is absolutely motionless in its vertical path, yet in a state of almost infinite potentiality.
And it is also the most destructive weapon our death culture has
yet created, which when wedded to the atomic bomb will make
our dream of total destruction reality. Weissman/Blicero (whiteman's-death) realizes this capability of the rocket, and satisfies
his sexual lust for death by firing the S-Gerät due north into the
total whiteness of the Arctic wastes—symbolic in our innermost
minds as the final escape from the blackness of the tomb.

But, like the rest of us, Blicero has been conned. The cargo of
the S-Gerät is Blicero's lover, a young man who has been told by
Blicero to expect a vision announcing that "he will never die,"

that he has transcended death by escaping gravity; instead he sees "a bright angel of death." He dies after all. Our like dreams of returning to the absolute stillness, perfect openness and total light of the timeless void, similarly lead only to annihilation.

In a section of *V.* set in the Southwest African desert in 1922, Weissman had puzzled over the meaning of some mysterious radio transmissions. Eventually, he decodes a message: "The world is all that is the case." (It is a quotation from Wittgenstein.) It might with equal justice have served as the "Message" of *GR.*

Is there any way out of this routine of endless death and the glorification of destruction? Can we avoid the apocalypse? These are questions we are entitled to demand that Pynchon consider. And throughout his work, the answer has always been a very qualified "maybe." Pynchon never allows his protagonists to succeed: Stencil and Profane in *V.* both fail, one in his quest, the other in life, and Oedipa's fate is left in doubt in *Lot 49.* But in *GR,* the case is more complicated, even though Slothrop fails, too.

It may help to look first at the opposition camp—Calvinists, Puritans, Pavlovians, businessmen, generals, Marxists, and Nazis. What they all share is a common approach to experience and life which sees in every case, no matter what the case, only two possibilities. For them it is always a situation of yes or no, zero or one, perfect certainty or perfect impossibility, all or nothing. Pynchon suggests that between the absolute extremes there are opportunities for those who see and make up the excluded middle, who have learned to compromise, and who know that at certain times anything can happen. Such times existed, in America in the seventeenth century, or in Germany after the war. Those, we know, were opportunities lost, "the fork in the road (we) never took." But this does not mean we will not have the chance again, personally and collectively. One of Slothrop's adventurers demonstrates how such an opportunity might be seized.

In Germany Slothrop briefly meets a boy named Ludwig, who has run away from home to find his pet lemming, Ursula, fearing she's left him to commit suicide. He finds her a few hundred pages later, but to keep the two of them alive he has had to become a prostitute for American servicemen: suffering, in Pynchon's carefully chosen phrase, "a fate worse than death." In Pynchon's world, we are all lemmings, racing to mass suicide. If we are to survive, like Ludwig, we must abandon our integrity and compromise ourselves, not in an act of transcendent escape, but of transcendent kindness. Accepting life in all its degradation, remaining fallible, mortal, and above all humane, is the "answer" to that original question — "To expect any more, or less," we are warned, "is to disagree with the terms of Creation." That Ludwig's story is extremely funny should not mislead us as to its importance. Pynchon's humour often masks serious intent: he seems compelled to "hide" himself in his fiction as he does in his life.

This theme of degradation is a major one in *GR,* and is linked to white man's fear of death, blackness, and excrement. In Pynchon's world, the deepest white fear is of being buggered by a black. Yet, it is waste matter, accumulating all around us deep beneath the earth, that offers us the possibility of regaining contact with life. Pynchon scatters a few hints for us: Herero women in Southwest Africa, we learn, are buried to the neck in the earth to cure sterility; Walter Rathenau, the industrialist who returns in the novel as a spirit, tells his listeners at a seance about how waste and excrement are compounded into coal in the depths of the earth; gravity not only pulls us down but pulls waste toward the centre of the earth, and is also the vital force which makes the very stuff of the planet adhere, and not fly apart in random disorder.

Of course, moving closer to fertile waste does not guarantee fertility. If we wallow in shit, like the coprophiliac General Pudding, for self-gratification alone, nothing is achieved. (Note that the first title of the novel was *Mindless Pleasures.*) But when it is done, as Ludwig demonstrates, out of love, selfless surrender on behalf of another, then life itself may be the result.

This theme of degradation is also crucial to another matter, the problem of Pynchon's language. It has always been idiosyncratic, and as long ago as 1963, reviewing *V.* in *The New Statesman,* Christopher Ricks pinpointed the question of Pynchon's tone, in other words, his attitude toward his own language, as the central one for an English reader. For example, was his American slang dead cliché or "freshly imaginative," Ricks wondered. And, I suspect, this is not a difficulty for English readers alone; Pynchon's language *is* difficult, and would be perceived as difficult by a reader of any nationality, American or otherwise. What may be of more moment is the resistance to this difficulty.

To allow oneself to be put off by this difficulty is in effect to state that one is not willing to work to read a novel. And to do this is to lose sight of the meaning embedded in the name of the form

—*novelty*. Novels, or at least the very best of them, have always been written in an attempt to say something new by making the language new. Novelists strive to make the word into the Word, and the text into the Text. There is something about this process which can and indeed should not make for easy reading, because it demands that the reader contribute actively to the reading experience, by following on his own the same paths the author has taken. Perhaps because of this there has always been an aliterary quality about the best novels too, requiring that one move from the word outward to the world, and henceforth experience it anew, with one's perceptions of it permanently altered. It is precisely this kind of effort in which Pynchon is engaged in *GR:* perhaps, then, the comparison with Joyce, or for that matter with another more explicitly social novelist, Dickens, would not be all that far-fetched.

It is in a kind of verbal waste and degradation, in popular song, advertising, slang and obscenity, that Pynchon finds the crucial linguistic energy for this enterprise. Here again, an important pointer is buried in a hilarious incident, when a German racketeer asks Slothrop to explain the American idiom "ass backwards." The German, typically, applies the powers of logic, those same rational powers that have been responsible for ruining our civilization throughout history. He reasons that if it means doing something backwards, since ass-forward is already backwards, why isn't the idiom "ass forwards?" The answer is simply that it isn't: language is a source of energy which will not be rationalised, which insists on the free and undelimited play of human creativity. Only that can create an idiom; and by implication, only that can create a novel as ingenious and inventive as *GR*.

At its very end, *GR* shifts dramatically from Germany in 1946 to Los Angeles (for Pynchon *the* modern conurbation) at the present moment. Suddenly, Pynchon draws us directly into the novel, and we find ourselves sitting in a movie theatre (the theatre of war, one wonders?) watching a film, which is perhaps the book itself.... But now the film has broken, or the power is shut off. The show is over. Overhead, the noise of a rocket, perhaps a nuclear rocket, is heard. A song starts, and after the first chorus we are invited to join in. And with that invitation, "Now everybody—," the novel ends.

This, I believe, is meant to make us realize that we are now in another opportune historical moment, when there are still choices

to be made; and the decision whether or not to make them is
wholly our own. But Pynchon will not be drawn into optimism.
It may be that already it is too late and that our lethal technology
has gone beyond control and is — like the descent of a rocket—
irreversible.

Jonathan Rosenbaum: A Reply

"Why is it that Pynchon is so highly praised in America but
not in England?" F. S. Schwarzbach asks,...adding, "There are
a number of possible explanations." As a London-based American
writer and *Gravity's Rainbow* enthusiast—a laboratory speci-
men, if one is needed—may I suggest that his entire treatment of
Pynchon, insofar as it seems characteristic of much literary
journalism in this country, inadvertently provides an explanation
of its own?

By attempting to reduce a very complex novel to the level of
plot and themes alone—and to limit "meaning" to a set of socio-
logical, political or strictly moral adages to be extracted or in-
tuited from the text—he bypasses so many crucial aspects that he
winds up with a virtually one-eyed appraisal. It is entirely symptomatic of his approach that he can state that the book's hero
Tyrone Slothrop "is unabashedly paranoid, and with good reason,"
a pure contradiction in terms that cleanly divorces Pynchon's evo-
cations of a "worldwide Plot" from the *formal* issue of Pynchon's
own plot-making when it is impossible to establish the former
without the latter. The facts that Slothrop literally disappears
from the narrative well before the book's end and that the whole
notion of a consistent, consecutive plot gradually collapses are so
inimical to Mr. Schwarzbach's mode of analysis that he simply
ignores them, brutally distorting and simplifying the novel in
the process.

To belabour the obvious, Pynchon's concern is not only with
"paranoia" (the myth that "everything is connected") but equally
with what he himself terms "anti-paranoia, where nothing is connected to anything," a vision of chaos that is no less important; to
omit this dialectic, which dictates his entire structure, is to overlook the work itself. For critics habituated to regarding prose as
a transparent medium rather than an artificial construction, a
sizable portion of the novel will undoubtedly remain incompre-

hensible, and Pynchon's efforts to deconstruct and expose his own artifices will continue to be glossed over or dismissed as an ironic subtext at best. But the lesson offered by such an anti-formalist bias is clear: attack a twentieth-century text with a nineteenth-century perspective and you will come up with a warped, old-fashioned reflection of a modern artifact—fiction reduced to the level of pseudo-fact. If this is the *Gravity's Rainbow* that Mr. Schwarzbach wants, he is welcome to it.

"Entropy" and Other Calamities

by Joseph W. Slade

Although Pynchon's reputation thus far rests principally on his three novels, he has also published six short stories in magazines. In chronological order they are: "The Small Rain," in the undergraduate magazine *Cornell Writer* (1959); "Mortality and Mercy in Vienna," *Epoch* (1959); "Low-lands," *New World Writing* (1960); "Entropy," *The Kenyon Review* (1960); "Under the Rose," *The Noble Savage* (1961); and "The Secret Integration," *The Saturday Evening Post* (1964). In addition, he has written an essay entitled "A Journey into the Mind of Watts," *The New York Times Magazine* (1966). "Under the Rose" is an early version of the third chapter of *V.*, and will not be considered here. (Nor will I do more than mention the two excerpts from *The Crying of Lot 49* which appeared in *Esquire* and *Cavalier;* these were probably placed by Pynchon's agent.) The remaining short stories are of interest as early examples of Pynchon's work, because they manifest themes and characters which appear later in his novels, and because they are interesting in themselves.

"The Small Rain," Pynchon's first story, is his most conventional, the product of an undergraduate perhaps drawing on his military experience. Yet it introduces a character type and a theme that will become constants in Pynchon's fiction: a potential "redeemer" who fails to rejuvenate a waste land because, like the paranoids of *Gravity's Rainbow*, he wants "to perfect methods of immobility." Immobility in Pynchon's world is the schlemiel's defense against entropy, the paranoid's means of copying with randomness, the decadent's denial of motion; it is, finally, the romantic's false notion of transcendence, the stillness at the apo-

"'Entropy' and Other Calamities." A revised and abridged version of Chapter I of *Thomas Pynchon*, by Joseph W. Slade (New York: Warner Paperback Library, 1974), pp. 19-47. Copyright 1974 by Joseph W. Slade. The present rewritten version was prepared for this collection by the author, and is printed by his permission and the permission of the publisher.

gee of a rocket's parabola. The comic, passive figure in "The Small Rain" is Nathan "Lardass" Levine, a pudgy graduate of CCNY gone deliberately to seed as an army recruit at Ft. Roach, Louisiana, partly as a protest against the phoniness of intellectuality. In contrast to most of his buddies, Levine enjoys the torpid mindlessness of army routine, which relieves him of responsibility; he has almost decided to re-enlist. While cultivating his "Sgt. Bilko" pose and reading pornographic novels, notably one called *Swamp Wench,* Levine is temporarily jostled from inertia by a hurricane that has devastated the bayou country of southern Louisiana. His communications unit is ordered into rescue operations with the National Guard.

From the college campus where the army sets up headquarters, Levine surveys a literal waste land whose metaphoric value is underscored by Pynchon's references to T. S. Eliot. Levine is the symbolic redeemer come to the swamps that now contain sterility and death. Whenever he appears someone exclaims "Jesus Christ!" A communications expert, Levine dreams of all humanity on "a closed circuit," much as Mucho Maas in *Lot 49* envisions multitudes joined in a "rich, chocolaty goodness." "A closed circuit," Levine says. "Everybody on the same frequency. And after a while you forget about the rest of the spectrum and start believing that this is the only frequency that counts or is real." His is a longing for human community without the diversity that would make the community human, and it attests to his incompetence as a healer. The July sun beats down on the swamp, but Levine is a "seed that casts himself on stony places, with no deepness of earth." He helps pick up corpses, tries to succor, and thinks of life-giving rain, but lacks fertility himself: he is a "Wandering Jew" without "identity" or potency. Even in what should be an oasis in this figurative desert, the college campus, there is no potential for salvation, only the trivial intellectuality Levine despises. Here Levine meets and sleeps with a coed who calls herself Little Buttercup and who has no "capacity to give." Having been conditioned by pornographic novels to regard women as objects, Levine can offer this "swamp wench" neither fertility, love, nor involvement; their union ends in statis. In what is his first statement about modern society's sexual love of death, Pynchon has Levine remark after intercourse, "In the midst of great death...the little death."

As the troops pull out to return to Ft. Roach, it begins to rain at last, yet the water seems to hold no more promise for the waste land than Levine. "Jesus Christ I hate rain," he says, "Funny ain't it," replies a buddy, "T. S. Eliot likes rain." Although "The Small Rain" does not explore, as Pynchon will explore later, the cultural forces that oppress the modern world, its theme is clear: Man has lost the capacity to revivify his landscape. Given the limitations of Pynchon's early methods, chiefly the near-audible clicks of motifs falling neatly into place, the story is fine and workmanlike. If it is a trifle superficial and a bit too sluggishly paced, Pynchon will earn, in his later fiction, to add historical dimension and to animate his plots with the excitement of lunatic quests.

In "Mortality and Mercy in Vienna," Pynchon alludes again to Eliot—and to Shakespeare and Conrad as well—so that while the setting, Washington, D.C., becomes a figurative waste land, it can also be thought of as the lawless Vienna of *Measure for Measure* or as the chaotic jungle of "Heart of Darkness." To a party in Washington comes another redeemer, Cleanth Siegel, a young diplomat recently returned from Europe. Part Catholic, part Jewish (an amalgam that will recur in Benny Profane of *V.*), Siegel's divided nature has apparently unbalanced him and caused him to equate healing with destruction. The party-giver, a strange Rumanian named Lupescu, startled by his *Doppelgänger*-resemblance to Siegel, deputizes the latter as his host and abandons the party to him with these instructions: "As host you are a trinity: (a) receiver of guests '—ticking them off on his fingers—' (b) an enemy and (c) an outward manifestation, for *them,* of the divine body and blood.' "

Lupescu designates Siegel a "fisher of souls." Cleanth soon learns that he shares more than a physical resemblance to the departed Rumanian. Something in their natures attracts the confidences of others; in the past each has served as confidant and confessor for a "host" (Pynchon plays on the word continually) "of trodden-on and disaffected" inhabitants of the modern waste land. Thus Siegel is not surprised when one by one the party guests tell him of his similarity to Lupescu and corner him in the Rumanian's "confessional," a bedroom decorated with crossed Browning Automatic Rifles on the wall. This mock priest hears confessions of decadent love affairs and emotional entanglements that increase his hysteria and convince him that the waste land is blighted indeed.

The instrument of healing turns out to be Irving Loon, an

Ojibwa Indian himself on the verge of hysteria. When Siegel sees the Indian standing in the apartment like a "memento mori," he recalls from his computer-like memory banks a Harvard anthropology professor for whom "all cultures were equally mad." According to the professor, the Ojibwa live so perpetually on the brink of starvation that the Indian brave succumbs to paranoia, convinced that the forces of nature are arrayed against him. The paranoia culminates in a peculiar psychosis, a personal identification with the "Windigo," a destructive, cannibalistic spirit. Once he believes himself to be the Windigo, the starvation-prone Ojibwa comes to regard even friends and relatives as "hosts" to be killed and eaten.

By whispering "Windigo" in Irving Loon's ear, Siegel triggers an irreversible chain of events which will lead to "a very tangible salvation" for the party guests: "A miracle involving a host, true, but like no holy eucharist." At his point the allusions to Eliot and Conrad begin to swell. Eliot's waste land requires the imposition of a new mythology, a new religion, before it can be cleansed and healed of its sterility. Ironically, the machine-like Siegel perceives in Irving Loon's primitive paranoia just the kind of healing the waste land needs. It will be a religion of retribution, of apocalypse—a destruction after the manner of Conrad's Kurtz, who wants to exterminate all the brutes. The miracle *was* in his hands after all, Siegel's Jesuit side says to him: "It was just unfortunate that Irving Loon would be the only one partaking of any body and blood, divine or otherwise." Spurred by Siegel and seen only by him, the Ojibwa takes a rifle down from the wall of Lupescu's bedroom and searches happily for ammunition. Siegel leaves the party without saying anything to the other guests, and hears the first reports of Irving Loon's celebration of the host from the street outside. By loosing the berserk Indian, he has acted as prophet and healer to the waste land; he has healed its sickness by annihilation.

Pynchon possesses the enviable ability to blend fact and fantasy in such a way that the facts seem less credible than the fantasies. The Windigo psychosis is well documented by anthropologists but appears more preposterous than Lupescu's leaving his party to a stranger or hanging BAR's on his walls. As Pynchon becomes more adept at incorporating his wide knowledge into his stories, the line separating the real and the ridiculous will grow thinner. Of continuing relevance also are several of the motifs of "Mortality and Mercy in Vienna." The weightiest is paranoia, which for Pynchon, as for many of his contemporaries, is a means of perception, a way of restructuring the world. While Irving Loon is probably the most extreme, other paranoids in Pynchon's fiction seem almost reasonable. In an insane world, call it waste land or whatever, paranoia represents an attempt to establish sanity, to create order out of chaos. To believe, however wrongly, that the world is hostile is to acquire a basis for action. A second motif is an assumed moral superiority of "primitive" cultures over the decadent, "civilized" type. Superseding the Ojibwas in later stories will be Maltese and Africans, from cultures which have been abused by colonialism but which still retain vitality. A third motif is a human penchant for annihilation as an alternative to a blighted world. Like Conrad's Kurtz, Cleanth Siegel suffers from a void within, made unbearable by the perception of a void without; Siegel and his successors in Pynchon's work cannot tolerate such a vacuum.

Still another redeemer appears in Pynchon's third story, "Low-lands," an explicit parody of *The Waste Land*. Dennis Flange, the protagonist, resembles both Lardass Levine of "The Small Rain" and Benny Profane of *V.*; more accurately, he is the prototype for Roony Winsome and Mucho Maas, the disaffected husbands of *V.* and *The Crying of Lot 49*. Another figure, Geronimo Diaz, a mad psychiatrist, prefigures the zany shrinks of the novels. "Low-lands" also marks the debut of Pig Bodine, the ubiquitous all-round pervert and good-natured if slightly sinister slob that his name suggests. And for the first time Pynchon makes use of what will become virtually a trademark: underground passages. Throughout his work tunnels serve as psychological and metaphysical arcs, as negative parabolas that will have positive counterparts in the flights of the V-2 in *Gravity's Rainbow*.

In "Low-lands," Dennis Flange's marriage is going sour. Behind the failure is his passivity. Since his days in the Navy he has retreated almost to a fetal state in his womb-like house on Long Island, in order to avoid responsibilities he vaguely associates with the sea. So strong is Flange's affinity with the sea that he cannot even talk about it, believing that

> it is all right to listen to but not to tell stories about that sea, because you and the truth of a true lie were thrown sometime way back into a curious contiguity and as long as you are passive you can remain aware of the truth's extent but the minute you become ac-

tive you are somehow, if not violating a truth outright, at least screwing up the perspective of things, much as anyone observing subatomic particles changes the works, data and odds, by the act of observing.

This invoking of the Heisenberg principle of physics, this refusal or inability to become involved—one of the things he admires about his psychiatrist—is the key to Flange's personality, as it is to those of many of Pynchon's other characters. Flange withdraws from experience. At moments he thinks of the sea as a "low-lands," a term he remembers from a seachantey. Viewed at certain times, the ocean seems "a waste land which stretches away to the horizen," a plain or desert that requires but one human figure "for completeness." Flange has come to think of his life as a flat surface, with "an assurance of perfect, passionless uniformity"; what he fears most is a convexity, a bulging of the planet's curvature that would leave him exposed. This vision of a flat surface, of course, is of a sea without water—in short, Eliot's waste land, arid and sterile. Flange imagines himself walking across this flat, solid sea from city to city. His psychiatrist considers this fantasy "a bizarre variation on the messiah complex," but Diaz is only partly correct. Flange is the traveler of the waste land, a mockery of the protagonist of Eliot's poem, the man who draws the Tarot card of the Phoenician Sailor.

When Flange's wife throws him out and tells him not to come back, he and Bodine fetch up at the city dump, a waste land ruled over, in lieu of Eliot's Fisher King, by a Negro named Bolingbroke (Shakespeare's Henry IV). Flange immediately perceives a predictable correspondence: the dump is a "low-lands," a flat surface slowly rising into convexity as garbage fills it. By the time Pynchon writes *Gravity's Rainbow*, the accretion of debris or detritus will serve as his principal metaphor for the history of civilization. It is a frightening image: the waste land, in this case a literal one, sifting deeper and deeper in accumulated sterility.

After a boozy conversation (in which Pynchon stresses comic parallels with *The Waste Land*), the men fall asleep in Bolingbroke's shack. Some hours later Flange is awakened by a siren voice (Eliot: "voices singing out of empty cisterns and exhausted wells") calling to his sailor image of himself. Outside the shack, before he can see who is calling, he "drowns" under a collapsing pile of snow tires. He is revived by a beautiful gypsy only three and a half feet tall, who leads him to her home in a tunnel complex built in the thirties by the Sons of the Red Apocalypse, the first of Pynchon's cabals, and now populated by gypsies.

The girl's name is Nerissa, which may derive from the Nereids, the nymphs of the sea. Who she really is becomes apparent when she introduces Flange to her pet rat—another prototype, for the rat Veronica of *V.* This rat's name is Hyacinth, and Nerissa is clearly a version of the Hyacinth Girl of the "Burial of the Dead" section of *The Waste Land.* Nerissa wants Flange to be her husband; she had been told by a fortuneteller named Violetta— Eliot's Madame Sosostris—that she would wed an Anglo like him. Flange considers. Noticing that Nerissa looks like a child, and the rat seems like *her* child, he wonders why he and his wife never had children. He decides to stay, because "a child makes it all right." The story ends with Nerissa holding the rat in her arms and with Flange visualizing her in sea images: "White caps danced across her eyes; sea creatures, he knew, would be cruising about in the submarine green of her heart."

Eliot's waste land suffers from failures of communication and love. Similar failures afflict Flange, and the dump, Pynchon's waste land, symbolizes his life. The dump is not, however, a particularly good paradigm for Flange's condition, if only because we know too little about him; but it does represent an amusing and imaginative attempt to unite the motifs of water and waste made so vivid by Eliot's poem. At the conclusion of "Low-lands," Nerissa, who has much in common with the loving females Pynchon will later develop, offers Flange love, admiration for the image he has of himself, and the potentiality of fertility, although the rat, an indication of decay and disease in *The Waste Land,* is here at best a mocking promise. No real healing or redemption seems forthcoming, even if we assume that Flange has symbolically died and risen; he is a miserable messiah. Considering his resemblance to Pynchon's other schlemiels, it is more likely that he has simply exchanged one kind of passivity for another, where, deep underneath the waste land, he is in Eliot's terms, neither "living nor dead." He prefers withdrawal underground to the void, the emptiness above. Flange is inert—paralyzed by surfaces Pynchon will convert into endless streets in his later fiction.

One of Pynchon's admirers, Richard Poirier, has observed that "the signal 'self-destruct' might be said to flash whenever a reader of Pynchon presses too confidently at a point where he thinks he's located the 'meaning.'"[1] While usually the ambiguity adds to appreciation, in "Low-lands" it seems merely the confusion of the author, the product of inexperience infatuated with cleverness in a manner which renders Black Humor frequently too academic. Pynchon himself has Fausto Maijstral remark in *V.* that "Shakespeare and T. S. Eliot ruined us all." If the story is pleasantly nutty, and considerably richer in its imagery than "The Small Rain," "Low-lands" is much less accomplished than "Mortality and Mercy in Vienna." In the latter, Pynchon's literary allusions bear the weight of his ambiguity without effort. In "Low-lands," because he too closely adapts Eliot's motifs, themselves highly complex and ambiguous, the result is fuzziness. Moreover, the story is essentially static; at the end Flange returns full circle to a fetal state, so that the plot does not advance, although it can be argued that from it Pynchon learns to use multiple plots to carry his themes. In any case, elements of "Low-lands" presage motifs and incidents in Pynchon's later works: failures of communication, underground networks, oddballs who enjoy Vivaldi, loving females, images of history, midgets. Considered together, the first three stories exemplify the extremes of response to the waste land of modern civilization: a desire for annihilation, for one's self or for others; and a desire for withdrawal, in order to protect one's self against the waste land's encroachment. Eventually Pynchon will couple similar responses to experience in a binomial pattern of ones and zeros borrowed from the "yes and no" language of computers. Most of his characters will vibrate between fear of incomprehensible, almost lethal motion and a longing for perfect, certain passivity, between the zero of chaos and the one of stasis, either of which leads to death; only the best of them will claim the ground of the excluded middle, the domain of compromise.

Compromise is the theme of "Entropy," Pynchon's fourth and most mature short story. With "Entropy," Henry Adams displaces T. S. Eliot as Pynchon's principal literary creditor, although references to de Sade, Faulkner, and Djuna Barnes crop up as well. If "Low-lands" demonstrates that the saturation of one's work with allusions is tricky business, "Entropy" re-establishes the method as a valid artistic approach. Here Willard Gibbs and Ludwig Boltzman are juxtaposed brilliantly with Henry Adams and Henry Miller. From Miller Pynchon takes a metaphor; "Entropy" begins with an epigraph from *Tropic of Cancer* in which Miller speaks of our age's depressing cultural and metaphysical climate as inclement weather. With this metaphor Pynchon associates a second, from *The Education of Henry Adams*: the concept of entropy as historical process. By updating Willard Gibbs, the physicist whom Adams leaned on, with references to Boltzman and Rudolf Clausius, who also contributed to theories of chemical and physical equilibrium, Pynchon can make use of entropy as a term denoting the unavailability of energy not just thermodynamically but generally; throughout his fiction it is the most pervasive of metaphors.

Clausius predicted that "heat-death" would occur when everything in the universe reached the same temperature, a prophecy Adams and Pynchon extend to human society, which, like the universe, is a system. According to Adams, over history entropy increases; the world is running down. One manifestation of an increase in entropy is mounting chaos within the system as energy begins to disperse more and more randomly. Systems in good repair function in orderly fashion, but as they succumb to entropy, order falls victim to chaos. Somewhat paradoxically, another manifestation of increasing entropy can be greater homogeneity among the system's parts. Healthy systems encompass diverse elements in relationship to each other, but as entropy increases those elements lose their differentiation. Thus it is possible to speak of entropy as a measure of disorganization and unpredictability, and also as a measure of sameness and conformity.

But there are other kinds of systems and another kind of entropy. Complicating Pynchon's story is his introduction of communication theory. Within a communication system, many things can cause information to deteriorate; the effect of distortion and noise, as when two people are speaking on a telephone, can act like friction or conduction on energy within a thermodynamic system. In communication theory, then, entropy can represent loss and decay. It can also be a measure of information, and here the ramifications of the term grow complex. Later, in *The Crying of Lot 49*, Pynchon will explore the abstruse relationship between communication theory and thermodynamics; in "Entropy," the term entropy in communications serves merely as counterpoint to the term as applied to the running down of the universe and society.

"Entropy" is skillfully constructed around the interlocking metaphors of weather and entropy in its double sense. Its structure can be visualized as parallel vectors pointing in opposite directions—tracks that provide compression and tension for the narrative. On one floor of a Washington, D.C., apartment house, Meatball Mulligan's lease-breaking party, now in its second day, has been disintegrating into a chaos steadily augmented by arriving guests. In this respect, the party as a system is not exactly closed, as thermodynamic systems usually are, since people do enter and leave; but Pynchon is probably suggesting that social systems are not entirely isolated: that would seem to be the point, that Meatball does not try to wall himself off from the outside. By contrast, on the floor above a man named Callisto has perfected an ordered existence in a hermetically-sealed, ecologically stable flat at the cost of isolation from the world. In fact, Callisto's apartment is a small-scale jungle, a "hothouse" in which he lives with a girl named Aubade, of French and Annamese ancestry—by which Pynchon may be hinting at exploitation by a technological colonialism. They do not go out, since Callisto fears the outside. He worries about the "heat-death" of the universe, a fixation abetted at the time of the story by the weather. For three days it has been 37 degrees outside; the weather will not change. Paranoiacally, Callisto seizes on the phenomenon as an omen of the end.

The significance of the story's title is amplified in Callisto's ruminations, which Pynchon intersperses with the events of the party below. Outside his room, Callisto believes, a decadent society has reduced people and things from healthy "differentiation to sameness, from ordered individuality to a kind of chaos." Until now Callisto, like the elder Stencil of *V.,* has been a disciple of Machiavelli, whose *The Prince* assumed that human agency *(virtu)* and chance *(fortuna)* governed the human condition in approximately equal proportions, but now the energies of history seem to have gone random. Callisto tries to resist entropy with love, manifested in his affection for a sick bird and for Aubade. It is the first such linkage of love and power in Pynchon's fiction; but, unlike his creator, Callisto does not realize how feeble a power love is, especially when it is coupled with stasis.

While Callisto treads his mental paces, below stairs Meatball Mulligan's party rollicks on. Meatball's guests range from the weird to the aimless, most of them pseudo-intellectuals, most of them employed by the government in some form of communications. Dominating the rest are the Duke di Angelis quartet, a spaced-out group of musicians sporting sunglasses and smoking marijuana—thoroughly decadent. At one point, the four decide to have a session without instruments. No one hears a note, of course, but this absurd exercise is very much a part of Pynchon's theme. By playing without instruments, the quartet try to avoid noise and distortion, to overcome entropy, to communicate on a purely mental level. If the attempt is fruitless, it is no worse than Callisto's experiment in divorcing himself from the world.

Only Meatball himself provides a possible approach to the problem of entropy in both communication and thermodynamics. Another of his guests, Saul, has just parted from his wife over an argument about communication theory. When Meatball does not understand, Saul explains part of the difficulty in terms relevant to Callisto's belief in love:

> Tell a girl: "I love you." No trouble with two-thirds of that, it's a closed circuit. Just you and she. But that nasty four-letter word in the middle, *that's* the one you have to look out for. Ambiguity. Redundance. Irrelevance, even. Leakage. All this is noise. Noise screws up your signal, makes for disorganization in the circuit.

Under Meatball's benign influence, however, Saul finally admits that nobody runs "at top effeciency," and marriages are "sort of founded on compromises." By extrapolation, so is communication and any human effort; one does the best one can to cope with entropy, and love *is* effective so long as it is active.

As the "system" of his party continues to decay, Mulligan does what he can to keep things functioning—not at top efficiency, but through compromise. Saul is dropping waterbags out the window, a girl is drowning in the bathtub, drunks are fighting, and horny sailors are gate-crashing in the belief that they have found a whorehouse. Unlike Cleanth Siegel at a similar chaotic party, Meatball responds humanely. He has two choices: he can crawl in a closet and wait till everybody leaves, or he can "try to calm everybody down, one by one." The former option is tempting, since the latter involves hard work, but Pynchon is suggesting that hard work is the only legitimate means to combat entropy in social systems. Hard as the job is, Meatball does restore order to his apartment.

Contrapuntally, Aubade senses Callisto's rising terror with alarm. As one who comes from a colonialized country, Aubade is no stranger to compromise either. Moreover, she apprehends the world through sound, as "music which emerged at intervals from a howling darkness of discordancy." In the past she has attempted to create a "closed circuit," using "feedback" in her efforts to maintain "the architectonic purity of her world." She has tried always to soothe Callisto, but now his anxious words mingle with car horns from the street outside and the wild music from Meatball's flat. Exhausted herself from keeping order in the "hothouse" by balancing the "signal-to-noise ratio," she perceives that Callisto is paralyzed with fear.

Like Meatball, Aubade must make a choice; but unlike him she elects to allow disorder to penetrate a closed system—because either way the system will decay. Too much order leads to stagnation; too little results in disintegration. With bleeding hands, Aubade smashes the windows of the hothouse and turns to wait

> until the moment of equilibrium was reached, when 37 degrees Fahrenheit should prevail both outside and inside, and forever, and the hovering, curious dominant of their separate lives should resolve into a tonic of darkness and the final absence of all motion.

Death may be the consequence, but at least the hothouse has been opened to the life of the street. One must face the possibility of eventual annihilation, not try to arrest time. Aubade's act is an acknowledgment of the limited choices available. Callisto's love is not enough; love, unless constantly and actively exercised, like power will decay. Mulligan shoulders responsibility for his life in time—and entropy is time's arrow. He merely retards the inevitable, but it is the only choice he has. The choice, the polarity between hothouse and street, and the concept of entropy will structure *V.* More sophisticated versions of the dilemma will figure in *The Crying of Lot 49,* which stresses the opening of closed social systems to retard entropy and deplores the inability of humans to perceive only the extremes of order and chaos, and in *Gravity's Rainbow,* which analyzes our culture in terms of a mania for order that prevents renewal and advocates embracing paradox and probability. Some of these concerns are anticipated in another short work.

"The Secret Integration," the first of Pynchon's stories to appear in a large-circulation magazine, is perhaps his least successful. Published after *V.*, it suffers from the very qualities that make the novel so engaging. *V.* is discursive and loose, but its diffusion is appropriate to its global setting. Equally loose, "The Secret Integration" is set in Mingeborough, Massachusetts, the Berkshire Mountain hometown of Tyrone Slothrop, protagonist of *Gravity's Rainbow;* and the small community cannot contain the multiple motifs of the plot. Nevertheless, "The Secret Integration" has its moments, and, more important, has elements of considerable relevance to Pynchon's other work. As one might expect, paranoia, technical terminology, and communication and its failures are prominent issues here.

Of a large assortment of characters, most of them oddball children, four are important: Tim Santora, through whose eyes the story's events are seen; Hogan Slothrop, at nine the youngest member of Mingeborough's Alcoholics Anonymous, who has renounced booze and got religion; Grover Snodd, a young math genius and ham radio operator; and Carl Barrington, a Negro boy new to the town and to the group of children. With few exceptions, the parents of Mingeborough's children are bigots, hysterical at the thought of a black family, the Barringtons, moving into town — and at the prospect of integration in general. "What's integration mean?" Tim asks Grover. The only kind the math whiz has ever heard of is

> "The opposite of differentiation," Grover said, drawing an x-axis, y-axis and curve on his greenboard. "Call this function of x. Consider values of the curve any little increments of x" — drawing straight lines from the curve down to the x-axis, like the bars of a jail cell — "you can have as many of these as you want, see, as close together as you want."
>
> "Till it's all solid," Tim said.
>
> "No, it never gets solid. If this was a jail cell, and those lines were bars, and whoever was behind it could make himself any size he wanted to be, he could always make himself skinny enough to get free. No matter how close together the bars were."

Grover has sketched the possibilities for human freedom in a highly "integrated" social system. Wiser than most of Pynchon's characters, Grover knows that the lines are artificial, mathematical conveniences, and he knows also that a paradox is involved: without integration there can be no differentiation in a healthy society. In a viable system, disparate elements function in concert. Despite his wisdom, however, Grover will be defeated by the cell bars of society's functions, for this is a story of childhood loss of innocence.

The children are a blend of sophistication and naiveté. Much of their time they spend listening to Grover's radio receiver, hearing "disembodied voices" which fill their dreams of the world beyond the mountains, or acting out Tom Sawyer adventure fantasies. Grover has organized the other kids into a conspiracy against the town's adults, which he names Operation Spartacus, after the Kirk Douglas movie. Most of their attempts at sabotaging the town's paper mill or at disrupting school are abortive, however, because the youngsters can be stopped by the lines of force the adults have drawn. In one raid on their school, the children are enthusiastic until they reach the playing field lines chalked around the perimeter; they cannot pass. Grover theorizes "that the line figure in the grass might have reminded the little kids of chalk lines on a greenboard." He tries to drill his troops by laying out lines on a practice field, but they lack adult authority.

Two events lead to the collapse of Operation Spartacus and an end to childhood. The first involves Hogan Slothrop, who is sent by the local Alcoholics Anonymous to help a transient, a Mr. McAfee, trying to kick the habit. When Hogan and Tim reach the alcoholic's hotel, they discover that he is a Negro; none of the adult A. A. members would have anything to do with a black, and have sent the boys as a joke, although the two take the assignment seriously. In the hotel room, they learn of isolation both racial and personal; the Negro's tale reminds Tim of the voices he has heard over Grover's radio, the voices of drifters and vagrants. So lonely is McAfee that the boys try to telephone a girl the man can hardly remember, but whose number he has been carrying in his wallet for years. As the telephone circuits open, Tim feels "the edge of a certain abyss" and realizes "how hard it would be, how hopeless, to really find a person you needed suddenly, unless you lived all your life in a house like he did, with a mother and father." When the adults run McAfee out of town the next morning, the Spartacists retaliate with a raid that is an affirmation of color.

The second event involves Carl Barrington. Tim and the other boys overhear their parents making hate-telephone calls to the black newcomers, the Barringtons. To compensate, the Spartacists accept Carl without reservation; it is a "secret integration." The point of the story, revealed at the end, is that the Barringtons have no children. Carl is imaginary, "put together out of phases, images, possibilities that grownups had somehow turned away from, repudiated, left out at the edges of towns, as if they were auto parts in Étienne's father's junkyard." Carl does not survive an adult counterattack. From a day of planning strategy, the youthful rebels return to find the Barrington lawn completely covered with garbage, and as the kids try to clean it up they discover garbage from their own homes. It is too much; they allow Carl to depart. He is discarded also, consigned to the junkheap of childish fantasies. And so is youthful rebellion. Each child leaves for "his own house, hot shower, dry towel, before-bed television, good night kiss, and dreams that could never again be entirely safe."

Indeed, those dreams will never be safe. Tim Santora has already discovered that his dreams are full of "struggle down the long, inexhaustible network of some arithmetic problem where each step led to a dozen new ones." For Pynchon, networks are reality, and humans stumble throught them.

Pynchon's fascination with junkheaps furnishes a focus for "A Journey into the Mind of Watts," his 1966 study of the slums of Los Angeles. The essay is a skillful piece of journalism in which Pynchon traces the ironies and absurdities of black life in a prosperous white city. It is an excellent tonic for the reader daunted by the difficulty of Pynchon's fiction. Although as journalism it is unremarkable, from the standpoint of continuity within Pynchon's work it is important, for it offers a sober and concise view of the Los Angeles he treats comically in *The Crying of Lot 49.* Pynchon constructs his essay around a real junkheap, a landmark in Watts erected by an Italian immigrant named Simon Rodia, who for thirty years gathered scrap and waste into "his own dream of how things should have been: a fantasy of fountains, boats, tall openwork spires, encrusted with a dazzling mosaic of Watts debris." Rodia's heap becomes a metaphor for the wasted lives in the waste land of the black ghetto.

Between that ghetto and the white metropolis are sharp divisions, says Pynchon; "Watts is country which lies, psychologically, uncounted miles further than most whites seem at present

willing to travel." Los Angeles and its subculture are different
states of mind, and Watts is quite simply paranoiac. That condition obtains in part because Los Angeles itself is "a little unreal, a little less than substantial. For Los Angeles, more than any
other city, belongs to the mass media." Watts lies "impacted in
the heart of this white fantasy," and as a consequence suffers from
aberration aggravated by the prevalence of the unreal. Paranoia assists the blacks in knowing who they are. For a time they
had accepted the white version of what blacks should be, but the
acquiescence has faded as the civil rights movement has flagged.
Nevertheless, "assorted members of the humanitarian establishment" continue in their efforts to mold the denizens of Watts in
the image of whites. Pynchon singles out the Economic and Youth
Opportunity Agency, a "bizarre, confused, ever in flux, strange-
ly ineffectual" organization characterized by internecine liberal
bickering and bureaucratic bungling. E. Y. O. A. begins the molding process with the young; its counselors tell black girls to trim
their afros and dress conservatively and advise black boys to
cultivate "Niceguymanship," to look and act as white as possible.
Strengthened by the rebellious spirit of the times, the young
blacks resent and resist efforts to change them. Nothing, however,
can fend off the fantasies of the mass media; television signals in-
vade Watts, continually reshaping reality.

   Paranoia flourishes in Watts for a second reason: *real* violence.
The violence in August 1965 turned Watts into "Raceriotland," a
literal battlefield strewn with the rubble of rage, the remnants of
a community that was never much to begin with. Pynchon's eye
instinctively picks out absurd details as he surveys the terrain.
For instance, when a storekeeper decides to rebuild his destroyed
business instead of fleeing the area, he breaks ground ceremo-
niously "in the true Watts spirit" by having his wife smash a bottle of champagne over a rock. Since this is a study after the fact,
Pynchon does not advance single causes for the riots. He does
review events afterward to suggest pattern to the violence and to
emphasize the possibility of recurrence.

   He begins "A Journey into the Mind of Watts" with an account
of a recent police killing of a black man, and observes that the
ever-present gun in the hand of the ever-present white cop en-
sures continual racial confrontation. Past experience and fear
make the roles of white and black inevitable, make "it impossible
for the cop to come on any different, or for [the black] to hate him

any less." Both cop and hassled black are caught up in a system which traps the two of them; neither wants the confrontation. Thus, when it comes, the violence follows the laws of physics: "for every action there is an equal and opposite reaction." Violence may also "be an attempt to communicate," since without it whites take no notice of the black individual beyond the role which the white system has assigned him.

The point Pynchon is making is not that the whites are necessarily wrong in asserting their values and standards, particularly since many whites genuinely want to give the blacks a place in the system. Nor is he saying that the police are necessarily wrong in enforcing the laws; he notes the "earnestness" of many policemen. If we borrow the math language of "The Secret Integration," the problem is that the whites attempt to force integration without allowing for differentiation, a mistake that rebounds, since it guarantees that the blacks will prize their differences. The more the blacks assert differentiation, the less regard whites have for it. The blacks thus become effectively isolated, part and no part of the system. Beyond that, the law the cop enforces is a reflection of the faulty system; the blacks get annoyance instead of justice. They receive no rewards even when they join the system and cooperate with the law. Whites are driven by the carrot, blacks by the stick. The citizens of Watts have been disinherited of America's bounty and disabused of their humanity. As Pynchon walks the streets he always finds so revelatory, he sees the poverty, the hopelessness, the blankness of Watts. Most of all he notices the absence of "surprise" to black life: "Watts is full of street corners where people stand, as they have been, some of them, for 20 or 30 years, without Surprise One ever having come along." Without surprise, life has little to offer.

Pynchon will return to the absence of surprise and the necessity of its possibility in his second and third novels. The blacks in Watts, however, may be preparing their own surprise. Pynchon ends his essay on an apocalyptic note, with an example of black Watts art, found objects plucked from the junkheap of the ghetto. It is a smashed TV set; inside the cavity that once held the picture tube, generator of white fantasy, sits a human skull. The title of the artwork is "The Late, Late, Late Show." It is an arresting image and a terrifying conclusion.

Several aspects of the article are germane to Pynchon's novels, not least of which is his grasp of authentic human suffering. For all his humor, Pynchon exhibits in his fiction, as he does here, an astute and sympathetic understanding of social and political realities that anchors his imagination and turns it toward the complex and very tangible dilemmas of this century. Systems— social, political, religious, economic—become his major concern, as do the paradoxes those systems generate. How is it possible, he will ask, for isolation and inhumanity to persist in the midst of the greatest potential for human community in history? The "media" in "A Journey into the Mind of Watts" hint at the approach he takes in his novels. In a sense, Pynchon is the world's first genuine technological novelist: he has evidently read, assimilated, and synthesized Lewis Mumford, Marshall McLuhan, and other theorists of the Second Industrial Revolution. In company with McLuhan in particular, he is preoccupied with all forms of communication, from language and mathematics to television, computers, films, and transportation, and with energy *as* communication, the definitive characteristic of the technological era. Pynchon knows that this energy is different from the energies of earlier eras, that it has disrupted our culture, but he knows also that historical momentum is powerful. While technological communication has the capacity not only to integrate Los Angeles but also to convert the entire planet into McLuhan's "global village," the historical forces of a linear, entropic, western culture fragment, divide, and disinherit. Rather than rejuvenating moribund systems, technology has been perverted to foster fantasies, "mindless pleasures." Technology, be it an alternative system of communication in *The Crying of Lot 49* or the flight of a rocket in *Gravity's Rainbow,* is Pynchon's ultimate "redeemer" for the waste land. So far, like all his other redeemers, it has failed; but the potential is still there.

An Anarchist Miracle:
The Novels of Thomas Pynchon

by Robert Sklar

We speak of writers as emerging, as if in our mind's eye the literary world were a stage and apprentice writers waited in the wings, or a sea where writers surface like submarines, or a world into which they are born from the womb of the muse. The stage, the surface sea, the world, belong to criticism and literary history: the wings, the depths, and the womb to sociology and the history of taste. Writers, in a different metaphor, make up an iceberg, with only a thin sharp edge showing in the open air, visible to the critics and the public unwilling to dive. But at the present moment no metaphor seems quite appropriate for the generation of American writers under 30. From this generation so far only one fiction writer, Thomas Pynchon, has emerged above the surface, and few could guess how vast or sturdy the iceberg is beneath him. This fact clashes so strongly both with historical precedent and with the contemporary experience of other art forms that it cannot help but illuminate the status and prospects of American fiction today.

From the 1890s on, every young American generation—until the present one—found its voice and proclaimed its special vision through the art of fiction. Of breakthroughs and new starts the sixties have seen many—but they have come from writers already past the age of 30, like Joseph Heller, Kurt Vonnegut, Jr., and John Barth. The children of the Great Depression have produced, astonishingly, almost no visible literature, nor have their younger brothers and sisters born during the Second World War. Graduate fellowships may have stolen the energies of young

"An Anarchist Miracle: The Novels of Thomas Pynchon," by Robert Sklar. From *The Nation*, 205 (25 September 1967), 277-80. Published under the title "The New Novel, USA: Thomas Pynchon"; the author's original title has been restored for this collection. Reprinted by permission of the author.

writers, the hippie ethic may have immobilized them, or activism pulled them into a different world. Perhaps they may come back from these diversions, like Conrads from the sea, to write mature and worldly novels.

The fact remains that young people read fiction but, on the whole, they do not write it. They do write poetry. They write songs and sing them. They paint, they sculpt, they play instruments, make films, dance, design happenings. Young people have made a considerable contribution, here and there a major contribution, to all the arts except the art of fiction. If fiction has not completely lost its relevance as an art form to creative young people, then it languishes in a period of biding time; since fiction is tied more closely to events and ideas than other arts, perhaps it stands in a fallow period, assimilating new configurations, as happened in the mid-nineteenth century after Darwin and in the early twentieth after Freud. In this perspective, Thomas Pynchon is far more than, dutifully recognized, the only known and therefore leading writer of the under-30s; for more than any other contemporary American novelist he has succeeded, in two interesting, intelligent, and serious novels, in absorbing and transforming new scientific and philosophical perspectives within his art.

Pynchon was born in 1937 and attended Cornell University, where as an undergraduate he published his first story, "Mortality and Mercy in Vienna," in *Epoch*. Soon after leaving Cornell he published three short stories—"Under the Rose," in *Noble Savage* #3; "Entropy," in *The Kenyon Review,* and "Low-lands" in *New World Writing* #16—which earned him an immediate reputation among the narrow but intense circle of short story readers. His novel *V.* won the Faulkner prize as the best first novel of it's year, 1963. His second novel, *The Crying of Lot 49,* published last year and received with far less warmth from reviewers and readers of fiction, won as compensation an award given annually to a meritorious novel that criticism and commerce have unjustly slighted.

Besides the novels, he has published in the past five years only one story, "The Secret Integration," in *The Saturday Evening Post,* and a magazine essay on Los Angeles in *The New York Times Magazine*. The critical point in Pynchon's career so far lies in the radical shift in literary focus he undertook to make from *V.* to *The Crying of Lot 49.* To say that the second novel is a better and more important novel than the first is not simply a way of scoring an easy victory over dull reviewers or doggedly insisting on a principle of growth. To grasp the nature of Pynchon's shift, for its artistic and intellectual value, and as a liberating gesture in its own right, is to take the measure of his wider significance for contemporary American fiction.

As a liberating gesture, Pynchon's shift from *V.* to *The Crying of Lot 49* broke him free from the constricting limitations of belonging to a "school" and writing in a genre. One reason the second novel proved disappointing to some admirers of the first, in fact, with its failure to fulfill the stereotyped expectations they had held for him. Yet even if *V.* wears a "black humor" label, and stands as one of the most intricate and elaborate novels in that genre, it accomplishes a good deal more than that. One who re-reads *V.* in the light of *The Crying of Lot 49* may come to feel that *V.* is itself a liberating gesture, a gesture of liberation from nearly all the styles and forms of fiction that have preceded it.

As *Catch-22* may be the first American novel truly to have attained a Cubist form in its treatment of space and time, so *V.* may be the first American novel of collage, an abstract composition put together with parodies of spy novels, political novels, adventure novels, decadent novels, romances, utopias and whatever other category the ingenious mind can find. *V.* may be doomed to the fate that befell *Finnegans Wake*, as Edmund Wilson described it, to go directly from the pen of the author into the hands of the schoolmasters. This is not the place to begin the task of critical dissection to which *V.* is foreordained; but when that job is done the attentive explicator will find that one of the principal subjects of parody in *V.* is the "black humor" style itself.

Read in the light of *The Crying of Lot 49*, then, *V.* does not appear as a launching platform for a style or a subject but rather as an isolated object or as an ending. That novel published in 1963 seems in 1967 not so much a contemporary work as a historical work, a novel that reflects the moods of the late fifties in America and the style of the early sixties. Part of this feeling, if it is an accurate one, may be attributed to a stylistic trait of the novel common to many works in the "black humor" genre, a style deliberately constructed to put a distance between the reader and the work, as if the novel were a game drawing on the reader's mental faculties but deliberately excluding his emotions.

The natural reaction to this sort of reading experience is to feel admiration for the author, for his ingenuity or his imagination or his nihilism or his guts, and to feel almost nothing for the novel itself. In contrast the reader, for example, of *The Sound and the Fury* invests his primary feelings into the matter of the work itself, and responds to the skill of the author only secondarily, as a deliberated afterthought. *V.* is like a riddle that, once correctly answered, never taxes the mind again; *The Crying of Lot 49* is founded in an emotion of mystery, an emotion which remains, inviolate and mysterious, even when the outward mystery is solved. *V.* is a complex novel that gets simpler with each rereading, *The Crying of Lot 49* a simple novel that, reread, grows more complex.

V. is chiefly memorable for what its earlier admirers called its vast warehouses of information, its immense knowledgeability, its prodigies of research. If one function of the novel, as Mary McCarthy once suggested, has been to provide facts, to let the reader know how to catch a whale or cut a field of hay, Pynchon's *V.* may rank as one of the most encyclopedic founts of facts in the history of the novel. In *V.*, the reader may find out how to perform a nose operation; how the Germans wiped out the native population of South West Africa before the First World War; how British espionage agents operated in the Middle East since the time of Kitchener; a good part of the history of Malta in this century; and much more. How much one may care to rely on Pynchon's facts is another matter; this reader, at least, has not yet taken the trouble to verify Pynchon's account of Wilhelmian Germany's African policies or of Maltese political life; and given Pynchon's propensity to parody the fictional styles which have conveyed this sort of subject in the past, it might be wise not to make any bets on the basis of what one reads in *V.* In any case, the truth of Pynchon's details, or even their significance, is not a matter that deeply engages the reader's concern.

Form and style in *The Crying of Lot 49* combine to give a far greater resonance to facts, but a much more striking comparison can be made between Pynchon's very good short story, "Under the Rose," and the chapter of *V.* into which that story later was transformed. "Under the Rose" is a poignant story of a few days in the life of a British spy in the Middle East, ending with his death. The story is far from simple, but it is tightly controlled, and the effect is tragicomic, an exceptionally fine fusion of emotional depth and historical breadth; more than anything else Pynchon has written, "Under the Rose" justifies the claims of some critics who link him to the tradition of Nathanael West. In the novel, the focus is fragmented among eight different narrative voices, and the culmination of the action is deliberately shrouded in mystery. Pynchon obviously was reshaping the material to fit the larger thematic purposes of the novel, but undeniably the narrative form diffuses the reader's attention and ultimately his concern for the character and their fate.

Nevertheless, Pynchon has created in *V.* an aura of formidable intellectual competence, and nowhere more significantly than in his mastery of scientific and technical subjects, particularly physics and electronic technology. It may be that no American novelist before Pynchon—science fiction writers not excepted—has brought so thorough and so prepared a scientific intelligence to bear on modern life; and this capacity to include in the novel the pervasive scientific and technological aspects of our day-to-day lives, rather than to neglect them through ignorance, may make *V.* a landmark of the novel in yet another sense.

It is true, though, that Pynchon dissipates this competence by expending it on a theme beloved of science fiction writers and their cousins among black humorists, the battle between men and machines, between the power of animation and the power of the inanimate. Perhaps the struggle of humans against the inanimate which pervades *V.* is one more aspect of Pynchon's satire, almost a self-parody of black humor thematic stock in trade. On a different level it is an aspect of Pynchon's even more pervasive concern with dualisms, with worlds and anti-worlds and worlds within worlds. At the heart of Pynchon's imagination lies not science and technology, nor the parody and wild humor which are so much a part of his style, but a sense of mystery, a vision of fantasy, that expresses itself in dualisms, in images of surface and depth, of mirrors, of secret societies and hidden worlds.

The prime mystery of *V.*, of course, is the mystery of V. herself, as a woman in many guises—Victoria Wren, Hedwig Vogelsang, Veronica Manganese, a mysterious woman in Paris, the Bad Priest killed in Malta—as a bald cipher that is charged with greater resonance with every repetition, until the eye responds to every capital letter V as if it were inked in red: Veronica the rat; Vheissu, the fantasy land beyond the deserts and the mountains;

Venezuela; the V-Note jazz club; Valletta, the capital of Malta; and the Vatican, Voce del Popolo, Birth of Venus, Ponte Vecchio, Via Cavour, Queen Victoria. Who is V.? The British espionage agent, Sidney Stencil, one of her lovers, in 1899 had written in his journal: "There is more behind and inside V. than any of us had suspected. Not who, but what: what is she? God grant that I may never be called upon to write the answer, either here or in any official report."

Pynchon, however, does feel called upon to write the answer, and he raises few mysteries in *V.* for which he does not quite openly and obviously provide the solution. But to answer who she is in her many masks is not to answer Sidney Stencil's question, what she is, and that question Pynchon leaves to his exegetes. It is true that a Freudian or a Jungian explication would serve the book quite comfortably, though Pynchon has dropped his broadest hints in the service of a historico-philosophical interpretation. One of the principal changes Pynchon made in revising "Under the Rose" for the novel, curiously, was rigorously to eliminate the word "apocalypse" each of the many times it appeared in the short story. Yet he still tosses "apocalypse" around so much in *V.* that its face is rubbed smooth, and one can barely make out its features.

The reverberations of that word, however, lead the attentive reader inexorably toward an historical interpretation for the novel, an interpretation that may encompass a meaning for twentieth-century history—history since that portentous day in "Under the Rose" when Kitchener and Marchand collided at Fashoda— and one that must come to terms with the revolutionary stances which Pynchon so noticeably adopts. All the answers to the puzzles of *V.*, and all the possible interpretations of its meaning and significance will one day be given to us in the scholarly studies for which *V.* seems almost to have been made: one leaves them here in a half-completed form because their completion may be found, not in an explication of *V.* but in Pynchon's second novel, *The Crying of Lot 49.*

Pynchon's radical shift in literary focus from *V.* to *The Crying of Lot 49* took the shape not of new themes and images but rather of changes in form and tone that significantly altered the value of old themes and images. His verbal playfulness, puns and jokes are reduced in quantity rather than intensity, and are made to serve the movement of the novel. Factual materials remain as important to the second novel as to the first; but where in *V.* the facts seemed to have been real but not necessarily true, Pynchon quite obviously invented the "historical facts" in *The Crying of Lot 49* for the purpose of the novel and thereby made them more plausible, artistically more true. The form of *V.*, moreover, exaggerated the sense of mystery and the aura of an exotic unknown, though Pynchon too often broke in and disengaged the mystery by providing explanations. In *The Crying of Lot 49*, the form of the novel centers on the normal and the everyday: strange events are explained earnestly and straightforwardly, yet the aura of mystery obstinately grows. And finally, whatever sense of mystery remained in *V.* was focused and contained by the past, where in *The Crying of Lot 49* the feeling of mystery that will not down comes inexorably to rest in the present and the future.

The Crying of Lot 49 is the story of how Mrs. Oedipa Maas discovers a world within her world, an anti-world, an adversary world—or invents one in her imagination. She has been named co-executor for the estate of a California financier named Pierce Inverarity, with whom, before her marriage, she had had a brief affair. In Mexico City with Pierce, she had seen a painting that had made her cry: a painting of frail girls held prisoner in a circular tower, that made her recognize that she too was imprisoned in a tower, "that what really keeps her where she is is magic, anonymous and malignant, visited on her from outside and for no reason at all."

When the novel opens, Oedipa is already primed to find a new magic to deliver her from the malignant magic that has her in its spell. Driving into the Southern California suburb where Pierce had lived, she looks down on the neat pattern of uniform houses and thinks of a time when she looked at a printed circuit inside a transistor radio—"there were to both outward patterns a hieroglyphic sense of concealed meaning, of an intent to communicate. There'd seemed no limit to what the printed circuit could have told her (if she had tried to find out); so in her first minute of San Narcisco, a revelation also trembled just past the threshold of her understanding. Smog hung all around the horizon, the sun on the bright beige countryside was painful; she and the Chevy seemed parked at the center of an odd religious instant." "*Shall I project a world?*" Oedipa writes later in her notebook. Oedipa comes upon her new magic—to adopt language which Pynchon's reference to religion validates—in an immanent world which gradually becomes more and more imminent.

The adversary world reveals itself to Oedipa through the symbol of a muted post horn and also by signs bearing the initials WASTE or w.a.s.t.e. These signs and symbols represent an underground postal system which operates parallel to or in direct subversion (through forged stamps and cancellations) of the U.S. Post Office. Oedipa pursues the long history of this secret system through investigations into the arcane byways of bibliography— a good part of the novel centers on the performance of a mock Jacobean revenge play, *The Courier's Tragedy*, and the tracing of its various texts and editions—and philately, giving Pynchon an opportunity to display his intellectual ingenuity in two fields he neglected to cover in *V*.

But the backbone of Pynchon's intellectual structure in *The Crying of Lot 49*, as in *V.*, is science; and in the second novel he develops a scientific metaphor far more rich and more original than the animate-inanimate dichotomy he borrowed or parodied in *V*. As with *V.*, Pynchon set down the new theme even more precisely in a preliminary short story, "Entropy," of which, however, only the theme carried over to the novel. In physics, the term entropy applies to the second law of thermodynamics. It describes loss of energy, or the amount of energy available for use in a thermodynamic system. Henry Adams borrowed this idea for his essay, "The Rule of Phase Applied to History," in which he calculated the running down of intellectual energy on earth—thought would reach the limits of its possibilities, he postulated, in the year 1921.

Henry Adams's concept of entropy lies at the core of Pynchon's story of that title; but the concept of entropy most important for *The Crying of Lot 49* derives from communications and information theory, particularly as that term was discussed by the mathematician Norbert Wiener. In *The Human Use of Human Beings* and in *Cybernetics*, Wiener argued against the pessimism which the second law of thermodynamics had engendered in Henry Adams and others. He agreed that the universe's energy would surely run down some day, but at a given moment in a given part of the system there were forces powerful enough to decrease entropy, to increase the amount of available energy in that part. "We may well regard living organisms," Wiener wrote, "such as Man himself, in this light." In *The Crying of Lot 49*,

Pynchon takes up not only the scientific significance of Wiener's viewpoint but its obvious social and political significance as well. The w.a.s.t.e. system puts to use moral and human energies that the surface system—the United States Government and the dominant American mode of life, as Pynchon makes explicit—lets go to waste.

The Crying of Lot 49 is a radical political novel. Where in *V.* and in "Under the Rose" Pynchon tossed out an idea of political apocalypse with bravado and as if to scare the liberals, in *The Crying of Lot 49* he never uses the word "apocalypse" but rather builds a concept and a structure of revolution right into the form of the novel. Unexpectedly, Oedipa runs across a Mexican anarchist she and Pierce had once argued with in Mexico. The anarchist says to her:

> You know what a miracle is. Not what Bakunin said. But another world's intrusion into this one. Most of the time we coexist peacefully, but when we do touch there's cataclysm. Like the church we hate, anarchists also believe in another world. Where revolutions break out spontaneous and leaderless, and the soul's talent for consensus allows the masses to work together without effort, automatic as the body itself. And yet, señá, if any of it should ever really happen that perfectly, I would also have to cry miracle. An anarchist miracle.

The Crying of Lot 49, too, in this sense, is an anarchist miracle, a novel which not only postulates another world but creates with the truth of art another world's intrusion into this one.

It is perhaps idle to talk of an American tradition in the novel, but one of the unmistakable virtues of *The Crying of Lot 49* is its success in making new and contemporary a traditional concern of the great American novelists—the creation, through the style and form of their fiction, of a social system more true to their national and social system. *The Crying of Lot 49* ends with Oedipa Maas awaiting the auctioning of the lot of postage stamps which will prove whether the muted post horn symbol and the w.a.s.t.e. signs form only a web to snare her paranoia or, in truth, form the communication network of another world.

For all his philosophical and scientific competence, for all his revolutionary political inclinations, Pynchon is above all an artist: and the ending of *The Crying of Lot 49* makes clear what the Argentine Jorge Luis Borges meant when he wrote in an essay,

"that imminence of a revelation that is not yet produced is, perhaps, the aesthetic reality." One would like to say of *The Crying
of Lot 49* what T. S. Eliot said of *The Great Gatsby*, that it represents the first step forward for American fiction in some time; for
if the road ahead for fiction lies in the direction Borges in his
stories has pointed, toward greater philosophical and metaphysical sophistication, Pynchon surely ranks as the most intelligent,
most audacious and most accomplished American novelist
writing today.

Pynchon's Tapestries on the Western Wall

by Roger B. Henkle

Lured to Mexico by the arch entrepreneur Pierce Inverarity, Oedipa Maas, the heroine of Thomas Pynchon's *The Crying of Lot 49*, comes across a triptych in which the central painting is of a group of frail girls with heart-shaped faces imprisoned in a tower, embroidering a tapestry. The endless tapestry spills out the slit windows of the turret "and into a void, seeking hopelessly to fill the void: for all the other buildings and creatures, all the waves, ships and forests of the earth were contained in this tapestry, and the tapestry was the world."[1] Pynchon's novels, *V.*, published in 1963, and *Lot 49* (1966), spill out, in the rich profusion of their historical inventions, philosophical ideas, literary parodies and grotesque characterizations, as if into the void that he suggests gapes below us. Like medieval tapestries, the novels lay out a field on which villains, heroes, and maidens romp and struggle in frozen moments of the cultural past or seek elusive grails in the dark green forests of imagined evils. His novels seem to recall in their scope the vast imaginative designs of a distant time, and even an earlier form of literature, the romantic epic.

The most readily discernible shapes and patterns we can discover in Pynchon's work, however, are those reminiscent of 20th-century novelists, especially Vladimir Nabokov. By analyzing *V.* and *Lot 49* in terms of their resemblances to Nabokov's novels (and others), we can identify Pynchon's themes and see why cer-

"Pynchon's Tapestries on the Western Wall," by Roger B. Henkle. From *Modern Fiction Studies*, 17, (1971), 207-20. Copyright © 1971 by Purdue Research Foundation, West Lafayette, Indiana U.S.A. Reprinted by permission of the author. The editor of this collection has made a slight cut in the text, with the consent of the author.

[1]Thomas Pynchon, *The Crying of Lot 49* (New York: Bantam Books, 1961), p. 10. All other citations to this edition will appear in parentheses in the text, *e.g.*, (*L.*, p. 170).

tain characteristics of the romantic epic—a loose structure, a highly fictionalized reinterpretation of a past culture, and an emphasis on literary invention almost for its own sake—seem appropriate to Pynchon's objectives. We can also move closer to an evaluation of Pynchon's use of imagination, the quality upon which so much of the strength of his work must depend.

Pynchon's first novel, *V.*, is made of two series of episodes, those of Benny Profane, Depression-child, "yo-yo," and *schlemiel*, and those which depict the quest of Herbert Stencil for a mysterious female figure (perhaps actually several figures) identified as "V.". Of the two strains in the novel, the V. episodes stand out most vividly.

Stencil first learns of V. from cryptic allusions in the literary remains of his father Sidney, who served as a minor British foreign intelligence officer in murky Continental cities at the turn of the century. V. and some larger pattern of events, involving her, materialize almost everywhere young Stencil looks. Stencil's inquiry into the hidden places of his father's life, requiring fanciful detective work that leads him bumbling into numerous false leads, is very Nabokovian,...and in fact *V.* and *Lot 49* contain frequent allusions to Nabokov's novels. Though Pynchon's V. is female, the use of that initial coyly reminds one that the narrator of Nabokov's *The Real Life of Sebastian Knight* (1941) is called simply "V." and stands perhaps for Vladimir; disguised and overt literary illusions are the most delightful tricks to borrow from and play against an old master. V. in *Sebastian Knight* engages in an elaborate posthumous investigation of his half-brother's secret life and in the process discovers that the half-brother's last lover assumed several identities, just as Stencil's father's mysterious woman does. Nabokov's V. alters the "real" past so extensively by his own subjective projections that in the end he confesses that perhaps his search has only been a conjuror's show. Pynchon, too, is intrigued with the notion that in re-creating the past we distort it, that it becomes our own fiction[2] and

[2]Pynchon expresses this problem in an early short story, "Low-lands," in which the protagonist, Dennis Flange, observes that the minute you try to tell someone about past events "you are somehow...screwing up the perspective of things, much as anyone observing subatomic particles changes the works, data and odds, by the act of observing." *New World Writing*, No. 16 (Philadelphia and New York: J. B. Lippincott Company, 1960), p.100.

with the idea that Nabokov so frequently works: our artifices have a reality as meaningful to us as any objectively verifiable event would have.

Indeed, all but one of the V. episodes in Pynchon's novel could very well be nothing more than young Stencil's "yarns." The Porpentine incident, for instance, is prefaced by the statement that Stencil had "only the veiled references to Porpentine in the journals. The rest was impersonation and dream."[3] The complex Mondaugen story was told to young Stencil in no more than thirty minutes, yet, "when Stencil retold it, the yarn had undergone considerable change, had become, as Eigenvalue put it, Stencilized" (*V.*, p. 211). Before Stencil renders the Florentine conspiracies, he admits that he had uncovered very little about V.; his discoveries, as one skeptical listener describes them, are a likely case of serendipity. But there is no such disclaimer about the Epilogue to the novel, which in mock Tolstoyan fashion fills in the story of V., carrying us to old Stencil's death in a waterspout, and amplifies the "historical theory" of the novel. Stencil's fictions have thus become the "reality" of the novel.

Like Nabokov—and James Joyce before him—Pynchon amuses himself by working into his fiction parodies of cultural and historical theories. Woven into the opening sentences of chapter three of *V.* is a reference to Robert Graves' *The White Goddess,* a thread which, if we pull it, seems to unravel much of the pattern of the V. episodes. For V. is Western man's conception of woman. She is even more than that; she is, as Graves' Goddess becomes, a symbol of the European humanist tradition. Graves' thesis is that the White Goddess in her many manifestations became the prevailing myth of most ancient European cultures. She represented fertility and the mysteries of feminity; she was the source of the power of early rulers and the mistress of the culture's fortunes by reason of her influence over the seasons. The myth was elaborated, Graves contends, in later Western religion and philosophy and became, in a sense, part of Western society's "cultural unconscious." The White Goddess was often a love goddess of the sea; Venus (V-ness) was such a one, and the Florentine episode revolves around an abortive attempt to steal Botticelli's

[3] *V.* (New York: Bantam Books, 1963), p. 52. All other citations to this edition will appear in parentheses in the text, *e.g.*, (*V.*, p. 52).

"Birth of Venus" from the Western wall of the Uffizi. Venus,
Graves notes, traditionally wore a five-figured comb,[4] and such
a comb is worn by Pynchon's V. figure. The Virgin was a White
Goddess,[5] and the Virgin, too, is associated with Stencil's mysterious woman. Stencil's V. is finally destroyed in Malta, on which,
we are told,[6] the cult of the female figure whom Graves calls the
White Goddess is thought to have been brought to its "highest,
purest and most fantastically elaborated form."

Graves associates the fall of Western culture with the debase-
ment of the religious and poetic myths which the White Goddess
embodied. If, he argues, the ascendency of technology and science
as pseudo-religions is not soon arrested, destruction awaits Western man. *V.* has been called an "apocalyptic" novel,[7] and Pynchon
keeps it flickering with images of world-consuming fire. But it
was something called "apocalyptic well-being" that prompted
Father Fairing to descend to the absurdity of trying to convert
the albino alligators in the New York sewers to Christianity.
Apocalyptic thinking is, as many victims of Colonialism in the
novel cynically observe, simply a grandiose penance devised by
Western Colonial rulers for their own spiritual comfort. The
Colonials don't take it seriously, and neither, perhaps, should we.
Pynchon undercuts such ready literary assumptions about his
vision.

Colonialism is the sickness that causes the feverish contortions
of the Western Europeans in the V. episodes. Young Stencil was
born in the year of Queen Victoria's death. The Queen, a secular,
debased White Goddess,[8] presided over the greatest extension of
British imperial control. V. first displays herself in the novel as
Victoria Wren, an idealization of English womanhood. Each of
the V. episodes takes place in a colony (except the Florentine
episode, which nonetheless involves a country subject to colonial
influence, Venezuela). As V. and the ruling culture that she represents degenerate, the colonial subjects progress from the impotent
anarchism of the Egyptians and the foolish heroism of a Vene-

[4]*The White Goddess: A Historical Grammar of Poetic Myth,* amended and
revised ed. (New York: Vintage Books, 1959), pp. 438ff.

[5]Graves, pp. 143ff.

[6]Jacquetta Hawkes and Sir Leonard Woolley, *Prehistory and the Beginnings
of Civilization* (New York: Harper and Row, 1963), p. 338.

[7]By R. W. B. Lewis in his *Trials of the Word* (New Haven: Yale University
Press, 1965), pp. 228-34.

[8]Graves, p. 453.

zuelan Gaucho to the bitter determination of the German South-West African Bondels, and then to the cool rationality of Malta's Fausto Maijstral. Fausto goes through four stages of personality development, and these transformations are intended to characterize the extreme and often agonizing metamorphoses the colonial native must undergo to liberate himself from oppressive European culture.

The colonial subjects form throughout most of the novel an underworld which haunts the Baedecker life of their occupiers; they live in the reverse, or mirror world—in what one European calls the "soiled South"—of the Equator and the Tropic of Capricorn. In terms of Graves' myths, they exist as the tanist of the ascendant European ruler, his twin who acts as deputy until the midsummer, at which time the ascendant ruler is destroyed and physically disassembled by his subjects and the tanist is brought to rule. Therefore, V. is hounded in her last days by hundreds of Maltese children, who can be heard as they run through the bombed-out cellars and caves in Valetta, but can be rarely seen. When V., now a debased and dehumanized symbol of Western European cultural hegemony, is pinned beneath the wreckage of a German bombing attack, the children of Malta converge on her, dismember her, and relieve her of the five-figured comb of the White Goddess. Paola Maijstral, Fausto's daughter, succeeds to that comb. Finally, the main body of the novel closes later on Malta, as British troops and planes go off to Egypt in the 1956 Suez crisis, felt by many at the time *V.* was written to be the last spasm of the Old Order.

Young Stencil's fantasies of V., then, project the decline of the cultural dominance of the European West. To comprehend V., Stencil is told, one has to "exorcise the city, the island...the continents, the world. Or the western part...we are Western men" (*V.*, p. 424).

Like Nabokov, Pynchon constructs his artifices through semi-parodic evocation of novelistic voices of a broad tonal range. The Porpentine episode is rendered by multiple observers, as is Lawrence Durrell's *Alexandria Quartet,* and the Alexandria and Cairo atmospheres of *V.* exude Durrell's intoxicating fumes. The Mondaugen story draws on the musical variations, the subliminal suggestiveness, the bizarreness and the nightmare quality of German Expressionism and alludes specifically to Hesse's semi-Expressionist *Steppenwolf.* When Stencil imagines Paris in 1913, he transposes onto that time expressionism and surrealism and onto it also a take-off on the tumultuous first performance of Igor Stravinsky's "Le Sacre du Printemps," in which the primitive rhythms of fertility cults were introduced into ballet. By that time, V. has become the Lesbian lover of a Hoffmanesque ballerina who dreams she is a wind-up doll. There are accents of T. S. Eliot, underground confessions, Proustian remembrances in the episodes, but most prevalent in the vignettes of the old world are the Eric Ambler settings and the Marx Brothers' madness of motion picture renditions of espionage abroad. The V. episodes conjure up not the distinctive and characteristic expressions of Western culture, but rather the most garish, absurd, and exotic renditions of those expressions—they often parody our cinematic travesties of the past. The cloak-and-dagger roles are carried out by Porpentine and "Old Soft-Shoe Sidney" Stencil with well-executed pratfalls, capers, shuffle steps, and bits of business. Sidney Stencil could easily have been worked into one of Sidney J. Perelman's scripts for Marx Brothers' movies.[9]

The novels of Perelman's brother-in-law, Nathanael West, seem—for most critics—to inspire the Profane episodes which make up the other half of *V.* The Profane episodes take place in a contemporary America that has inherited Western Europe's degeneracy but none of its panache. Benny Profane roams the fringes of the Whole Sick Crew, a dismal group of the barely living, who cannot create, cannot love, and cannot respond. The Crew seek to merge with the objects in their lives: one, Fergus Mixolydian, has become an extension of his television set; another, Rachel Owlglass (who later breaks away from the Crew) is literally auto-erotic: she copulates with her MG. Each of the Crew wills his own immobility so as not to have it foisted upon him. Only Benny Profane seems to be free of this curious identification with objects, although even he yearns at times for the all-electronic wom-

[9]The following paragraph is pure Perelmanese: "Dudley Eigenvalue, D.D.S., browsed among treasures in his Park Avenue office/residence. Mounted on black velvet in a locked mahogany case, showpiece of the office, was a set of false dentures, each tooth a different precious metal. The upper right canine was pure titanium and for Eigenvalue the focal point of the set. He had seen the original sponge at a foundry near Colorado Springs a year ago, having flown there in the private plane of one Clayton ('Bloody') Chiclitz. Chiclitz of Yoyodyne, one of the biggest defense contractors on the east coast, with subsidiaries all over the country" (*V.*, p. 138).

an: "Any problems with her, you could look it up in the main-tenance manual" (*V.,* p. 361).

The division of *V.* into two series of episodes, comparing no-tions of European culture with American life, calls to mind Nabokov's ironic confrontation of the two cultures in *Lolita* and *Pnin.* Structurally, though, *V.* has a slyly calculated resemblance to Joyce's *Ulysses.* Stencil, like Stephen Dedalus, is engaged in a Jesuitical search of the past for its "meaning"; Benny, like Bloom, is immersed in the experience of the everyday. It is as if Benny, the son of a Jewish mother and Catholic father, were a degenera-tion from Bloom, for Benny's mind has completely and lazily succumbed to the profane; it has none of the rich imaginative variety of Leopold Bloom's. And the science that so fascinated Bloom has really got Benny down. There are other superficial resemblances to motifs and incidents in *Ulysses* — Bloom's *Photo Bits* picture of a Nymph comes "alive," changes, as V. does, into an object and cracks open like a plaster cast — but they are impor-tant only as reminders of the literary self-consciousness of the artifice-maker. We should recall that when Stephen Dedalus' pretentious aestheticism was at its height, he proposed to title all his novels with a single letter of the alphabet: "Have you read his F? O yes, but I prefer Q"[10] — or V.

The Profane episodes can be most fruitfully approached from the vantage of the American realistic novel. Benny Profane, though modeled partly on absurd literature's bum, is a *reductio ad absurdum* of that favorite American novel device, the "honest, neutral" protagonist-observer who is sensitive but nearly inert; he is a logical step down from Fitzgerald's Nick Carraway and West's Tod Hackett. Pynchon, like many writers in the realistic tradition, has a genuine compassion for those in America who are left out, for the lonely, the grotesque, the uprooted, and the for-gotten. While the underworld of the European V. episodes is at least peopled by colonial subjects and by anarchists who seem to be only biding their time, the demimonde of Pynchon's America is inhabited by the flotsam and jetsam for whom time holds no promise.

Whereas *V.* depicted America as the near-dead progeny of a diseased European culture, Pynchon's second novel, *The Crying*

---

[10]*Ulysses* (New York: The Modern Library, 1961), p. 40.

of Lot 49, sees America in terms of its own cultural assumptions. As Oedipa Maas sets out on a depressing and dizzying investigation of a secret organization known as Tristero, she discovers that the dazzling California sub-culture is made up largely of derelicts, who have been discarded like so many used cars, and of intensely suspicious and unhappy people who are convinced that they have been robbed of the promises of the American Dream. Paranoid and frustrated, many Americans adopt conspiracy theories— there is pathetic communion in that. They suspect that they are being programmed; somewhere there are computer tapes, printed circuits, and record grooves that pattern and prefigure their lives. In a kind of pathetic self-assertion, each of these despairing souls opts out of the life of the Republic into a personal retreat, and in doing so, cuts himself off from love and communication. Oedipa's husband Mucho floats away on LSD. Her former lover Inverarity dies leaving only a mocking legacy to her. Metzger, her one extra-marital affair, elopes with a nymphet, and Randolph Driblette, who might help her uncover Tristero, walks into the sea. Oedipa exists in the landscape that Benny Profane has nightmares about: a plain where nobody lives but herself.

Pynchon's literary descriptions of America read in many ways as unconscious parodies of the distorted American concepts that Leslie Fiedler writes about in his *Love and Death in the American Novel* (1960). Oedipa Maas is the little girl, the fair-haired maiden that Fiedler contends is idealized and sentimentalized in American literature. Mucho is his Rip Van Winkle who cannot function as a husband.[11] Benny, Pig Bodine, and Pappy Hod are the Good Bad Boys. Tristero is another rendition—comic, of course—of what Fiedler sees as the American Faustian theme: an urge to set up controls and intricate systems in order to acquire overweening power. And, of course, there is the good old American violence, wrought to surrealistic extremes. I have no reason to believe Pynchon sought to put Fiedler's elements into his novels, as we can fairly assume he put in Nabokovian and Joycean elements. Pynchon, though, like Fiedler, does have an eye for the Freudian pattern and he puts society's ills in what appear to be Freudian terms. Pynchon's diagnosis of the modern human condition (which he shares with a number of other contemporary

---

[11]Pynchon's story "Low-lands" also deals with such a character.

novelists, such as Joseph Heller and Günter Grass) is that man
is becoming more inanimate, and, at the same time, more child-
like and self-protective. Benny Profane, for instance, is often
described as a "yo-yo"; Oedipa's lover Metzger is only a larger
version of Baby Igor, the child star he used to be. This notion
perfectly fits (and perhaps is distantly derived from) Freud's
theory that there is in man a compulsion to avoid all outer stimuli,
to repress the libido, and revert to an insular, nearly inorganic
state. Pynchon's solution—or, at least, basis for hope—lies in an
affirmation of love for others. Both of Pynchon's novels end with
small celebrations of individual, domestic love, as also do the
novels of so many other American writers of the sixties. The downward slide of Western culture can be reversed, Pynchon seems to
say, by the love that Paola Maijstral is capable of giving to Pappy
Hod and that Rachel Owlglass expresses for Benny Profane.

There are two additional grounds of affirmation that are especially evident in Pynchon's novels. In *V.*, the rise of former colonial subjects offers promise of redemption of the Western world.
The five-figured comb of V. is passed to a Maltese native who is
capable of love: Paola. Paola's father Fausto, who was once nearly
inanimate by reason of imitating the European style of life, experiences a slow rising curve from non-humanity to humanity. He
observes that there is in process an inversion of the "mirror
world"; when Malta is bombed by the Germans, it is the European-
occupied street which is death, and the underground of the Maltese is life.

The other ground of affirmation is Pynchon's nostalgic personal attachment to aspects of his own past culture, a feeling that
also seems particularly Nabokovian. At times—especially in its
last pages—*Lot 49* staggers under the weight of the narrative's
invocation of the American dream. Although we have witnessed
throughout the novel the irony and pathos of Oedipa's attempt to
merge herself into the fiction of some irretrievable America (as
young Stencil tried to do with a disintegrating European tradition), Pynchon, like Nabokov, nonetheless asserts the importance
of an individual relationship with a culture and its mythos. If
Pynchon's America seems at times to fit the various formulae of
the self-deluding fantasies that Fiedler says inhabit much American literature—for the America Pynchon evokes is often the one
of sentimental masculine camaraderie: three-day vodka- and

wine-swilling sieges of working-girls' apartments or roaring trips
through the American night with a six-pack in the back seat—
there is still no denying his intense feeling about it.

Unfortunately, in neither of the novels do the affirmations carry
compelling power. In part this is a consequence of the shift of the
weight of his imagination onto those themes from which we can
get no affirmation; in part this is due to weakness to realizing
character. Paola Maijstral, who has barely come alive in *V.,* is
too frail a phoenix; she is lost amid the collapse of so rich and
imaginatively intriguing an edifice as European culture. Benny
Profane, good-hearted *schlemiel,* and McClintic Sphere, a Negro
jazz musician who tells us to "keep cool but care," do not stand out
against the bleak and sepulchral twilight of the America of the
Whole Sick Crew. Oedipa Maas, for all Pynchon's obvious affection for her, is too slight a little housewife to lead us out of the
labyrinths of paranoid California.

Oedipa, in fact, illustrates the failure of Pynchon's characters
to carry the heavy themes of his novels. She is supposed to enact
the desperate and possibly self-destructive drive of Americans
to understand the causes of the meaninglessness of their lives,
but instead she haplessly stumbles through a Byzantine literary
maze. And, more important, she fails as a character to *dramatize*
her own supposed compulsions and needs. The source of the
problem lies in novelistic strategy. A novelist like Pynchon is
intent upon abstracting invalid or absurd philosophical, historical
and cultural ideas of our time and putting them in the richest
possible comic framework. He begins with the premise that such
ideas are no longer adequate guides or interpretations of modern
human life; the European humanistic tradition is moribund, so
we presumably don't live by it any more—it is only Stencilian
fantasy. Similarly, the American dream has become a nightmare
(even though we may be, like Pynchon himself, still nostalgically
attached to that dream). Such comic abstraction poses two difficulties. First, there is usually, as in these novels, a great dis-
crepancy between the imaginative power with which the comedy
of the ideas is rendered on the one hand, and the strength of the
depiction, on the other hand, of ordinary life's muted values of
domestic love, good fellowship, and considerateness. Secondly,
since the ideas have been abstracted from the lives of the characters, the ideas cannot be dramatized and the characters hence
are not realized. For instance, Herbert Stencil says that he him-

self used to be an aimless yo-yo, but that once he began his search into the causes of the breakdown of Western humanism, his life took on some purpose. Yet his personal fate does not seem to the reader to be tied up in any way with the deterioration of Western Europe's culture. Stencil does not live by those precepts, which have become invalid. Perhaps he is searching for the reason his life is now so empty, but there is still no tragedy—and very little drama—in the spectacle of an empty man idly fantasizing (in motion picture terms, at that) about the glory of a past life that he neither lived nor attains to. Nor can we be moved by the assertion that characters with comic book names who have not been brought by their creator to a believable level of humanity are in danger of drifting into inanimateness.

It is fair to take Pynchon to task for his failures to dramatize his themes through characterization because it is clear that at certain points in both his novels he is trying to achieve that dramatization. This is most apparent as we near the end of *V.*, and Pynchon attempts to portray both Rachel and Paola as women who have the emotional intensity to be potentially redemptive influences. Benny Profane, despite his inertness, is intended to be acting out—albeit in a nightmarish setting—a felt spiritual malaise, trying, in Rachel's words, to amplify his own flabby, clumsy soul into a Universal Principle. The poignancy of *Lot 49* depends to a great extent on our response to Oedipa's anguish and need. Despite the type names of his characters and the sustained parodic structures of both novels—and despite the precedence given to comic rhetoric—Pynchon is trying unsuccessfully to attain, at crucial moments in his novels, social realism and full realization, through character, of philosophical themes.

Yet most of us, as readers, respond favorably to the novels despite these faults. The conventional expectations of realism seem to be too narrow a critical focus to put on Pynchon's vivid novels, especially *V.*, for they don't allow for the power and the gusto of the comic invention that is so impressive in Pynchon's work. Few writers are able to create so detailed a fabric of purely imaginary and comic scene and action as Pynchon is in the *V.* episodes that take place in early 20th-century Egypt, Florence, or German South-West Africa. One never loses consciousness of the fact that these scenes are artifice, yet one gets great reading joy from the denseness, variety, and, indeed, the blatant artificiality, with which they are rendered. Nabokov's novels, and Joyce's too, have showed us that we can potentially draw as much personal delight and understanding from structures of artifice as we can from novels that give us the shock of recognition. Thus, although Pynchon is clearly straining intermittently to make his characters realistic and to dramatize his ideas through them, we are willing to overlook his failures along that line because we are aware that Pynchon's subject matter—the illusions that one has about his past and present culture—and Pynchon's objectives— to create highly elaborate and comic fiction—demand a more open novelistic expression than we are used to.

The structure that Pynchon's novels themselves seem to suggest is close to that of the romantic epics of the late middle ages and the Renaissance. One thinks of Ariosto, Tasso, and Spenser when one reads a novel of the profusion and intricacy of *V.* The romantic epic writers often projected the dim or confused historical and mythical events of their own cultures, transmuting them by imagination into stories by which ideas could be tested. A series of tales (like Stencil's yarns) was held together loosely by a quest and sustained by the wonder of a purely imaginative world. Evil grew and spread with an inexhaustible luxuriance as it does in the Mondaugen story, metamorphosizing before the reader's eyes and taking on hallucinatory forms. Love was one of the few constants in the epic's mutable world, as it is in Pynchon's. *V.* almost openly evokes the romantic epic in Stencil's fantasized quest for the legendary woman V., and Oedipa Maas observes at the beginning of *Lot 49* that she feels like a "captive maiden" imprisoned in a tower by the force of magic, with no knight to deliver her of its spell. These resemblances are not sufficient in themselves to indicate that Pynchon is intentionally remodeling the already highly malleable novel form in the image of the romantic epic—as John Barth and J. P. Donleavy have turned it back toward the picaresque in their novels—but they suggest that for what writers like Pynchon want to do in fiction—for the cultural and imaginative sweep they want to achieve—the structural looseness and imaginative freedom of a prose romantic epic may be the most congenial form.

For, as we have noted, Pynchon wants a structure than can accommodate a far-ranging and energetic comic mind. The release of creative energy, which Pynchon shares with other novelists of the sixties, seems, indeed, to belie the very "sickness" that Pynchon insists is with us. He is not the only novelist of his time to describe this sickness with great vitality, to draw energy from ennui, to render a supposedly sterile world with a fecund literary imagination. For a time when skepticism reigns, Pynchon shows there are remarkable ideational riches to work with.

Such a welling forth of creative energy—seen before in the early Victorian period as well as the Renaissance—may be an attempt to deal with the proliferation of objects in the world. Pynchon's novels often catalogue the mass of things with which modern life is inundated. The code of Tristero is W.A.S.T.E. Pynchon has great curiosity for all the things there are about us and for how they work, and at times one thinks he is trying to subsume them all by dint of literary imagination. Again, there is nothing new in this attempt—Joyce was doing it in *Ulysses*—but it is significant that it is still being made with such determination.

V. and *Lot 49* also seem to reflect the outpouring of information in modern life. It is unkind but intriguing to suggest that Pynchon elaborated a metaphor for his own efforts when he devised Maxwell's Demon, a little black box with a piston on the top. The demon, Oedipa is told, must be fed information by someone who is "sensitive" and then it converts that into energy which drives the piston. The Demon realizes the theory of entropy, which is a "figure of speech...a metaphor. It connects the world of thermodynamics to the world of information flow" (*L*, p. 77).

Sometimes one feels that Pynchon is feeding into his novels all the data he has, consuming it, and converting it into literary material. As one tries to cope with the plethora of literary concepts, philosophical ideas, all the snippets of information in these novels, he sometimes suspects that the following passage from Pynchon's short story, "Mortality and Mercy in Vienna," is part confession:

> Siegel began flipping over a stack of mental IBM cards frantically. There was something he knew, something he had had in college. It irritated him not to be able to call the information up because most of the courses he had taken had served no other function—at least such had been his undergraduate protests—than to provide material for conversation at parties like this one.[12]

The choice of the metaphor of IBM cards is apt for Pynchon because his literary invention draws heavily from science. The con-

[12]*Stories from Epoch: The First Fifty Issues* (1947-1964), ed. Baxter Hathaway (Ithaca, New York: Cornell University Press, 1966), p. 193.

cept of entropy that operates in Maxwell's Demon is played with at length in a short story entitled "Entropy." In the middle of *V.* is a suture-by-suture description of a nose job operation. SHROUD and SHOCK, the plastic dummies in *V.,* are described with technical thoroughness. Pynchon wrote *V.* while he was working as a technical writer for Boeing in Seattle, and his bent of mind is toward technical, complex structures, even when he is creating a mock Jacobean play or working out parallels of Graves' theory of the White Goddess. There are other writers who seem to yield to the same fascinations—Kurt Vonnegut, Jr., for example—and writers like John Barth who relish displays of technically intricate virtuosity. Pynchon is acute enough, of course, to detect the comic qualities of the amateur scientist or hobbyist as literary creator. The use of the Thurn and Taxis stamps in *Lot 49* parodies Nabokov's involuted artifices with lepidoptery in his novels.

Pynchon's own technical bent of mind, however, explains something of the quality of literary creation in his novels. For, rich and witty and crafty as Pynchon's imagination is, it is closer to invention than to what we normally consider imagination. We expect imagination to work in the Coleridgian way: to transform its material so that new relationships are created and new insights can be achieved by the use of the transmuting, molding power of the human mind. Pynchon, in the final analysis, does not achieve this kind of transformation. his character Fausto Maijstral states at one point that poets live in a world of metaphor and that metaphor has no value apart from its function as a "device, an artifice" to delude people into believing that the objects outside them reflect their human qualities. These metaphors work like the brilliant one in *Lot 49:* when Oedipa and her seducer Metzger reach a sexual climax, the Paranoids, an electric guitar playing rock group, reach a kind of musical "climax" themselves and blow all the fuses in the motel. Pynchon reiterates that metaphor—that our machines sometimes ludicrously mimic us, and vice-versa—throughout his novels. The common theme of *V.* and *Lot 49* is the failure of our cultural assumptions, our philosophies, and even our imaginative constructs, to transform our lives. We are prisoners in a world of phenomena, able only, at best, to devise cinema scenario parodies of the literary excesses of the past or to project elaborate conspiratorial fantasies that crackle out like bizarre short circuits of the brain. And, as if to illustrate his theme, Pynchon's own art turns frequently to purely mechanical and sometimes accidental resemblances for its source of metaphor and relies upon complicated invention to do its work.

Even his parodies are often contrivances. They are not reductive because they draw upon material that is usually self-parodying. They are not close enough to the works they mimic to be analytical, and they do not, as Joyce's parodies do, show us the relation of literary language to its content. Nor, despite Pynchon's closeness to Nabokov, do they succeed in shutting us off from the comfortable referents to experience that we bring to the reading of a book, thus compelling us, as Nabokov does so often, to respond simply to the artifice, to build up a series of emotional and critical relationships to something that we know is involuted and unrealistic—to force us into relativism. Pynchon pulls in and out of parody and half-hearted realism too often to achieve the polished surface of Nabokov's best novels; Pynchon parodies seem to be there largely to satisfy the novelist's pleasure in constructing them. They are usually simply elaborate amusements.

This may be why we sense that Pynchon's intricate novels do not realize their *imaginative* potentiality, even though we are quite willing to forego social realism, subtle characterization, and dramatization of ideas. His books may have brought romantic epic grandness and openness into the novel form, but they have, because of the nature of Pynchon's "metaphorical approach" to this material, failed to carry the romantic epic's transfiguring vision. To return to my own "metaphor," Pynchon's novels are more like tapestries—in which human beings in action are rendered as uncannily vivid figures in ornate scenes of heightened posing. They are colorful and varied and subtly woven. Their profusion of patterns and scenes recalls the aesthetic revels of the thirteenth-century tapestries which depicted a wild, elaborate world of dragons, fools, beggars, questing knights, angels, Apocalyptic flames, and crashing cities. At times we think we witness mutations of the patterns, but for all the winking eyes, the leering faces, and the startling juxtapositions that we momentarily discover, the world that is depicted has become only stylized, not transformed. Thus we return to our initial observation that the knight is two-dimensional, and he and his rearing horse, though delightful to behold, are frozen in their stances.

The Sacred, the Profane,
and *The Crying of Lot 49*

by Edward Mendelson

I

Pynchon's first two novels (a third has been announced at this writing) are in many ways inverted mirror images of each other. *V.* entered the world to almost universal praise. Although the book is enormous in its range of knowledge and incident, its sustained explosions of verbal and imaginative energy, its ability to excite the emotions without ever descending into the easy paths of self-praise or self-pity which less rigorous writers had been tracking for years, *V.* now seems less various, more single-minded, as readers become more familiar with it. By now it is clear—as it was not when the book was published—that *V.* explores a single action, although that action is repeatedly articulated in dozens of variants. That action is the decline, both in history broadly conceived and in individual characters, from energy to stasis, from the vital to the inanimate. *The Crying of Lot 49,* in contrast, at first received a relatively muted welcome. Compact where *V.* was expansive, consistent in style where the earlier book was virtually a compendium of rhetorics, *Lot 49* now proves to have hidden complexities and depths which its first readers almost entirely missed. And the complexities of the second book have illuminated some of the simplicities of the first. *Lot 49* clarified many of the issues in *V.* by inverting and developing them. *Gravity's Rainbow* will probably sort out some of the difficulties of *Lot 49*. The present essay is an attempt at an interim

"The Sacred, the Profane, and *The Crying of Lot 49,*" by Edward Mendelson. From *Individual and Community: Variations on a Theme in American Fiction,* edited by Kenneth H. Baldwin and David K. Kirby (Durham, N.C.: Duke University Press, 1975), pp. 182-222. Copyright 1975 by Duke University Press. Revised and slightly abridged for the present collection by the author.

progress report, with some new observations, on the reading of Pynchon's second book.

Both of the novels describe a gradual revelation of order and unity within the multiplicity of experience, but the kinds of order that the two books discover are almost diametrically opposed. Despite its cosmopolitan variety of incident and character, *V.* develops around a unifying principle that is ultimately constricting and infertile. The book's central metaphor is the thermodynamic concept of entropy, which for the moment may be defined loosely as the slowing down of a system, the calcifying decay of life and available energy on a scale that may be minute or global. Entropy is the principle within irreversible processes, the principle that, in Freud's words, opposes the undoing of what has already occurred. By extending this principle one may speculate that the universe itself must eventually suffer a "heat-death," reduced and simplified to a luke-warm system in which no energy may be used for any purpose. Pynchon used "Entropy" as the title and theme of one of his first published stories,[1] and the concept recurs, in a significantly different form, in *The Crying of Lot 49*. In Pynchon's hands entropy serves as a metaphor of exceptional range and emotional power, and in this Pynchon is not alone. The concept of entropy, whether or not it is named as such, has informed much fiction and philosophy for centuries: it is a central motif in satire, and is the historical principle behind Plato's account of four types of unjust society in the *Republic*.

The Crying of Lot 49, although slighter in scale than *V.,* finds the intrusive energy that is needed to reverse the process that *V.* describes. In *Lot 49* a world of triviality and "exitlessness"[2] becomes infused with energy and choice, and Pynchon seems to be demonstrating that he can balance the 500 pages of decline recounted in *V.* with some 200 pages of possible recovery in *Lot 49*. The ostensible subject of the latter novel is one woman's discovery of a system of communication, but the system refers to something far larger than itself: it fosters variety and surprise, and offers a potential access to "transcendent meaning" and "a reason that mattered to the world" (181). Extend the world of *V.*

[1]In *The Kenyon Review*, 20 (Spring, 1960), 277-292.

[2]*The Crying of Lot 49* (Philadelphia: Lippincott, 1966), p. 170. Further references to this novel are inserted parenthetically into the text. To find page references in the 1967 Bantam paperback edition, subtract 8 from the reference given and multiply the result by four-fifths.

beyond the book's final chapters, and you eventually intrude on the unlit, motionless world of the later Beckett. Extend *The Crying of Lot 49,* and you soon come in sight of Prospero's island and the seacoast of Bohemia. The processes of *V.* isolate; those of *Lot 49* create community.

Almost all the incidents in *V.* enact a decline of available energy, a hardening of living beings into artificial ones, a degradation from vitality to mechanism, a transfer of sympathy from human suffering to inanimate, objective existence. In the world of *V.* there can only be few alternatives to decline, and those few are weak: some understated temporary acts of escape and love, a sudden dash into the sea as all the lights go out in a city, the reconstruction of a marriage. All the rest leads to stasis—although the book's scale and exuberance suggest that mass decline is a principle of existence in the novel but not in its creator. The central plot from which the book's various historical fantasies depend—Egypt in 1898, Florence in 1899, Paris in 1913, Malta in 1919 and again in the 1940s, South-West Africa in 1922, and glimpses of a score of other settings and moments—involves the search made by one Herbert Stencil for traces of the woman V., who may have been Stencil's mother, as she moves through Europe and the twentieth century, becoming ever less vital and more artificial as she grows older. In her final manifestation as "the Bad Priest" at Malta during the Second World War, V. advises young girls to become nuns, to "avoid the sensual extremes —pleasures of intercourse, pain of childbirth"—and to stop the creation of new life. To young boys she preaches "that the object of male existence was to be like a crystal: beautiful and soulless."[3] And before her death she gives up much of her own body to inanimate surrogates: a wig, artificial feet, a glass eye containing a clock, false teeth. A jewel is later found sewn in her navel. Increasingly lifeless and crystalline, finally killed by the mechanical engines of war in the sky over Malta, the woman V. is the most vividly realized victim of the book's pandemic processes of inanition and decline. The other victims include a ruined product of failed plastic surgery, a man with a knife-switch in his arm, a synthetic body used for radiation research, a girl reduced to a fetish, a character named Profane who is constantly victimized by hostile objects. The book implies a conclusion that

[3]*V.* (Philadelphia: Lippincott, 1963), p. 340. Further references are given parenthetically in the text.

lies beyond itself: an ending where all life and warmth have declined and disappeared, an apocalypse that arrives in total silence.

"There is more behind and inside V. than any of us had suspected. Not who, but what: what is she," asks Stencil's father in his diary (*V.*, 53). The novel *V.* is an elaborate gloss on an earlier account of a woman whom history replaced with an object: the chapter on "The Dynamo and the Virgin" in *The Education of Henry Adams.* Pynchon's Stencil, who like Adams talks of himself in the third person, searches for a symbol even more inclusive than Adams's; V. is the virgin who *became* the dynamo. The woman V. is Stencil's reconstruction of scattered and ambiguous clues and symbols, gathered into episodes told by narrators—often obviously flawed and unreliable—whom Stencil creates for the occasion. Half the novel consists of Stencil's indirect narration of the life of V., who is seldom central to the story, but slips in sideways when she is least expected. Stencil's reconstruction of V.'s fragmentary signs—an enactment in reverse of her physical disintegration—is a paradigm of Pynchon's reconstruction of twentieth-century history, a reconstruction in which he establishes the novel's background. The woman V., like Pynchon's history, is put together by design. In his Spenglerian sweep through the century (Stencil, born in 1901, is "the century's child" [*V.*, 52] as well as, perhaps, V.'s) Pynchon invents coincidences and patterns which suggest historical design in the novel's world. "If the coincidences are real then Stencil has never encountered history at all, but something far more appalling" (*V.*, 450).

This suggestion of will and design in history is analogous to Stencil's own "design" of V., but Pynchon makes the analogy even more complex and suggestive than a simple equation can be. First of all, V. is not entirely a product of Stencil's reconstructions. The frame of the novel *V.* is a narrator's direct account of events in 1955 and 1956, events which include Stencil's *in*direct narrations of the life of V. (Pynchon makes certain that Stencil's narratives, compelling as they are, will be taken as speculative and suspect: people speak and understand languages which they could not understand "in life," and characters in the book occasionally point out such improbabilities.) The direct framing narrative is, unlike Stencil's, apparently reliable, and it gradually and increasingly provides its own, un-Stencilled, evidence of V.'s existence. "The Confessions of Fausto Maijstral," an apparently reliable narrative

written by the last person who saw V. alive, has a chapter to itself, unmediated by Stencil; it presents a plausible account of
V.'s final moments. And a relic of V., an ivory comb which in
Stencil's invented narrative she had perhaps acquired decades
earlier, later appears both in Maijstral's confessions and, in the
hands of Maijstral's daughter, in Pynchon's direct narrative. The
comb serves as a kind of optical proof that V. once existed in the
world of the book. But by the time the evidence appears in the direct narrative, Stencil has gone off to Stockholm to pursue other
and more tenuous threads, and the authentic clue eludes him,
presumably forever. The moment when the comb reappears is a
heartbreaking one, not only because the reader knows then that
one neat and satisfying conclusion to the novel—a reasonably
successful conclusion to Stencil's search—has been irrevocably
denied, but also because the incident makes a faint and reticent
suggestion of the limits of human knowledge: a suggestion which,
perhaps because of its reticence, rings true.

This leads back to the matter of historical design. For the characters in the direct narration of the book, V.'s existence is never
more than speculative: their evidence of her is always partial.
It is only the narrator, who has no *use* for it, who has thorough
knowledge of the evidence and of the "truth." The characters
have only partial knowledge of what in the book "in fact" exists.
Now, the book's Spenglerian speculation on historical design is
also a reconstruction from partial evidence, for even the narrator's historical knowledge is severely limited. But by analogy
with the "real" coherence of the woman V. (and the book softly
but insistently presses the analogy), there may, the book suggests,
be a real order and coherence to history in the world of phenomena that lies outside fiction's garden. But, as the genuine signs
of V. elude Stencil—though they do exist, and Stencil has partial
knowledge of some of them—so there may be a genuine transcendent coherence in the world's history, although the signs of that coherence either refuse to cooperate with our preconceptions, or
elude us entirely. *V.* is finally a tragedy of human limitation,
and like all tragedy it points towards the larger frame in which
the tragic action occurs. The contradiction between human ignorance of the frame, and the frame itself, is tragedy's ultimate source,
its mode of being.

II

In contrast with the absconded signs of *V.*, the signs that appear throughout *The Crying of Lot 49* are not elusive at all. They intrude iteratively on the book's heroine until they entirely supplant the undemanding world with which she had once been familiar. In *Lot 49* the systems of interrelation and commonality that inform the book's world have consequences entirely different from the superficially similar systems in *V.* To participate in the processes of decadence in *V.* you have only to become passive, inanimate and selfish; history, which simplifies *V.*'s world, will do the rest. But in *The Crying of Lot 49* the revealed pattern offers "maybe even...a real alternative to the exitlessness, to the absence of surprise to life that harrows the head of everybody American you know" (170), an alternative to physical crowding and ethical vacancy, an alternative that reveals itself quietly but persistently to the passive listener, yet will not allow that listener to remain passive for long. In this second novel, published only three years after *V.*, a hidden order reinfuses Pynchon's world with energy, adds to the world's complexity and demands not acquiescence but conscious choice.

Described briefly, in the sort of bare outline that makes any serious plot sound ridiculous, *The Crying of Lot 49* recounts the discovery by its heroine, Mrs. Oedipa Maas, of an ancient and secret postal system named the Tristero. The manifestations of the Trystero (an alternative spelling), and all that accompanies it, are always associated in the book with the language of the sacred and with patterns of religious experience; the foils to the Trystero are always associated with sacrality gone wrong. As every person and event in *V.* is implicated in the general decline into the inanimate, everything in *Lot 49* participates either in the sacred or the profane. A major character in *V.* is named Benny Profane; in *Lot 49* there are wider possibilities (including someone named Grace). As Pynchon's work avoids the weightlessness of Nabokovian fantasy, so it avoids the self-important *nostalgie de la boue* of the social and psychological novels that occupy most of the fictional space in postwar America. Oedipa has "all manner of revelations,"

but they are not in the manner of most recent fiction, and certainly not the kind of revelations that her name might suggest: they
are "hardly about...herself" (20). Pynchon writes at the end of
an era in which the Freudian interpretation of an event served as a
more than adequate succedanium for the event itself: it was an act
of courage to name his heroine Oedipa (I shall have more to say
later about the courage to risk facetiousness), for the novel contains not even a single reference to her emotional relations with
her parents or her impulses towards self-creation. The name instead refers back to the Sophoclean Oedipus who begins his search
for the solution of a problem (a problem, like Oedipa's, involving a dead man) as an almost detached observer, only to discover
how deeply implicated he is in what he finds. As the book opens,
and Oedipa learns that she has been named executor of the estate of
the "California real estate mogul" Pierce Inverarity, she "shuffl[es]
back" in her memory "through a fat deckful of days which seemed...
more or less identical" (11). But as she begins to sort out the complications of Inverarity's estate she becomes aware of moments
of special significance, repeated patterns of meaning, which had
not previously been apparent. Driving into the town where Inverarity's interests had been centered, she looks down from the freeway
upon "the ordered swirl of houses and streets" and senses the
possibility of a *kind* of meaning that is, for the moment, beyond
her comprehension:

> she thought of the time she'd opened a transitor radio to replace
> a battery and seen her first printed circuit. The ordered swirl of
> houses and streets, from this high angle, sprang at her now with the
> same unexpected, astonishing clarity...[T]here were to both out-
> ward patterns a hieroglyphic sense of concealed meaning, of an in-
> tent to communicate...[Now,] a revelation also trembled just past
> the threshold of her understanding...[She] seemed parked at the
> centre of an odd religious instant. As if, on some other frequency,
> or out of the eye of some whirlwind rotating too slow for heated
> skin even to feel the centrifugal coolness of, words were
> being spoken.   (24-25)

At this point Oedipa's revelations are only partly defined. In the
next paragraph the narrator dismisses Oedipa's experience by plac-
ing it in distancing quotation marks: "the 'religious instant,' or
whatever it might have been."

But a few pages later an "instant" of the same kind occurs, this time more clearly defined. Oedipa sees in a television commercial a map of one of Inverarity's housing developments, and is reminded of her first glimpse of the town in which she is now: "Some immediacy was there again, some promise of hierophany" (31). This "promise of hierophany," of a manifestation of the sacred, is eventually fulfilled, and her "sense of concealed meaning" yields to her recognition of patterns that had potentially been accessible to her all along, but which only now had revealed themselves. In the prose sense, what Oedipa discovers is the Trystero, "a network by which X number of American are truly communicating whilst reserving their lies, recitations of routine, arid betrayals of spiritual poverty"—that is, everything profane—"for the official government delivery system" (170). But across this hidden and illegal network information is transmitted in ways that defy ordinary logic: often, the links in the system cross centuries, or move between the most unlikely combinations of sender and receiver, without anyone in the world of routine ever recognizing that something untoward has occurred. The Trystero carries with it a sense of sacred connection and relation in the world, and by doing so it manifests a way of comprehending the world. By the end of the novel Oedipa is left alone, out over seventy thousand fathoms, left to decide for herself whether the Trystero exists or if she has merely fantasized it, or if she has been hoodwinked into believing in it. On that all-or-nothing decision, everything—her construing of the world, and the world's construction—depends:

> how had it ever happened here, with the chances once so good for diversity? For it was now like walking among matrices of a great digital computer, the zeroes and ones twinned above, hanging like balanced mobiles right and left, ahead, thick, maybe endless. Behind the hieroglyphic streets there would either be a transcendent meaning, or only the earth. ... Ones and zeroes. ... Another mode of meaning behind the obvious, or none. Either Oedipa in the orbiting ecstasy of a true paranoia, or a real Tristero. For there was either some Tristero behind the appearance of the legacy America, or there was just America. ...   (181-182)

As in all religious choices, no proof is possible: the choice of ones or zeroes presents itself "ahead ... maybe endless," and the watcher is left alone.

Pynchon uses religious terms and hieratic language not simply as a set of metaphors from which to hang his narrative, not merely as a scaffolding (as Joyce, for example, uses Christian symbols in *Ulysses*). The religious meaning of the book does not reduce to metaphor or myth, *because religious meaning is itself the central issue of the plot*. This creates difficulties for criticism. The Trystero implies universal meanings, and because universal meanings are notoriously recalcitrant to analysis, it will be necessary to approach the holistic center of the book from various facts and fragments. I hope the reader will bear with an argument that may, for a number of pages, ask him to assent to resolutions of issues which have not yet been discussed.

The book refers at one point to "the secular Tristero," which has a plausible history and a recognizable origin in ordinary human emotion and human society. During one of the few areas of the narrative in which nothing extraordinary happens—a "secular" part of the book—Oedipa compiles, with the help of one of the book's prosier characters (an English professor, alas), a history of the system, a history which is somewhat speculative, but more plausible than the mock-theorizing in *V*. The history of the Trystero intersects with authentic history in a manner taken from historical novels like *Henry Esmond* or *The Scarlet Pimpernel,* where an extraordinary, fictional pattern of events, one which almost but not quite alters the larger course of history, is presented behind the familiar, public pattern. Pynchon's Trystero, then, began in sixteenth-century Holland, when an insurgent Calvinist government unseated the hereditary postmaster, a member of the Thurn and Taxis family (here Pynchon blends authentic history with novelistic fantasy—the counts of Taxis did hold the postal monopoly in the Empire), and replaced him with one Jan Hinckart, Lord of Ohain. But Hinkart's right to the position, which he gained through political upheaval, not through inheritance, is disputed by a Spaniard, Hernando Joaquín di Tristero y Calavera, who claims to be Hinckart's cousin and the legitimate Lord of Ohain—and therefore the legitimate postmaster. Later, after an indecisive struggle between Hinckart and Tristero, the Calvinists are overthrown, and the Thurn and Taxis line restored to postmastership. But Tristero, claiming that the postal monopoly was Ohain's by conquest, and therefore his own by blood, sets up an alternative postal system, and proceeds to wage guerrilla war against the Thurn and Taxis system. The rallying theme of Tristero's struggle: "disinheritance" (159-160).

So far, the story, though a fantasy, is still historically plausible, requiring only a relatively slack suspension of disbelief. However, the word Calavera (skull, Calvary) in Tristero's name already suggests some emblematic resonances, and the theme of disinheritance joins the Tristero's history to Oedipa's discovery of it while executing a will. Later in the history, the Trystero system takes on, *for its contemporaries,* a specifically religious meaning. Pynchon invents a severe Calvinist sect, the Scurvhamites, who tend toward the gnostic heresy and see Creation as a machine, one part of which is moved by God, the other by a soulless and automatic principle. When the Scurvhamites decide to tamper with some secular literature (specifically, the play *The Courier's Tragedy,* of which more shortly) to give it doctrinal meaning, they find that the "Trystero would symbolize the Other quite well" (156). For Thurn and Taxis itself, faced with the enmity of the anonymous and secret Trystero system, "many of them must [have] come to believe in something very like the Scurvhamite's blind, automatic anti-God. Whatever it is, it has the power to murder their riders, send landslides thundering across their roads...disintegrate the Empire." But this belief cannot last: "over the next century and a half the paranoia recedes, [and] they come to discover the secular Tristero" (165). The Trystero returns from its symbolic meanings into a realm which is historically safe and believable. In this passage Pynchon offers an analogously safe way to read his own book: the Trystero is a symbol for a complex of events taking place on the level of a battle in heaven, but it is merely a symbol, merely a way of speaking with no hieratic significance in itself. But the novel, while offering this possibility, does so in a chapter in which nothing strange happens, where the world is Aristotelian and profane, where the extraordinary concrescenses of repetition and relation which inform the rest of the book briefly sort themselves out into simple, logical patterns. The book offers the possibility that its religious metaphor is only metaphor: but if the book were founded on this limited possibility, the remaining portions of the book would make no sense, and there would be little reason to write it in the first place.

The potted history near the end of the novel describes the discovery of the "secular Tristero" behind the demonic one; the book itself describes the progressive revelation of the sacred significance behind certain historical events. It should perhaps be pointed out that the frequent associations of the Trystero with the demonic do not contradict the Trystero's potentially sacred significance: the demonic is a subclass of the sacred, and exists, like the sacred, on a plane of meaning different from the profane and the secular. When Pynchon published two chapters from the book in a magazine he gave them the title, "The World (This One), the Flesh (Mrs. Oedipa Maas), and the Testament of Pierce Inverarity":[4] it is through Inverarity's will that Oedipa completes this proverbial equation, finding her own devil in the agonizing ontological choice she has to make as the novel ends. The revelation of the sacred gets underway when Oedipa sees in the map of one of Inverarity's interests "some promise of hierophany." The sense of the word "hierophany" is clear enough—it is a manifestation of the sacred—but the word itself has a history which is informative in this context. The word is not recorded in the dictionaries of any modern European language (the related "hierophant" is of course recorded, but "hierophany" is not), and it appears to have been invented by Mircea Eliade,[5] who expands most fully on the word in his *Patterns in Comparative Religion* but gives a more straightforward definition in his introduction to *The Sacred and the Profane*: "Man becomes aware of the sacred because it manifests itself, shows itself, as something wholly different from the profane. To designate the *act of manifestation* of the sacred, we have proposed the term *hierophany*. It is a fitting term, because it does not imply anything further; it expresses no more than is implicit in its etymological content, *i.e.*, that *something sacred shows itself to us*. ... From the most elementary hierophany... to the supreme hierophany...there is no solution of continuity. In each case we are confronted by the same mysterious act—the manifestation of something of a wholly different order, a reality that does not belong to our world, in objects that are an integral part of our natural 'profane' world."[6] This later condition, that the objects in which the sacred manifests itself be part of the natural world, is central to *Lot 49*, because everything in the novel that points to a sacred significance in the Trystero has, potentially,

---

[4]*Esquire*, 64 (Dec., 1965), 171. This title is noted on the copyright page of the novel, while the title of another excerpt published elsewhere is pointedly omitted.

[5]Reinvented, actually: the word seems to have had a technical meaning in Greek religion.

[6]New York: Harcourt, Brace, 1959, p. 11. Eliade's italics.

a secular explanation. The pattern and the coherence may, as Oedipa reminds herself, be the product of her own fantasy or of someone else's hoax. She is left, at every moment, to affirm or deny the sacredness of what she sees.

When, as she begins to uncover the Trystero, Oedipa decides to give, through her own efforts, some order to Inverarity's tangled interests, she writes in her notebook, "Shall I project a world?" (82). But her plan to provide her own meanings, "to bestow life on what had persisted" of the dead man, soon confronts the anomaly that more meanings, more relationships and connections than she ever expected begin to offer themselves—manifest themselves. And these manifestations arrive without any effort on her part. When, by the middle of the book, "everything she saw, smelled, dreamed, remembered, would somehow come to be woven into The Trystero" (81), she tries to escape, to cease looking for order. "She had only to drift," she supposes, "at random, and watch nothing happen, to be convinced that it was purely nervous, a little something for her shrink to fix" (104). But when she drifts that night through San Francisco she finds more extensive and more varied evidence of the Trystero's existence—evidence far more frequent and insistent than she found when she was actually looking for it. Like the mystic whose revelation is dependent on his passivity, Oedipa's full discovery of the Trystero depends on her refusal to search for it. In the last chapter even the most surprising events leave her only in expectant passivity: "Even a month ago, Oedipa's next question would have been 'Why?' But now she kept a silence, waiting, as if to be illuminated" (152).

Recent criticism has devoted much energy to finding detective-story patterns in fiction, and *The Crying of Lot 49*, with its heroine named after the first detective of them all, lends itself admirably to this method. However, Pynchon's novel uses mechanisms borrowed from the detective story to produce results precisely the opposite of those in the model. Where the object of a detective story is to reduce a complex and disordered situation to simplicity and clarity, and in doing so to isolate in a named locus the disruptive element in the story's world, *The Crying of Lot 49* starts with a relatively simple situation, and then lets it get out of the heroine's control: the simple becomes complex, responsibility becomes not isolated but universal, the guilty locus turns out to be everywhere, and individual clues are unimportant because neither clues nor deduction can lead to the solution.

"Suppose, God, there really was a Tristero then and that she *had* come on it by accident. ...[S] he might have found The Tristero anywhere in her Republic, through any of a hundred lightly-concealed entranceways, a hundred alienations, if only she'd looked" (179). What the detective in this story discovers is a way of thinking which renders detection irrelevant. "The Christian," Chesterton writes somewhere, "has to use his brains to see the hidden good in humanity just as the detective has to use his brains to see the hidden evil." This, in essence, describes Oedipa's problem: she never discovers the alienation and incoherence in the world—those were evident from the start—but she stumbles instead across the hidden relationships in the world, relations effected through and manifested in the Trystero.

Near the middle of the book Oedipa stops searching. From this point on she becomes almost the only character in the novel who is *not* looking for something. While hierophanies occur all around her, almost everyone else is vainly trying to wrench an experience of the sacred out of places where it cannot possibly be found. As everyone in *V.* worries constantly about the inanimate, everyone in *The Crying of Lot 49* suffers from some distortion of religious faith, and almost everyone in the book eventually drops away from Oedipa into some religious obsession.[7] Their examples demonstrate the wrong turnings that Oedipa must avoid.

Mucho Maas, for example, Oedipa's husband, who works as a disc jockey, suffers "regular crises of conscience about his profession[:] 'I just don't believe in any of it'" (12). This sounds at first like a suburban cliché, but the religious language soon develops in complexity and allusiveness. Oedipa's incomprehension during her first "religious instant" reminds her of her husband "watching one of his colleagues with a headset clamped on and cueing the next record with movements stylized as the handling of chrism, censer, chalice might be for a holy man...[D] id Mucho stand outside Studio A looking in, knowing that even if he could hear it, he couldn't believe in it?" (25). His previous job had been at a used car lot, where although "he had believed in the cars"

---

[7]One character who drops away from Oedipa, but without any religious significance to his actions, is her coexecutor, the lawyer Metzger, who goes off to marry a sixteen-year-old girl. Metzger, who never takes the slightest interest in the other characters' preoccupations, seems to serve in the novel as the representative of the entirely profane. His name, appropriately enough, is the German word for butcher.

he suffered from a nightmare of alienation and nothingness (which also provides Pynchon with a send-up of Hemingway's "A Clean, Well-Lighted Place"): "'We were a member of the National Automobile Dealers' Association. N.A.D.A. Just this creaking metal sign that said nada, nada, against the blue sky. I used to wake up hollering'" (144). His escape from a nihilistic void takes him into the impregnable solipsism granted by LSD, and he leaves Oedipa behind.

The drug had previously been urged on Oedipa herself by her psychiatrist, Dr. Hilarius, who conducts an experiment he calls the Bridge — not a bridge across to community but "the bridge inward." Oedipa, who seems to merit her revelations through her knowledge of what does *not* lead to revelation, knows that she "would be damned if she'd take the capsules he'd given her. Literally damned" (17). Hilarius himself distorts the purpose of faith. In an attempt to atone for his Nazi past he tries to develop "a faith in the literal truth of everything [Freud] wrote. ... It was ...a kind of penance. ... I wanted to believe, despite everything my life had been" (134-135). The strain finally sends him into paranoia and madness: fantasies of vengeful Israelis, a wish for death.

Randolph Driblette, who directs the play in which Oedipa first hears the name Trystero, suffers from the nihilistic pride that thinks itself the only possible source of order in the universe. In the play he directs, "'the reality is in *this* head. Mine. I'm the projector in the planetarium, all the closed little universe visible in the circle of that stage is coming out of my mouth, eyes, sometimes other orifices also'" (79). (It is from Driblette that Oedipa borrows the metaphor of her notebook-question, "Shall I project a world?") In directing plays Driblette "felt hardly any responsibility toward the word, really; but to...its spirit, he was always intensely faithful" (152). The logical response to a world where one creates, alone, the only order — where one ignores the *data* of the word — is nihilistic despair. And the logical culmination of an exclusive devotion to the spirit is the sloughing-off of the flesh. Driblette commits suicide by walking into the sea.

John Nefastis, the inventor of a machine which joins the worlds of thermodynamics and information theory (of which more later) through the literal use of a scientific metaphor known as Maxwell's Demon is "impenetrable, calm, a believer" — in whose presence Oedipa feels "like some sort of heretic." Nefastis, the book's

fundamentalist, believes his scientific metaphor is "not only verbally graceful, but also objectively true." His language recalls
similar moments in the rest of the book when he refers to the
visible operation of his machine as "the secular level" (105-106),
and the photograph of the physicist James Clerk Maxwell that
adorns the machine is, oddly enough (though the narrator does
not remark on the oddity), "the familiar Society for the Propagation of Christian Knowledge photo" (86). Nefastis's unbalanced
science is endorsed, shakily, by the language of belief.

At least one character, however, has something of the enlight-
enment that Oedipa is approaching. A Mexican anarchist whom
Oedipa meets on her night of drifting, and whom she and Inverarity had first met in Mexico some years before, is named
Jesus Arrabal. When he talks politics his language quickly shifts
to the language of religion:

> You know what a miracle is...another world's intrusion into this
> one. Most of the time we coexist peacefully, but when we do touch
> there's cataclysm. Like the church we hate, anarchists also believe
> in another world. Where revolutions break out spontaneous and
> leaderless, and the soul's talent for consensus allows the masses to
> work together without effort. ... And yet...if any of it should ever
> really happen that perfectly, I would also have to cry miracle. An
> anarchist miracle. Like your friend [Inverarity the real-estate
> mogul]. He is too exactly and without flaw the thing we fight. In
> Mexico the privilegiado is always, to a finite percentage, redeemed,
> one of the people. Unmiraculous. But your friend, unless he's
> joking, is as terrifying to me as a Virgin appearing to an Indian. (120)

The intersection of two worlds in miracles is a theme we shall return to. For the moment, it should be noted that Arrabal admits
the possibility that the "miraculous" Inverarity may be "joking"
—just as Oedipa has to admit the possibility that the miraculous
Trystero may be a hoax, a joke written by Inverarity into his will.

Compared with the obsessions and confusions that surround
most of the other characters, the religious language associated
with Oedipa herself is on a different and much clearer level.
The word "God" occurs perhaps twenty times in the book (it appears hardly at all in *V.*), and on almost every occasion the word
hovers near Oedipa or her discoveries. In her very first word, on
the first page of the book, she "spoke the name of God, tried to
feel as drunk as possible." When she first encounters the Trystero's emblem, a drawing of a muted post horn, she copies it into

her notebook, "thinking: God, hieroglyphics" (52)—a double iteration, through the prefix *hiero,* of the Trystero's sacrality. In an early passage that anticipates the book's later, culminating reference to "a great digital computer [with] the zeroes and ones twinned above," Oedipa tries to elude a spray-can gone wild: "something fast enough, God or a digital machine, might have computed in advance the complex web of its travel" (37). When she sees the Trystero symbol in one more unexpected place she feels "as if she had been trapped at the center of some intricate crystal, and say[s], 'My God'" (92). "Suppose, God, there really was a Tristero," she considers; and faced with her final choice of ones and zeroes, of meaning or nothingness, she thinks, "this, oh God, was the void" (171). There are other examples. What would simply be a nagging cliché in another kind of novel becomes here a quiet but insistent echo, a muted but audible signal.

III

The Crying of Lot 49 is a book partly *about* communications and signals—Oedipa's discovery of the Trystero involves the interpretation of ambiguous signs—and, logically enough, its central scientific metaphor involves communication theory (alternately called Information Theory). It is through information theory, in fact, that Pynchon establishes in this novel an imaginative logical link with the world of his first novel, *V.* The two novels share some superficial details on the level of plot—one minor character appears briefly in both, a Vivaldi concerto for which someone is searching in *V.* is heard over muzak in *Lot 49*—but their deeper connection lies in *Lot 49's* extension and transformation of *V.'s* central metaphor. *V.* describes the thermodynamic process by which the world's entropy increases and by which the world's available energy declines. But the equations of thermodynamics and the term "entropy" itself were also employed, decades after their original formulation, in information theory, where they took on a wider and more complex function than they had ever had before. By using information theory as a controlling pattern of ideas in his second book, Pynchon is in one way simply extending the metaphor central to his first book: but the extension also adds immeasurably to the complexity and fertility of the original idea. Thermodynamic entropy is (to speak loosely) a measure of stagnation. As thermodynamic entropy increases in a system, and its available energy decreases, information about the system increases: the system loses some of its uncertainty, its potential. In the language of information theory, however, entropy is the measure of *un*certainty in a system. As you *increase* thermodynamic entropy, therefore, you *decrease* information entropy.[8] In information theory, also, the *entropy rate* of a system is the rate at which information is transmitted. Entropy increases in *V.,* and the world slows down; in *The Crying of Lot 49* Oedipa receives more and more surprises, more and more rapidly, and entropy still increases—but now it is information entropy rather than thermodynamic entropy, and the effect of the increase is invigorating rather than stagnating.

Metaphorically, then, the two meanings of the term "entropy" are in opposition, and it is precisely this opposition which John Nefastis tries to exploit in his machine. Oedipa finds Nefastis's account of his machine confusing, but

> she did gather that there were two distinct kinds of this entropy. One having to do with heat-engines, the other to do with communication. The equation for one, back in the '30's, had looked very like the equation for the other. It was a coincidence. The two fields were entirely unconnected, except at one point: Maxwell's Demon. As the Demon sat and sorted his molecules into hot and cold, the system was said to lose entropy. But somehow the loss was offset by the information gained about what molecules were where.
>
> "Communication is the key," cried Nefastis. ...   (105)

When Maxwell's hypothetical "Demon" (a received term that fits neatly into Pynchon's hieratic language) sorts hot and cold molecules, he can apparently raise the temperature in one part of a system, and lower the temperature in the other part, without expending work—thereby *decreasing* the system's thermodynamic entropy, in violation of the second law of thermodynamics. But the decrease of thermodynamic entropy is balanced by an *increase* in information entropy, thereby supposedly making the whole thing "possible," when a person whom Nefastis calls a "sensitive" transmits information to the Demon that Nefastis believes is actually in his machine.[9] Nefastis mixes the language of science with that of spiritualism. The "sensitive" has to receive data "at

[8]This usage conforms to that of the founder of the theory, Claude Shannon, but is disputed by other scientists. For a full discussion see Leon Brillouin's *Science and Information Theory* (New York, 1956), to which I am deeply indebted.

[9]The real scientific problem behind this fantasy is described by Brillouin (ch. 13).

some deep psychic level" from the Demon; the "sensitive" achieves his effects by staring at the photo of Maxwell on the machine; and so forth. The whole effect is one of Blavatskian mumbo-jumbo, but Nefastis also uses the language of belief which Oedipa is learning to understand. Feeling "like some kind of heretic," she doubts Nefastis's enterprise: "The true sensitive is the one that can share in the man's hallucinations, that's all" (107). But the implied question, raised by Oedipa's doubt, is whether Oedipa's sensitivity to the Trystero is also the product of hallucinations.

The Nefastis machine is based on the similarity between the equations for information entropy and those of thermodynamic entropy, a similarity which Nefastis calls a "metaphor." The machine "makes the metaphor not only verbally graceful, but also objectively true" (106). Pynchon has much to say elsewhere in the book about the relation between truth and metaphor, but Nefastis's error is based on the confusion of language and reality, on an attempt to make two worlds coincide. Nefastis, the "believer," has faith in his metaphor, and believes that the truth of that faith can objectively be demonstrated and confirmed. Oedipa, on the other hand, receives no confirmation. Faith, wrote Paul to the Hebrews, is "the evidence of things *not* seen."

Besides using the association of entropy and information theory, Pynchon also exploits the theory's rule concerning the relation of surprise and probability in the transmitting of data. Briefly, the rule states that the more unexpected a message is, the more information it contains: a series of repetitive messages conveys less information than a series of messages that differ from each other. (Of course there must be a balance between surprise and probability: a message in language the receiver cannot understand is very surprising, but conveys little information.) In *The Crying of Lot 49* there are *two* secret communications systems: the Trystero, and its entirely secular counterpart, the system used by the right-wing Peter Pinguid Society. Both circumvent the official government delivery system, but, unlike the Trystero, the Pinguid Society's system cares less about transmitting information than about nose-thumbing the bureaucracy. Oedipa happens to be with a member of the Society when he receives a letter with the PPS postmark:

> *Dear Mike,* it said, *how are you? Just thought I'd drop you a note. How's your book coming? Guess that's all for now. See you at The Scope* [a bar].

> "That's how it is," [the PPS member] confessed bitterly, "most of
> the time."   (53)

The Pinguid Society's letters, bearing no information, are empty
and repetitive. With the Trystero, in contrast, even the stamps
are surprising:

> In the 3¢ Mothers of America Issue...the flowers to the lower left
> of Whistler's Mother had been replaced by Venus's-flytrap, bella-
> donna, poison sumac and a few others Oedipa had never seen. In
> the 1947 Postage Stamp Centenary Issue, commemorating the great
> postal reform that has meant the beginning of the end for private
> carriers [of which the Trystero is the only survivor], the head of a
> Pony Express rider at the lower left was set at a disturbing angle
> unknown among the living. The deep violet 3¢ regular issue of
> 1954 had a faint, menacing smile on the face of the Statue of
> Liberty....   (174)

This delicate balance of the familiar and the unexpected (note,
for example, that there are enough surprising poison plants, on
one of the stamps, to indicate that the even more surprising ones
which "Oedipa had never seen" are also poisonous) produces a
powerful sense of menace and dread—a sense no less powerful
for its comic aspects—while the secular Pinguid Society messages are capable only of conventionality, of repetition without
any sense of the numinous.

The unit of information in communication theory is the *bit*,
abbreviated from *b*inary dig*it*. Theoretically, all information can
be conveyed in a sequence of binary digits, i.e., ones and zeroes.
By the end of the novel, in a passage quoted above, Oedipa perceives the dilemma presented to her by the possible existence of
the Trystero in terms of the choice between one bit and another
(Pynchon always provides the possibility that the Trystero is
"only" Oedipa's fantasy, or that the whole system is a hoax written into Inverarity's will): "For it was now like walking among
matrices of a great digital computer, the zeroes and ones twinned
above...Behind the hieroglyphic streets there would either be a
transcendent meaning, or only the earth" (181). The signs themselves do not prove anything: the streets are "hieroglyphic"—
an example of sacred carving—but behind the sacred sign *may*
lie what is merely profane, "only the earth." The religious content of the book is fixed in Oedipa's dilemma: the choice between

the *zero* of secular triviality and chaos, and the *one* which is the *ganz andere* of the sacred.

In Pynchon's novel, as in life, there are two kinds of repetition: trivial repetition, as in the monotony of the Pinguid Society letters, and repetition that may signify the timeless and unchanging sacred. In *The Sacred and the Profane* Eliade writes that "religious man lives in two kinds of time, of which the more important, sacred time, appears under the paradoxical aspect of a circular time, reversible and recoverable, a sort of mythical present that is periodically regenerated by means of rites" (70).[10] Oedipa's first experience (in the book, that is) of trivial repetition occurs when she encounters a debased version of Eliade's "circular time, reversible and recoverable." In the second chapter, before she has any evidence of the Trystero, she watches television in the Echo Courts motel (the name is a grace-note on the main theme), with her coexecutor Metzger—a lawyer, once a child actor. The film on the screen turns out to star Metzger as a child, and when the film-Metzger sings a song, "his aging double, over Oedipa's protests, sang harmony" (31). At the end of the book, Oedipa wonders if the Trystero system is simply a plot against her; here, at the beginning, she suspects that Metzger "bribed the engineer over the local station to run this[:] it's all part of a plot, an elaborate, seduction, *plot.*" Time, on this occasion, seems to become even more confused and circular when one reel of the film is shown in the wrong order: "'Is this before or after?' she asked."

In the midst of the film Oedipa glimpses a more significant form of repetition: in a passage I discussed earlier, a map in a television commercial reminds her of the "religious instant" she felt on looking over the town where she is now. But this significant repetition occurs in the midst of reports of other, sterile ones. For example, Metzger, an actor turned lawyer, describes the pilot film of a television series on his own life, starring a friend of his, a lawyer turned actor. The film rests isolated in its own meaningless circular time, "in an air-conditioned vault...light can't fatigue it, it can be repeated endlessly." Outside the motel room, a rock-music group called the Paranoids, who all look alike, seem to be multiplying—"others must be plugging in"—until their equipment blows a fuse.

[10]Compare Malta, in *V.,* "where all history seemed simultaneously present" (481).

In contrast, the recurring evidence of the Trystero which Oedipa later discovers suggests that something complex and significant has existed almost unaltered for centuries, in Eliade's "mythical present that is periodically reintegrated." Many of the events, linked with the Trystero, that occur in the Jacobean *Courier's Tragedy* which Oedipa sees early in the book, recur in the midst of the California gold rush, and again in a battle in Italy during the Second World War. The Trystero's emblem, a muted post horn (suggesting the demonic aspect of the system: it mutes the trumpet of apocalypse), recurs in countless settings, in children's games, in postmarks, lapel pins, tattoos, rings, scrawled on walls, doodled in notebooks—in dozens of contexts that cannot, through any secular logic, be connected. Each of these repetitions, each evidence of the Trystero's persistence, seems to Oedipa a link with another world. As the Nefastis machine futilely tried to link the "worlds" of thermodynamics and communications, Jésus Arrabal talks of a miracle as "another world's intrusion into this one" (120). Those who joined the Trystero, Oedipa thinks, must have entered some kind of community when they withdrew from the ordinary life of the Republic, and, "since they could not have withdrawn into a vacuum...there had to exist the separate, silent, unexpected world" (92). To enter the Trystero, to become aware of it, is to cross the threshold between the profane and sacred worlds. "The threshold," Eliade writes in *The Sacred and the Profane,* "is the limit, the boundary, the frontier that distinguishes and opposes two worlds—and at the same time the paradoxical place where those two worlds communicate, where passage from the profane to the sacred world becomes possible" (25). Oedipa wonders if she could have "found the Trystero...through any of a hundred lightly-concealed entranceways, a hundred alienations" (179).

Yet in the middle of the fifth chapter of the book the entranceways, the alienations ("Decorating each alienation...was somehow always the post horn"—123), suddenly disappear: the repetitions stop. For perhaps thirty pages Oedipa receives no immediate signs of the Trystero, nothing more than some historical documents and second-hand reports. Until the middle of the fifth chapter (131, to be exact) Oedipa consistently sees the post horn as a living and immediate symbol, actively present in the daily life around her. From that point on she only hears about its past existence through documents, stamps, books—always second-hand. (This distinction is nowhere mentioned in the book, but the clean break after page 131 is too absolute to be accidental.) And at the same time, all her important human contacts begin to fade and disperse: "They are stripping from me, she said subvocally — feeling like a fluttering curtain, in a very high window moving ...out over the abyss. ...My shrink...has gone mad; my husband, on LSD, gropes like a child further and further into the rooms and endless rooms of the elaborate candy house of himself and away, hopelessly away, from what has passed, I was hoping forever, for love;...my best guide to the Trystero [Driblette] has taken a Brody. Where am I?" (152-153). Without signs, without the repetition which all signs embody, she is left to her own devices. Until now, the repetitions *told* her of the Trystero ("the repetition of symbols was to be enough...*She was meant to remember. ...* Each clue that comes is *supposed* to have its own clarity, its fine chances for permanence" — Pynchon's italics), but the simple reception of signs is insufficient for the revelation she is approaching: "she wondered if each one of the gemlike 'clues' were only some kind of compensation. To make up for her having lost the direct, epileptic Word, the cry that might abolish the night" (118).

Pynchon's reference to epilepsy recalls its traditional status as a sacred disease. A few pages earlier, Oedipa had encountered another repetition of one of the book's motifs: the destruction of a cemetery for a freeway. When she hears the cemetery and freeway mentioned again, "She could, at this stage of things, recognize signals like that, as the epileptic is said to. ... Afterward it is only this signal, really dross, this secular announcement, and never what is revealed during the attack, that he remembers." She had been given a glass of wine made from dandelions picked once from the destroyed cemetery. "In the space of a sip of dandelion wine it came to her that she would never know how many times such a seizure may already have visited, or how to grasp it should it visit again" (95). The "message" of the epileptic seizure, the sacramental content of the wine, the persistence of mythical time behind the profane world, becomes explicit when she receives the wine once again:

> He poured her more dandelion wine.
> "It's clearer now," he said. ... "A few months ago it got quite cloudy. You see, in spring, when the dandelions begin to bloom

again, the wine goes through a fermentation. As if they remembered."

No, thought Oedipa, sad. As if their home cemetery in some way still did exist, in a land where you could somehow walk, and not need the East San Narciso Freeway, and bones still could rest in peace, nourishing ghosts of dandelions, no one to plow them up. As if the dead really do persist, even in a bottle of wine.   (98-99)

This splendid passage combines almost all the book's central motifs: the alternate world "where you could somehow walk," the persistence of the world of the sacred present, the *tristesse* of the illumination that accompanies the Trystero.

The Trystero's illuminations are conveyed through miracles, sacred versions of what Oedipa thinks of as the "secular miracle of communication" (180). The one traditional miracle most close-ly involved with communication is the miracle of Pentecost:

> When the day of Pentecost had come, [the Apostles] were...all filled with the Holy Spirit and began to speak in other tongues, as the Spirit gave them utterance.... [T]he multitude came together, and they were bewildered, because each one heard them speaking in his own language.... And all were amazed and perplexed, say-ing to one another, "What does this mean?" But others mocking said, "They are filled with new wine."   (Acts 2)

Pynchon names Pentecost only once, in the play-within-the-novel *The Courier's Tragedy*, where the novel's use of the Pen-tecost motif is parodied darkly. The gift of tongues is perverted, amidst a scene of Jacobean horror, into the tearing out of a tongue. The torturer gloats:

> Thy pitiless unmanning is most meet,
> Thinks Ercole the zany Paraclete.
> Descended this malign, Unholy Ghost,
> Let us begin thy frightful Pentecost.
>   (68)

The feast of Pentecost is alternately called Whitsunday, after the tradition that on that day baptismal candidates wear white. The final scene of the book—a stamp auction held, surprisingly, on a Sunday—is a parody of Pentecost: "The men inside the auc-tion room wore black mohair and had pale cruel faces.... [The auctioneer] spread his arms in a gesture that seemed to belong to the priesthood of some remote culture; perhaps to a descending angel. The auctioneer cleared his throat. Oedipa settled back, to await the crying of Lot 49." And the book ends. The auctioneer prepares to speak; Oedipa awaits the forty-ninth lot of the sale, a lot whose purchaser "may" turn out to be from the Trystero, thus forcing the system to reveal itself. But why the *forty-ninth* lot? Because Pentecost is the Sunday seven weeks after Easter — forty-nine days. But the word Pentecost derives from the Greek for "fiftieth." The crying — the auctioneer's calling — of the forty-ninth lot is the moment before a Pentecost revelation, the end of the period in which the miracle is in a state of potential, not yet manifest. This is why the novel ends with Oedipa waiting, with the "true" nature of the Trystero never established: a manifestation of the sacred can only be believed in; it can never be proved beyond doubt. There will always be a mocking voice, internal or external, saying "they are filled with the new wine" — or, as Oedipa fears, "you are hallucinating it...you are fantasying some plot" (170-171).

Oedipa's constant risk lies in that nagging possibility: that the Trystero has no independent existence, but is merely her own projection on the world outside. The center of Pierce Inverarity's interests is a town named San Narciso, and the name insistently mocks Oedipa's quest. (There is a Saint Narcissus in *The Courier's Tragedy*, so the narcissism in question is not limited to mid-century America.) The novel describes, however, Oedipa's progress away from the modes of narcissism. At the end of the first chapter Pynchon writes that Oedipa was "to have all manner of revelations[,h] ardly about Pierce Inverarity, or herself." Oedipa recalls, a few lines later, a past moment with Inverarity in Mexico when she saw an emblem of solipsism to which she responded in kind. They had

> somehow wandered into an exhibition of paintings by...Remedios Varo; in the central painting of a triptych...were a number of frail girls...prisoners in the top room of a circular tower, embroidering a kind of tapestry which spilled out the slit windows and into a void, seeking hopelessly to fill the void: for all the other buildings and creatures, all the waves, ships and forests of the earth were contained in this tapestry, and the tapestry was the world.[11]

(Driblette's vision of himself as director is a later version of this image.)

---

[11]Some critics have invented pedigrees for this painting out of English literature, but Varo *was* a Spanish painter, and the painting exists. For a reproduction see *Remedios Varo* (Mexico: Ediciones Era, 1966), plate 7.

Oedipa...stood in front of the painting and cried.... She had looked down at her feet and known, then, because of a painting, that what she had stood on had only been woven a couple thousand miles away in her own tower, was only by accident known as Mexico, and so Pierce had taken her away from nothing, there'd been no escape.

The tower of isolation, though an expression of the self, is not a product of the self, but one of the conditions of this world:

Such a captive maiden...soon realizes that her tower, its height and architecture, are *like her ego only incidental*: that what really keeps her where she is is magic, anonymous and malignant, visited on her from outside and for no reason at all. ... If the tower is every-where and the knight of deliverance no proof against its magic, what else?   (20-21)

With this gesture towards hopelessness the chapter ends. But to its final question, the remainder of the book—with its partial revelation of what the Trystero might stand for—offers a tenta-tive answer.

Near the end of the novel, when Oedipa stands by the sea, "her isolation complete," she finally breaks from the tower and from the uniqueness of San Narciso. She learns, finally, of a continuity that had been available, but hidden, from the beginning:

She stood...her isolation complete, and tried to face toward the sea. But she'd lost her bearings. She turned,...could find no moun-tains either. As if there could be no barriers between herself and the rest of the land. San Narciso at that moment lost (the loss pure, instant, spherical...), gave up its residue of uniqueness for her; became a name again, was assumed back into the American con-tinuity of crust and mantle.   (177)

At this point the uniqueness of her experience matters less than the general truth it signifies: "There was the true continuity.... If San Narciso and the estate were really no different from any other town, and any other estate, then by that continuity she might have found The Tristero anywhere in her Republic...if only she'd looked" (179). Her choice now is either to affirm the existence of the Tristero—through which continuity survives, renews, reintegrates itself over vast expanses of space and time— or to be entirely separated, isolated, an "alien...assumed full circle into some paranoia" (182). San Narciso or America.

IV

Like every sophisticated work of fiction, *The Crying of Lot 49* contains within itself guides to its own interpretation. The book offers synthesizing critical methods which are integral with the very material the methods propose to organize. Certainly this is a book that needs a *vade mecum*: its reader finds himself continuously in a dilemma analogous to its heroine's. Both are given a series of clues, signs, interconnecting symbols, acronyms, code words, patterns of theme and variation which never *demand* to be interpreted, but which always offer themselves as material that is available for synthesis and order.

The play-within-the-novel, *The Courier's Tragedy* "by Richard Wharfinger," offers in concentrated and often inverted form the main concerns of the novel as a whole. The plot of the play is quite as elaborate as that of any genuine Jacobean tragedy, and any summary here would be almost as long as Pynchon's account in the novel (q.v.). One or two points, however, call for special attention. As on every occasion when a work of art appears within another, Pynchon offers his readers the possibility that their "attendance" at the novel is analogous to Oedipa's attendance at the Wharfinger play. In the performance that Oedipa attends, and, it later develops, *only in that performance*, the director, Driblette, alters the text to conform with the version produced by Scurvhamite tampering (as discussed above), the version which actually names the Trystero. (The other editions of the play, all discussed later in the book, omit the name altogether.) The implication of this is that the naming of the Trystero on one particular night may have been directed *at* Oedipa— that the production was not simply made available to whomever happened to buy a ticket. Underneath this suggestion (and the implications are developed in another passage which I shall discuss shortly) is the implied possibility that the relationship of a reader and a work of art may perhaps not be simply an aesthetic relationship—that the work has, potentially, a *purposive* effect.

In the action of the play itself one event casts special light on the meaning of the Trystero system within the rest of the novel. The eponymous hero of the tragedy, a rightful prince deposed (disinherited, like the founder of the Trystero) and now disguised

as a courier at the court of his enemy, is sent by that enemy with
a lying message to another court. But this enemy then sends out
agents—from the Trystero, in Driblette's production—after the
disguised prince, with orders to murder him. Later, the lying
message is found on the dead body, but "it is no longer the lying
document...but now, miraculously, a long confession by [the
prince's enemy] of all his crimes" (74). In an unexplained manner
the Trystero has been associated with a miracle: though murderers,
they have somehow produced the miraculous transformation of
lies into truth. And this transformation, in which a message is
miraculously different when sent and when received, is a version
of the miracle of Pentecost—which the play has already named.
The patterns of the novel are here sketched for the novel's heroine.

But how is she—and by analogy the reader—to construe these
patterns? Is Oedipa to interpret the signs she discovers merely
as she would interpret a play in performance—or do the signs have
a meaning that "mattered to the world"? The performance of
The Courier's Tragedy which she attended *may* have been directed specifically at her: her relationship with it was either potential or actual. Pynchon elaborates on these two possibilities
in another metaphor derived from theatrical performance, this
time strip-tease:

> So began, for Oedipa, the languid, sinister blooming of The Tristero.
> Or rather, her attendance at some unique performance...something
> a little extra for whoever'd stayed this late. As if the breakaway
> gowns, net bras, jeweled garters and G-strings of historical figura-
> tion...would fall away...; as if a plunge toward dawn indefinite
> black hours long would indeed be necessary before The Tristero
> could be revealed in its terrible nakedness. Would its smile, then,
> be coy, and would it flirt away harmlessly backstage...and leave
> her in peace? Or would it instead, the dance ended, come back
> down the runway, its luminous stare locked on to Oedipa's,
> smile gone malign and pitiless; bend to her alone among the des-
> olate rows of seats and begin to speak words she never want-
> ed to hear?   (54)

Pynchon here uses a metaphor from performance to describe
the demands that may be made by the Trystero, and the metaphor thus transfers the problem of belief to one of its analogues,
the problem of literary meaning. Pynchon joins the problem
posed by the novel's *content*—the meaning of the Trystero to
Oedipa—to the problem posed by the book's *presentation*—the

the meaning of the novel to its reader's nonliterary experience. What the passage delineates, in a version of the one-zero alternative that pervades the book, are two different concepts of art. In the first, according to which art's function is *to delight*, a novel is a superior form of entertainment which never intrudes into the world of decision and action, and whose structure and texture aspire to illuminate nothing but themselves (one might think of the later Nabokov or the stories of Borges's middle period). According to the second concept, art's purpose is *monere*, to instruct, and a novel offers to its reader an example of coherence and order which rebukes the confusion of life and offers an alternative example: "the dance ended," its meaning taken out of the aesthetic realm it offers to a reader "words she never wanted to hear."

These two extremes suggest a scale along which any work of fiction may be placed, a scale which measures the degree to which a work illuminates (at one end of the scale) the nature of the world outside the work, or (at the other end) the nature of the work's own language and structure. At the latter extreme is that which may be called *subjunctive fiction*, works concerned with events that can occur only in language, with few or no analogues in the phenomenal world. At the other extreme is *indicative fiction* (which includes *imperative fiction*), works which transmit, through no matter how elaborate a transformation, no matter how wide or narrow a focus, information about the emotional and physical world of nonliterary experience, including, but not limited to, the experience of language. Of course all indicative fiction has subjunctive elements, or it would be formless and not "fiction"; and all subjunctive fiction has indicative elements, otherwise it could not be understood at all.[12]

When read superficially, *The Crying of Lot 49* seems to fall near the subjunctive end of the scale. One often finds the book compared with Nabokov or Borges, and Pynchon's invention of an alternate "world," an alternate system of organization revealed through the Trystero, appears to justify these comparisons. If Van Veen can live in Anti-Terra, then Oedipa can find a Trystero.

[12]This issue is related, of course, to the issue of probability and surprise in information theory. But while subjunctive fiction *apparently* has more "surprise," and indicative fiction more "probability," the matter in fact is far more complex. Information theory is not in any way concerned with the *value* of information — only with its quantity and the clarity of its transmission. Information theory and aesthetics are indeed related, but only tangentially.

But a "subjunctive" reading accounts for too few of the novel's details and complexities, and is finally insufficient. Where Nabokov and Borges create a novelistic equivalent to *la poésie pure*, Pynchon strives to remain as *im*pure as possible. His novel insists on its indicative relation to the world of experience; and its proposal of "another mode of meaning behind the obvious" is not a tentative aesthetic proposal, but "words [one] never wanted to hear."

A story by Borges, from which Pynchon may have jumped off into the deeper themes of his novel, offers a subjunctive version of *The Crying of Lot 49*. Borges's "The Approach to al-Mu'tasim," in *Ficciones,* poses as a review of a novel published in Bombay (and described with the usual Borgesian panoply of sources, analogues and scholarly commentary). The "reviewers" of the novel point out its "detective-story mechanism and its undercurrent of mysticism." The central figure of this novel, a student, goes in search of a woman whom he has heard about, vaguely, from a particularly vile thief. In the course of his search the student takes up "with the lowest class of people," and, among them, "all at once...he becomes aware of a brief and sudden change in that world of ruthlessness—a certain tenderness, a moment of happiness, a forgiving silence." The student guesses that this sudden change cannot originate in the people he is among, but must derive from somewhere else: "somewhere on the face of the earth is a man from whom this light has emanated," someone for whom he now begins to search. "Finally, after many years, the student comes to a corridor 'at whose end is a door and a cheap beaded curtain, and behind the curtain a shining light.' The student claps his hands once or twice and asks for al-Mu'tasim [the object of the search]. A man's voice—the unimaginable voice of al-Mu'tasim—prays him to enter. The student parts the curtain and steps forward. At this point the novel comes to its end."[13]

The structural analogies to *The Crying of Lot 49* are clear. The hero who sets out in search of one thing, as Oedipa sets out to give order to Inverarity's legacy; the discovery of something else entirely, as Oedipa begins to be made aware of the Trystero; the revelation of happiness and forgiveness, informed by and

[13]The translation quoted here is the one by Borges and Norman Thomas di Giovanni in *The Aleph and Other Stories* (New York: Dutton, 1970), pp. 45-52. An earlier translation appeared in *Ficciones* (New York: Grove Press, 1962). I am indebted to Professor Frank Kermode for pointing out this story.

originating from a semi-divine object; the "detective-story and [the] undercurrent of mysticism"—all these are common to Pynchon's novel and to Borges's novel-within-a-story. But Pynchon inverts the playful superficialities in Borges to create a pattern of greater intellectual depth and one deeper in emotional resource. In Borges, for example, the student *hears* his evidence of love and coherence amidst a scene of evil and degradation. In a corresponding episode in *Lot 49*, Oedipa herself *enacts* the love and charity that Borges's hero can only witness. Oedipa's action occurs when she sees, on the steps of a dilapidated rooming house, an old sailor with a "wrecked face" and "eyes gloried in burst veins," who asks her to mail a letter bearing a Trystero stamp. After a night in which she has seen scores of signs of the Trystero, she is now flooded by a vision of the old man's whole experience of suffering, futility and isolation. She pictures to herself the mattress he sleeps on, bearing the "vestiges of every nightmare sweat, helpless overflowing bladder, viciously, tearfully consummated wet dream, like the memory bank to a computer of the lost."

> She was overcome all at once by a need to touch him.... Exhausted, hardly knowing what she was doing, she came the last three steps and sat, took the man in her arms, actually held him, gazing out of her smudged eyes down the stairs, back into the morning.   (126)

Here Oedipa performs an act in which she takes personal responsibility for the patterns of correlation and coinherence which she has found in the world outside. Her embrace of the old sailor is a tangible manifestation of the unlikely relations for which the Trystero is an emblem. Through the Trystero, Oedipa has learned to comfort the book's equivalent of that helpless figure to whom all successful quest-heroes must give succour.

But the Trystero is not simply a vehicle by which unseen relationships are manifested. Its name hides not only the unseen (and, to the secular world, illicit) relationship of the *tryst*, but also the *tristesse* that must accompany any sense of coherence and fullness. For if even the smallest event carries large significance, then even the smallest loss, the most remote sadness, contains more grief than a secular vision can imagine. When Oedipa helps the old sailor upstairs she imagines the enormous loss that must accompany his death (which she imagines occurring when a spark from his cigarette will ignite his mattress):

She remembered John Nefastis, talking about his Machine, and massive destructions of information. So when this mattress flared up around the sailor, in his Viking's funeral: the stored, coded years of uselessness, early death, self-harrowing, the sure decay of hope...would truly cease to be, forever, when the mattress burned. She stared at it in wonder. It was as if she had just discovered the irreversible process.   (128)

The final metaphor, borrowed from information theory and thermodynamics, here becomes a compelling metaphor for a crucial aspect of human experience and human loss.

"She knew," Pynchon continues, "because she had held him, that he suffered DT's. Behind the initials was a metaphor, a delirium tremens. ..." The metaphor is *itself* a "delirium": a violent dissociation of what it describes. Oedipa recognizes now how deep and how complex is the indicative power of language, how much deeper than she had imagined. Remembering a college boyfriend studying calculus, she forms a pun on the man's disease: "'dt,' God help this old tattooed man, meant also a time differential, a vanishingly small instant in which change had to be confronted at last for what it was, where it could no longer disguise itself as something innocuous like an average rate;...where death dwelled in the cell though the cell be looked in on at its most quick." For Oedipa the possibilities of *seriousness* have now multiplied: each moment, each event, "had to be confronted at last for what it was." The movement from one element of a pun to the other is at once a comic slide and a movement towards real relation: "there was that high magic to low puns." And metaphor is at once a verbal trick and a way of talking about the truth of the world: "The act of metaphor then was a thrust at truth and a lie, depending on where you were: inside, safe, or outside, lost. Oedipa did not know where she was" (129). The problem of metaphor is here transferred in part to the reader. Metaphor—carrying over, across—is a way of signifying the true but not immediately accessible relations in the world of experience: "a thrust at truth." But metaphor acts this way only when one is "inside, safe," joined to the world in which moral and metaphoric connections, links of responsibility across time and among persons, endorsed by a hieratic vision, actually exist. If one is "outside, lost," damned to isolation and incoherence, then metaphor is nothing but a "lie," a yoking together by violence of heterogeneous concepts.

Yet metaphor is, potentially, *both* a thrust at truth and a lie: the one-or-zero choice remains.

As metaphor can have either a subjunctive or an indicative meaning, so the Trystero will either leave Oedipa in peace or compel her to decision. Pynchon's novel points outside itself: the act of reading it (to use terms from communications and thermodynamics) can be either adiabatic or irreversible, either, that is, locked in the unchanging garden of fiction, or open to the shifting and uncertain world of choice, emotion, and community, either a verbal spectacle which leaves its reader in peace, or words you never wanted to hear.

The achievement of *The Crying of Lot 49* is its ability to speak unwanted words without a hint of preaching or propaganda. The book's transformation of the impersonal language of science into a language of emotional power is a breathtaking accomplishment, whose nearest rival is perhaps Goethe's *Elective Affinities.* Equally remarkable is the book's ability to hover on the edge of low comedy without ever descending into the merely frivolous. The risks Pynchon takes in his comedy are great, but all the "bad" jokes, low puns, comic names, and moments of pure farce that punctuate the book have a serious function: the book, through its exploration of stylistic extremes, constantly raises expectations which it then refuses to fulfill. Its pattern of comic surprises, of sudden intrusions of disparate styles and manners, is entirely congruent with the thrust of its narrative. As Oedipa is caught unaware by the abrupt revelations that change her world, and is thus made attentive to significance she never recognized before, so the variations in the book's texture alert a reader to the book's complexity. High seriousness is difficult to sustain—nor, clearly, would Pynchon ever want to do so. A serious vision of relation and coherence must include comic relationships, and recognize comic varieties of attention.

Pynchon recognizes the limits of fiction—his comedy is in part a reminder of the fictional quality of his world—but he never lets his book become therefore self-reflective. Although he shares the painful knowledge wrought by modernism of the limits of art, and although he knows that no work of quotidian fiction—neither social nor psychological—can ever again persuade, he devotes himself to the effort that leads from pure fiction to a thrust at truth. The effort is difficult and complex, and most of the modes in which the effect has previously been attempted now seem exhausted. Pynchon's search for a new mode of indicative fiction is a lonely and isolated one, but it leads to a place where fiction can become less lonely, less isolated than it has been for many years.

Postscript (1973)

Gravity's Rainbow — all 760 pages of it — has now appeared, and tends to confirm this essay's reading of Pynchon's earlier work. The themes and methods of *V.* and *The Crying of Lot 49* also animate this third novel, yet they do so with far greater profundity and variety. *Gravity's Rainbow* is eight times as long as *The Crying of Lot 49,* and it includes at least three hundred characters, all joined to a plot that on a first reading appears uncontrolled, but which, on a second reading, reveals an extraordinary coherence. ...

It is now possible to state that Pynchon's subject is the response made by men and women to their recognition of the connectedness of the world. In *V.* the decline into entropy is the universal norm. But the central issue of the book is not this decline *per se* — if it were, the book would be little more than an ingeniously articulated conceit — but the possibility of a transcendent coherence and connectedness by which the same process of decline occurs in everything and at every scale. What Stencil finds "appalling" at the end of *V.* is the possibility that there is a design to history, that the world functions according to processes that lie outside the comfortable parameters of science or the humanistic arts. Similarly, in *The Crying of Lot 49* Oedipa recognizes the continuity that informs the apparently disconnected elements of the world, a continuity of which the Tristero is the emblem, as the woman V. was the manifestation of the earlier book's continuity. Both novels, however, oppose to their "real" connectedness the alternative possibility of false or merely mechanical relationships: in *V.,* the relations between human beings and machines, or the international conspiracies imagined or created by the people among whom V. moves; in *Lot 49,* the possibility that the Tristero is Oedipa's fantasy or an elaborate practical joke. In each case the false continuity is a symptom or cause of paranoia.

Gravity's Rainbow is reticulated by more systems and genuine conspiracies than one likes to imagine, ranging from an electrical grid to the bureaucracy of dead souls. Paranoia is the book's endemic disease, but Pynchon writes that paranoia "is nothing less than the onset, the leading edge, of the discovery that *everything is connected,* everything in the Creation." The book's examples of debased or mechanical connections, the analogues to the possibility of conspiracy in *The Crying of Lot 49,* involve international cartels and spy rings, even the cause-and-effect networks established by behaviorists and Pavlovians. Yet the book's final coherence, like that of the earlier book, is religious. The focus of all relationships in *Gravity's Rainbow*—its V., its Tristero, its Rome to which all hidden catacombs and public highways lead—is the V-2 rocket. The process enacted throughout the book, the analogue of entropy in *V.,* is the process (described by Max Weber) through which religious charisma yields to economic and pyschological pressure to become rationalized and routinized, to become reduced to bureaucracy. *Gravity's Rainbow* is a book about origins, and, in Weber's account, charisma in its pure form exists only in the process of originating. This process Pynchon describes most vividly in terms of the first few moments of the rocket's ascent, the originating moments through which its entire trajectory is irrevocably determined. The action of the book takes place in 1944 and 1945 (it is remarkable that the finest novel yet written of the Second World War should be the work of an author whose eighth birthday occurred on V-E Day), the originating and perhaps determining moments of contemporary history. The moral center of the book is the difficult but required task of recognizing the secular connectedness of the present scientific and political world—and the even more difficult requirement to act freely on the basis of that recognition. The secular patterns of the present, Pynchon indicates, are the product of originating moments in the past, but free action must take place here and now. The book's one-or-zero choice is the choice whether to live in the contingency and risks of freedom, or to remain trapped by the same determinism that binds the inanimate (though charismatic) rocket. The V-2 is the real descendant of the woman V.

The Crying of Lot 49 has a story by Borges as its concealed and unacknowledged source; in *Gravity's Rainbow* Borges's name at last surfaces, and it appears often. Both Borges and Pynchon write fantasies, but while Borges's fantasies are built upon curiosities of language or mathematics, Pynchon's are extensions of man's capacity for evil and for love. Borges's language is one that is triumphantly capable of delight and astonishment, but Pynchon writes from the knowledge that language can also hurt and connect. *Gravity's Rainbow* cataclysmically alters the landscape of recent fiction, and it alters the landscape of our moral knowledge as well. It is a more disturbing and less accessible book than its predecessor, and demands even more intelligent attention, but its difficulties are proportional to its rewards. *The Crying of Lot 49* is an exceptional book, *Gravity's Rainbow* an extraordinary, perhaps a great one. The enterprise of Pynchon's fiction, its range and profundity, remain unparalleled among the novelists of our time.

Pynchon's Paraclete

by James Nohrnberg

...Near the end of T. S. Eliot's *Four Quartets,* in a passage to whose symbolism Pynchon seems to have been especially receptive, there is a description of what the poem had earlier called a "calamitous annunciation"—the Axis blitz of London during World War II. In the poem this follows the description of the aftermath of an air raid—"After the dark dove with the flickering tongue/ Had passed below the horizon of his homing"—and repeats the earlier symbol of the dove:

> The dove descending breaks the air
> With flame of incandescent terror
> Of which the tongues declare
> The one discharge from sin and error.
> The only hope or else despair
> Lies in the choice of pyre or pyre—
> To be redeemed from fire by fire.

A character in the epilogue to *V.,* Stencil Sr., speaks of "Paracletian politics"—the politics of the Holy Ghost—by which he means the alleged willingness of the Church to exploit the revolutionary movements that threatened the British Empire at the end of World War I. Stencil's notes include:

> The matter of a Paraclete's coming, the comforter, the dove; the tongues of flame, the gift of tongues: Pentecost. Third Person of the Trinity.... Would the Paraclete also be a mother? Comforter,

"Pynchon's Paraclete," by James Nohrnberg. Published here for the first time; the present text is excerpted by the editor from a long unpublished essay of the same title, with the permission of the author. Copyright © 1977 by James Nohrnberg. The earlier portions of the essay are devoted to a study of the form of *The Crying of Lot 49,* particularly in terms of the "Menippean satire" defined by Northrop Frye in his *Anatomy of Criticism.* Parenthetical page references are to the Bantam paperback edition of *Lot 49.* The author wishes to acknowledge his indebtedness to Maria Di Battista and James Earl.

true. But what gift of communication could ever come from a woman. ...

This old idea, that the Holy Spirit was Jesus's *mother*—it appeared in the lost apocryphal Gospel of the Hebrews—informs the central pieta of *The Crying of Lot 49*.

Analogous meditations in *V.* are also given to Fausto Maijstral, a Maltese follower of T. S. Eliot:

> Mothers are closer than anyone to accident. They are most painfully conscious of the fertilized egg; as Mary knew the moment of conception. ...The same forces which dictate the bomb's trajectory, the deaths of stars, the wind and the waterspout have focused somewhere inside the pelvic frontiers without their consent, to generate one more mighty accident. It frightens them to death.

The bomber-Paraclete symbol is first introduced into *Lot 49* in burlesque form, as a berserk can of hair-spray that caroms around Oedipa's motel bathroom—its course seemingly comprehended only by "God or a digital machine"—to the accompaniment of a World War II movie sound-track: "a slow decrescendo of naval bombardment...screams and chopped-off prayers of dying infantry" (23).

Oedipa is seduced upon this occasion, while the Paranoids' serenade describes the moon filling a beach with a "ghost of day" and pulling the tide over the singer "like a comforter" (24ff.). The scene of the Annunciation is suggested iconographically, by the emblem of the motel, Echo Courts: Its sign is a thirty foot nymph (or pinup), holding a white blossom, her gauze chiton being kept in constant agitation by a concealed blower system. The sight reminds Oedipa of an immediately prior "religious instant" in which sacred words seemed to be being spoken "on some other frequency, or out of the eye of some whirlwind rotating too slow for her heated skin even to feel the centrifugal coolness of" (13, 15).

The peculiar circumstances of Oedipa's seduction at the motel —her *piercing* or *penetration,* in the diction of the book—sensitize her to the signs of the Tristero that she begins to notice shortly thereafter. However, the Paracletian Tristero hardly comes to Oedipa as a comforter; it appears rather as a spiritual terrorist, a courier that combines, in one "hierophanic" or "miraculous" intrusion into her reality (18, 88, 92, 97), the angel of a calamitous annunciation, the angel of death, and the angel who

will blow the last trumpet—or posthorn. On the sinister postage
stamp illustrating "Columbus" (the name means dove) "Announcing his Discovery of America," the audience is in the stunned
posture of victims. The "zany Paraclete" that descends in the
revenge play, *The Courier's Tragedy,* is both a revenger who
ignites his enemy's mutilated tongue and a group of assassins who
leave behind them a miraculous testament written in blood and
bone ash. ...

In the Tristero, Oedipa is "faced with a metaphor of God knew
how many parts," but also simply with a metaphor of God (80).
Although she is not in the least virginal, Oedipa's story receives
a Marian configuration from the moment that Pierce Inveriarity,
a former lover, telephones his promise to the heroine that "the
Shadow" will be paying her a visit (cf. Luke 1:35: "The Holy
Spirit will overshadow thee"). Her appointment as an executor of
Inveriarity's will causes her to speak "the name of God" on the
story's first page, and this significant response is repeated twice
in contexts of revelation: in the play, where the "wedlock whose
sole child is miracle" (the testament left by the Tristero) causes
"all to fall to their knees" and "to bless the name of God" (52);
and in the scene at Vesperhaven House with Mr. Toth, when
Oedipa discovers the Tristero symbol on the ring that Mr. Toth's
grandfather, as a Pony Express rider, hacked from the finger of a
desperado masquerading as an Indian:

> She looked around, spooked at the sunlight pouring in all the
> windows, as if she had been trapped at the centre of some intricate
> crystal, and said, "My God."
> "And I feel him, certain days, days of a certain temperature,"
> said Mr. Toth, "and barometric pressure. Did you know that? I
> feel him close to me."
> "Your grandfather?"
> "No, my God." (67)

Vesperhaven House is a home for senior citizens, and the dreamy
Mr. Toth is effectively its Simeon. Dismissed from the story at
virtually the point at which he is introduced, he departs from
Oedipa's world before what the Gospel of Luke calls the piercing
sword of the word comes into it. ...

Neither virgin nor mother, Oedipa nonetheless shows the
naiveté of the one, and the maternal instinct of the other. Grace
Bortz assumes that Oedipa is a mother, like herself; and shortly

after their encounter Oedipa uses Mrs. Bortz's name when she arranges for pregnancy tests. Mary is addressed as "full of grace" by the angel; "Your gynecologist has no test for what she was pregnant with," the narrator comments, speaking of Oedipa (131). Oedipa herself compares her sensitivity to the Tristero to the "secular announcement" felt by an epileptic, the "pure piercing grace note announcing his seizure" (69). At another moment of aborted insight, Oedipa "felt briefly penetrated, as if the bright winged thing had actually made it to the sanctuary of her heart"; "She waited for the winged brightness to announce its safe arrival" (121-22).

Considered in terms of metaphysics or the preternatural, the Word may be associated with silence or dumbness or deafness, as there is a difference between hearing the Word and taking it to heart or writing it down. The play director Driblette feels free to disregard the script's words, in order to bring out its spirit: "'To give the spirit flesh. The words, who cares?'" (56). ... Similarly, the taciturnity of the Tristero obliges it to speak in hieroglyphics and acronyms: Its sign is the muted posthorn. The fullest revelation of the Tristero's activity to Oedipa is directly followed by her temporary induction into a society of deaf-mutes—a society which proves to be a quasi-Pentecostal community of the spirit.

The revelation of the Tristero to Oedipa constitutes the Annunciation of *Lot 49,* but the Tristero also functions in a second Paracletian capacity in the story, uniting its diverse satiric languages through a Holy Spirit of coincidence.

Coincidences never seem entirely accidental, since a "correlation" is always formed in observing them (67). It is when one part of the coincidence becomes the sign of the other that the curious part begins, for the curious is what contains hidden significance, or exhibits an involuted design. The first coincidence in *Lot 49* occurs when Oedipa meets the co-executor of Inveriarity's will on the same night that he appears on the TV screen as the child-star of an old movie the two watch together. This coincidence, playing into the hands of her seducer, seems prearranged by a higher power, that is, by a maker of plots or a giver of signs.

The TV movie also creates a fold in time: The repetition of experience on the plane of illusion suggests that the occult penetration or occupation of the present by the past, as if the present had fallen into the control of its own ghost or shadow. Oedipa is "interpenetrated by the dead man's estate" (80), much in the way that Mary is overshadowed by the Holy Ghost. Similarly, the dandelion wine Oedipa shares with Ghengis Cohen seems infused by the memory of springtime in the graveyard where the dandelions once grew: The late fermentation of the wine shows the elegiac nexus of remembrance by means of a quasi-sacramental metamorphosis. A related image in *Lot 49* is the lakeside death of men in uniform, along with their subsequent transubstantiation into something strange. The image might be repeated in Oedipa's experience only coincidentally, except for its appearing on two planes: in recent history, and in an old play, as if occurring on a second, controlling register of experience. Since the play director compares his projections to those in a planetarium, we may compare the way that a sign appears in the heavens: In Pynchon's work, the dove and the rainbow are two such signs which we will meet again.

The movement in Oedipa's mind from a correspondence between experiences to a conspiratorial collusion among them requires the animation and pluralization of her coincidences by the discovery of a secret community existing among them. The coincidences become "Legion," once their "breathing together" has been accepted. The belief that everything has a design points two ways: either towards the unity and universality of the divine counsel (the Spirit is the Counselor), or towards paranoia (the belief of the subject that he or she is the sole *object* of the conspiracy). The coincidence is an unused piece of design, a fragment of the Scholastic postulate of a universal coherence, reflecting either the mind of the Designer, or the mind of subject. Thus Pynchon places in apposition "the clairvoyant whose lapse in recall is the breath of God" and "the true paranoid for whom all is organized in spheres joyful or threatening about the central pulse of himself" (95). The correspondence handled by the Tristero is either a universal one, or it is the illusory mutualization of solipsism — people talking to themselves. ...

The same list that includes the seer and the paranoid begins from "the saint whose water can light lamps" (95). This is Saint Narcissus, the Bishop of Jerusalem whose image has figured fatally in the history preliminary to the action of the terrible revenge play (45), and whose picture is to imply a hope for grace in the later episode of Oedipa and the sailor. A song Mucho Maas whistles, "I Want to Kiss Your Feet," refers to the worship of the saint (12, 45), and it introduces the second chapter and thus The Paranoids. *Lot 49* thus begins by associating paranoia not with communal collusion, but with narcissism: The paranoia found at the motel is merely the heroine's and her lover's marked tendency towards self-parody, a mimicking of themselves as persons by themselves as actors and spectators of themselves as actors. But the bomb of hair-spray that shatters Oedipa's bathroom mirror announces the impending blitz of her self-satisfaction and confidence, and the development in her of a receptivity to a true otherness. In the "secular" sense, of course, this may not differ much from a satirical mocking of a subject by his own unknowable self. Oedipa may gain no more than an enhanced awareness of her own subjectivity and self-ignorance.

The Paranoids of the story are succeeded by the Tristero, a disinherited and beleagured organization that has much more reason to feel paranoid than the imitation London rock-group. The Tristero system might well induce paranoia in the agencies charged with repressing it, but an anonymous "they" exists for both parties to the rivalry (see 31, 124). More than a rival of the official post, however, the Tristero is also its "other." It forges postage stamps which travesty orthodox ones: The Tristero is fighting a losing battle against history, especially history of the official or panegyrical kind commemorated on postage stamps, of which the Tristero takes a satirist's cynical view.

Oedipa's construction of the rival history involves her in various agonizing reappraisals of her present, but it also promotes in her a more generalized sense of the sadness or tearfulness of historically understood things—their *tristesse*. The labyrinthine lines on Driblette's eyes seem to be "a laboratory maze for studying intelligence in tears" (54). Oedipa recalls her own marked tendency to well into tears: Once, crying before a Rapunzel-like image reflecting her own situation, she imagined a way of perpetuating her maudlin state by means of sealed glasses. ... Thus the mock-cathexis of narcissism at the Echo Courts Motel is paralleled by the earlier mock-grief of melancholy or depression Oedipa experienced in Mexico. Self-parody has succeeded self-pity. But neither mourning for the self nor self-love can satisfy what *V.* called "the need to care." It is the remembering of others, and especially remembering the dead, which seems to be the important unselfish work of love in *Lot 49*. ... Thus Oedipa's tears over Oedipa at the end of the first two chapters are replaced at the end of the fourth by her sadness over the shared glass of elegiac wine. A similar kind of grief infuses the colloquy over beer when Oedipa learns of Driblette's suicide, an end Oedipa herself half-heartedly attempts on her own. . . .

The memorial work of love also lurks in the background of the climactic episode of the story, where Oedipa's tears reappear in the sobbing of the derelict sailor—his eyes "gloried in burst veins" (92). Overwhelmed by "the need to touch" (93), Oedipa shares the ebbing life of this human wreck out of a concern that displays no trace of condescension and a sorrow that lies deeper than all her earlier tears. The emblem over the dying sailor's bed, "a picture of a saint, changing well-water to oil for Jerusalem's Easter lamps" (94), recalls the metamorphic dandelion wine which had symbolized a memorial communion with what was past and lost.

The saint's miracle, however, also suggests the interpenetration of two worlds, one fiery and sacred, and the other waiting for a miraculous sign of a spiritual power able to redeem it. All of her education in the Tristero seems to have been preparing Oedipa to touch an untouchable, as a saint might touch a leper. Thus Oedipa and the sailor form a pietà, with the sailor's obscurity being precisely the point. That is how the play of sympathy works, abolishing for a miraculous moment the differences and distances between members of an otherwise atomized universe. The Tristero is the means whereby a group of isolates can "keep in touch" (64).

Oedipa now carries what is probably the sailor's last letter to his wife to a Tristero mailbox in the shadow of a San Francisco freeway. The letter appears to have been written long ago—like other Tristero mail, it will be a message out of the past. In carrying this letter, Oedipa is symbolically conscripted into the Tristero system; she becomes yet another "private carrier" (68). This scene thus leads directly to the end of the story, where Oedipa seems ready to pray (in Eliot's words again) the "barely prayable/ Prayer of the one Annunciation," a prayer of perfect surrender to to the Other. In effect, such a prayer is an answer to her original seclusion at the Echo Courts motel: "Be unto me according to thy Word" is the petition of Mary, and the repetition of Echo.

In Christian iconography, the Holy Ghost is shown entering Mary through her ear. Oedipa's radio announcer husband cannot believe in his vocation, but he is also a priestlike "holy man" whose program goes out to all the faithful (13), effecting the seduction of young girls. The addressee of the words that Oedipa once imagined that she never wanted to hear (36)—"the direct epileptic word," "the cry that might abolish the night" (87)—is not only symbolically a Mary, but also a Paul. Paul enjoyed an "abundance of revelation" (II Cor. 12:7—Oedipa is to have "all manner of revelations" [9; cf. 28, 58]). Paul's revelations took the form of apparently epileptic ecstatic seizures, and Pynchon emphasizes Oedipa's own epileptic receptivity.

The content of revelation in the New Testament is necessarily esoteric, for faith is the evidence of things unseen. As Pynchon's reference to it suggests, the Bible records not the search for the "historical Jesus" (113), but rather the signs of Jesus's spititual power. But these were experienced in the corporate life of the primitive Christian community. The existence of the historical Tristero raises analogous problems of verification, since its existence is chiefly manifested in the signs of hieroglyphs employed by the various "communions" that communicate through its offices and that are formed under its signs.

The Tristero is called a system, but it is really somewhat charismatic as organizations go, and hence is rather an anti-system, or what *Gravity's Rainbow* will call a Counterforce. The anthropologist Victor Turner, developing a model he takes from initiation rites, speaks in *The Ritual Process* of "liminal communities," that is, groups of neophytes who are temporarily deprived of the status and support of the more established society that they are on the threshold of joining, and who exist peripherally and in a critical polarity to that society, in a "limbo" of the virtually preexistent. Over the course of her story, Oedipa herself becomes such an initiate, beginning as a "Young Republican" (53), even while sharing later in the Tristero's "calculated withdrawal from the life of the Republic" (92). At the climax of this withdrawal, she shadows a Tristero mailman through a long isolating night, thus sharing the isolation of the Tristero existence and experiencing (in Turner's words) "the structural invisibility of novices undergoing life-crisis rituals. ... Secluded from the spheres of everyday life...they may be disguised in pigments or masks, or rendered inaudible by rules of silence." This recalls not only Oedipa's nominal disguise behind the badge of "Arnold Snarb," but also her sequestration in the Echo Courts Motel—and the Tristero agents who disguised themselves as American Indians.

Turner notes that because of the enhanced vulnerability of such groups, their "rule" typically emphasizes the need for human-kindness. This is the lesson of *Lot 49*'s deepest encounter, Oedipa's pietà with the sailor. But the Tristero, like the Franciscans, is a perpetual rather than a temporary liminal community, and also a floating link between many other such communities. The instatiation of the Tristero ideal is accomplished indirectly, through Oedipa's discovery of the analogous secret societies. These tend to arrange themselves in pairs, as if every alternative to the visible and audible America of the TV set might take either a "negative" or "contrary" form. In one episode, for example, the Mafia seems to be contrasted with the Fangoso Lagoons Security Force. "'It does not do to be seen helping those the organization does not want helped,'" a character says of the Mafia; the Security Force, on the other hand, is "a garrison against the night made up of one time cowboy actors and L.A. motorcycle cops," and it proves to be genuinely helpful (40, 44).

The first liminal community encountered in *Lot 49* is the Peter Pinguid Society (PPS), founded as a kind of late post script to the history of Russian-American relations, and named after a non-martyr to the Utopian cause of a pre-industrial but slave-owning America. "You're so right wing you're left-wing," Metzger protests to the proselytizer for the PPS (64). This group's inauthenticity appears in its mode of defying the government's monopoly on mail delivery: Its system (within its San Narciso chapter) is a parasite on the inner-office mail of the arms manufacturer Yoyodyne. Its counterpart on the far left (as the rightist initials might suggest) is the CIA, the Conjuracion de los Insurgentes Anarquistas, exiled from the so-called permanent revolution in Mexico. The CIA's spokesman believes that "the soul's talent for consensus" will make possible a spontaneous and leaderless revolt of the masses (88). Significantly, CIA mail is delivered sixty years late, making it another postscript to history.

Another such group is the Inamorati Anonymous, a "society of isolates" (83) that takes the Tristero sign for its emblem, without ever knowing its meaning. IA is dedicated to keeping its members out of love; it was founded by a cuckolded executive who was saved from a fiery death — suicide — by the timely delivery of letters from other would-be suicides. He discovers the Tristero's watermark: "'A sign,' he whispered, 'is what it is.' If he'd been a religious man he would have fallen to his knees" (85). The mysterious communion of failed suicides that communicates under

this sign forms, in effect, a *contrapositive* to a society of isolates—
a liminal community at a threshold.

Then there is the communion of the obsessed individualistic
inventors who can always instinctively recognize one of their own
(64). These isolates from teamwork, whom modern corporate
policy has dispossessed of patent rights, also communicate via
the Tristero system. If they have a positive contrary, it is found
in the inscrutable photograph of James Clerk Maxwell affixed to
the Nefastis machine. Inside this crackpot invention, "Maxwell's
Demon" converts information flow into energy flow—a work of
the spirit and work for a familiar spirit. The picture is the "familiar Society for the Propagation of Christian Knowledge photo"
(62), virtually a silent rebuke of Nefastis's endeavor to procure
a mechanical operation of the spirit.

The radio audience of teenage girls addressed by Mucho Maas
also parodies a community of the spirit. Apparently Mucho sends
the story's second letter by the Tristero system. Later he takes
LSD, and thereafter he seems, ecumenically, "like a whole room-
ful of people" (106), "a walking assembly of man" (104). His "vision
of consensus" is a couple of hundred million people saying in
unison "rich chocolaty goodness" (106); his audition of unanimity
emphasizes only uniformity. The gift of tongues, for Mucho,
would be everyone speaking the same tongue.

Mucho's contrary is found in the frenetic party of the California
chapter of the American Deaf-Mute Assembly, in which Oedipa
is caught up as she enters her Berkeley hotel the morning after
her principal ordeal. The assembly delegates are all in the spirit,
being drunk (cf. Acts 2:13), and they combine unity with diversity:
Each dances a different dance to the same music, and though unable to hear the tune, they all break off dancing simultaneously,
"by mysterious consensus"—"an anarchist miracle" (97).

In Golden Gate Park during the same night of ordeal, Oedipa
encounters a group of AWOL dream children whose games utilize
broken down rimes and reminiscences of the Tristero, about which
they are able to impart no knowledge ("The night was empty of
all terror for them, they had inside their circle an imaginary fire,
and needed nothing but their own unpenetrated sense of community" [87]). Their contrapositive is the boy who leaves his mother
in order to open negotiation in Miami with the dolphins;...his
mother urges him to write her by Tristero (91).

The most ancient of the book's liminal communities is the seventeenth century "sodality of the Scurvhamite," whose morbid fascination with the Manichean "opposite Principle" running the damned majority of the universe causes the whole group to commit spiritual suicide (116). "'They felt Trystero would symbolize the Other quite well'" (117). The Simeon-figure among the dying at Vesperhaven House, in contrast, feels himself nearing a more complete communion with God.

One last communicant is the director, Randolph Driblette, around whose death Professor Bortz's students gather. Driblette is notable for his intense fidelity to the "invisible field surrounding the play, its spirit" (113; cf. 115)—in this case, the "preapocalyptic" expectation of its original, jaded, seventeenth century audience. Driblette divines the spirit of the Tristero too, and his suicide in the "comforter" ocean parallels Oedipa's later impulse. Pregnant with her incommunicable conception (131), Oedipa forms Driblette's contrapositive, a spiritual community of one—the mother in communion with her unborn child, each inhering in the other.

A successful novelist is distinguished by the number of novels he is able to finish, and by the finish he is able to give his novels. No such rule holds for the satirist. Conformable to satire's parody of finished forms, many satires, from the *Satyricon* to *Dead Souls*, exist in a fragmentary or unfinished state. One satiric convention, in fact, is the lost and recovered manuscript, which provides a formal explanation for satires lacunae, problematic authority or authorship, unverifiability, and incompleteness. This convention of the satiric *apocryphon* appears in *Lot 49* as the last will and testament of Inverarity. An absconding or absent mode of authorship seems endemic to satiric forms, and many satirists are known only through the texts of their satires. Possibly Pynchon's aversion to personal publicity may be understood in light of the convention of the satirist's anonymity.

Large satiric works are generally receptive to a pastiche of a variety of other forms: Such a receptivity might also mark a satiric author's work as a whole, with separate works being assimilated as installments to the larger oeuvre. And though works like those of Rabelais and Sterne conclude, they do not conclude at all conclusively. The tendency we are discussing is present in Pynchon's oeuvre: Characters reappear from book to book, symbols

prove equally migratory; and when his books end, they end in a form which we may designate as the "penultimate preposterous."...
Each of Pynchon's books ends "recursively," that is, focused on a direct antecedent of what is on the first page, "before" the book began. This reversion to what is essentially the book's foreconceit turns the book into a kind of speculation upon its own existence. The delayed noise of the rocket launched in the final passage of *Gravity's Rainbow* is heard on the first page, after the rocket itself has hit, making what follows "all theatre." The epilogue of *V.*, dated "1919," takes the reader back a generation, to the point where Stencil Sr. seems to lose track of V., the quest for whose history Stencil Jr. has followed through the preceding pages: All of Pynchon's stories entail a researching of things past and lost. *V.* actually ends with a character (Mehemet) disappearing through a fold in the fabric of time, reverting to the Middle Ages, from which he seems to have strayed in the first place. *The Crying of Lot 49* ends on the verge of a scene analogous to the aboriginal one that we must posit in order for the story to have taken place, namely the reading of a will and the announcement of its executors in a courtroom—it is the "crying" of "lot 49" by the auctioneer that will make public to the survivors the nature of the "legacy" that Oedipa has pursued throughout the story. In a more literal way, also, *Lot 49* ends on the page before the one on which it began, that is, upon the words of the title-page, which conclude the last sentence....

If the ending of *V.* and the beginning of *Gravity's Rainbow* are "preposterous," the endings of *Lot 49* and *Gravity's Rainbow* are "penultimate": As Edward Mendelson has suggested, forty-nine is one number short of the Pentecostal number fifty. [See p. 135 above.] Each of Pynchon's works is penultimate with respect to the next; each new book turned the last into the last but one, and into the successor book's foreconceit. The epilogue of *V.* has the reverse effect: Historically speaking, it is a prologue, not an epilogue, and it almost suggests the aging of the reader, as if the characters had grown a generation older during the reading of the book.

At their outset, Pynchon's books display a manic and almost mindless invention, while an ultimately entropic and depressive quality gradually engulfs the development. As information about the subject of the book enlarges, the action is dissipated in speculation upon the accumulating mass of possibility. At the beginning of Oedipa's quest, she embraces the manic and erect child-actor Metzger, who is the opposite of the exhausted and powerless sailor she reaches out to touch much later. The sailor has the "dts," that is, he is dying, and by doing so is entering the fixed and terrible frame of the still point in time, the time differential, "a vanishing small instant in which change had to be confronted for what it was" (95). The fate of Mucho Maas is symptomatic of the same development: He goes the way of V., pluralizing and receding "farther and farther into the endless rooms of the elaborate candy house of himself and away...from what had passed...for love" (114). The spending of the initiative of the "novel," the fading of its charisma in the elaboration of its satiric "anatomy," is epitomized by V.'s own gradually revealed obsession with incorporating bits of inert matter in her body: V. and *V.* are both reduced to the sum of their detachable parts or members, each member or chapter constituting a digression upon the title cipher. The incorporation of the Peculiar Polymer, the erectile plastic, into the rocket of *Gravity's Rainbow* is based on a Frankensteinian inversion of the same *dejecta membra* motif. The degeneration of Slothrop into Rocketman, and his migration into the "Zone," exhibits the same entropic tendency as V.; but the Zone, unconditioned by laws of cause and effect, is also (however nihilistic) a ground for a new creative evolution, or a new Becoming. Thus the triumph of entropy that overtakes Pynchon's fictions is countered by a *ricorso* at their end, where the process of the book shows signs of beginning anew. The final register at which the book thus arrives prophesies or announces a new book. The one we have read is the *last* book in contradictory senses: Both the final one and the previous one.... The legacy motif becomes important here, because the study of Pynchon's mutually entailed endings and beginnings is motivated by a search for substitutes for novelistic form in this author, and because of the relation between *canon*, the legal instrument for restricting a text, and *testament*, the legal instrument for assigning a legacy. Some notable units of the Biblical canon either form or end upon last wills and testaments, and Pynchon's title for an excerpt from *Lot 49* had as its last third "the Testament of Pierce Inverarity."...

We can, as usual, find this theme in *Lot 49*'s central pietà, for the letter Oedipa delivers for the sailor appears to have been prepared in advance of the sailor's death: If it is mailed upon that death, it is essentially testamentary—unlike any other writing

160 James Nohrnberg

that survives the writer, it is the testator's dying breath that activates his testament (cf. Heb. 9:15-17). But Inverarity's cryptic testament might be apocryphal: "hidden" or secret. It may be important, then, that in the actual chronology of the Pynchon canon, *Lot 49* occupies what the Biblical scholar would call an "interestamental" position, in which the apocryphal or deutero-canonical books are often placed. The meditation of the interval between *V.* and the V-2 rocket of *Gravity's Rainbow* thus becomes one more of the courier functions of Pynchon's Paraclete. The Annunciation brought by the Holy Ghost is intertestamental in the sense that it is not so much the beginning of the gospel as the preparation for it. Correspondingly, the ending of *Lot 49* (according to Professor Mendelson again; see p. 134 above) recalls the closed room at Pentecost; but just as we do not see the courtroom scene in which it was announced that Oedipa was to be co-executor of Inverarity's will, neither do we see the ultimate auction-room scene in which the mysterious portion of his estate is disposed of. Thus *Lot 49* is kept intertestamental.[1]

The paralegal aspect of Oedipa's quest to determine the authentic contents of Inverarity's mysterious testament is shadowed by the problem of whether his final gesture towards Oedipa has been a blessing or a curse. Either Oedipa has been blessed with a new critical knowledge, or she has been mocked as the victim of a hoax—that is, as the victim, rather than the beneficiary, of a satirist. Oedipus will finally discover all the evil he is heir to, but Oedipa is deserted "on the brink of fearful knowledge" with nothing finally or definitively disclosed. The ending of *Lot 49* hangs upon the expected epiphany and the expected annunciation, with the auctioneer gesturing either like a priest or a descending angel.

[1][*Editor's note:* There is another sense in which *Lot 49* is "apocryphal" in Pynchon's work, and that is Pynchon's otherwise incomprehensible refusal to incorporate characters from *Lot 49* into *Gravity's Rainbow*. Elements of *V.* are carefully fitted into both the later books; but nothing that first appears in Pynchon's second book reappears in his third—even though the Buchenwald experiments of Dr. Hilarius would fit there with perfect logic and propriety. Since it is clearly Pynchon's practice to make connections between his books, the absence of Dr. Hilarius from *Gravity's Rainbow* amounts to its author's rejection of *Lot 49*, the book that introduced Hilarius, from his own canon; while at the same time the extensions of *V.*'s stories in *Gravity's Rainbow* amount to a confirmation of the canonical status of the earlier work. In effect, the prophecies of *V.* are fulfilled in *Gravity's Rainbow*, while *Lot 49* is restricted to an apocryphal, intertestamentary position.]

This ending is consistent with what we know of *Lot 49*'s genre. Among the brief forms of satire is the quizzical or unresolved debate, which concludes without concluding anything. Such endings appear in larger satiric forms as the projection of the reality of an immense fantasy, on the threshold of assent to which we are pointedly abandoned. We are left with "compiled memories of clues, announcements, intimations, but never the central truth itself" (69), for the satirist is occupationally skeptical about such a truth, or verity.... The reader's sense of being defrauded of what becomes a consistent or cherished illusion actually signals the fulfillment of the satiric design. But even if such works as Apuleius' *Golden Ass* posit no more than the existence of virtual worlds, the imminence of conversion on their last pages gives them the force of testaments, as well as apocrypha. That is why Pynchon's narrative, having reached a point that is more of an impasse than an end, may also seem to pause—as if to validate and complete such a narrative there only wanted some miraculous intrusion: the descent of the dove.

Decoding the Trystero

by Frank Kermode

...Perhaps some readers may have been induced, by the fore-going, to think of a more familiar book—one that contrives, with-out explicit advertisement, to raise the question of suspended meaning and ask questions which cannot be answered by an ap-peal to some incontrovertible, unproblematic structure. In *The Crying of Lot 49,* Pynchon's Oedipa, as her name implies, is also confronted with riddles and with the obligation to discover an order. The origin of these riddles is in doubt; it may be the nature of the human world, viewable as waste or as system; it may be a man called Inverarity, who in turn may be either untruth or *dans le vrai.* The book is crammed with disappointed promises of significance, with ambiguous invitations to paradigmatic con-struction, and this is precisely Oedipa's problem. Is there a struc-ture *au fond,* or only deceptive galaxies of signifiers? Like California itself, the text offers a choice: plentitude or vacuity. Is there a hidden plot concerning an almost Manichaean con-flict, which makes sense, whether evil or benign, of the random-ness of the world?

Consider the opening: we find Oedipa returning from a Tup-perware party; I understand that on these occasions goods are sold outside the normal commercial system. She stands in her living-room before a blank television set (communication sys-tem without message) and considers the randomness she projects on the world: thoughts about God, a Mexican hotel, dawn at Cornell, a tune from Bartók, a Vivaldi concerto for kazoo. Soon

"Decoding the Trystero," by Frank Kermode (editor's title). From "The Use of the Codes" in *Approaches to Poetics,* edited by Seymour Chatman (New York: Columbia University Press, 1973), pp. 68-74. Reprinted with permission of Columbia University Press and the author. The present excerpt takes up the argument at the end of a discussion of texts whose meanings are, in effect, "sus-pended"—not unquestionably determined by their author, but susceptible to "production" by their readers.

we hear about the coded voices of Inverarity, the culinary jumble of a Southern California supermarket, her husband's life as a used-car salesman, systematizing, giving meaning to, the trash in old cars. Now he works on a pop radio station, the communication system—without content—of another culture. Later he will start *listening* to Muzak, another type of the empty system. In a world where the psychiatrists provide material for paranoid fantasies, and lawyers are locked in imaginary rivalries with Perry Mason, everybody is tending toward his own dissident universe of meaning; Oedipa is Rapunzel, her own reality let down like hair from her head. Minority cultures, bricolaged from pop, old movies, astrology, coexist in a world whose significances, if any, relate to no conceivable armature.

But Oedipa has "all manner of revelations," and a shadowy armature seems to be taking shape. Is she still in her head, or is the great plot real? If so, is it malign? To discover it may be the same thing as inventing it. What Peter Berger and Thomas Luckmann call "the social construction of reality" proceeds because there are phenomena we cannot simply wish away; death is one, but there are others. The construction is what our social situation permits—say, the national limits, the limits of California, ultimately the limits of dissident groups and our protestant selves. As we plot against reality we comply with or deviate from the institutionalized plots; a great deviation is called a sect if shared, paranoia if not. There is always a way of coding the material, even that which in other views is simply waste. Having instituted a system, one keeps it intact either by legitimating extraneous material or, if that is too difficult, or the threat too great, by nihilating it.

Making sense of other somewhat arbitrary symbolic universes, understanding their construction, is an activity familiar to all critics. Certainly it involves choices, a limitation of pluralities. The activity of the critic, thus understood, is nomic. It seeks order, and is analogous to the social construction of reality. What Oedipa is doing is very like reading a book. Of course books can be read in very strange ways—a man once undertook to demonstrate infallibly to me that *Wuthering Heights* was an interlinear gloss on Genesis. How could this be disproved? He had hit on a code, and legitimated all the signs. Oedipa is afraid she may be like that man, or that she is drifting into paranoia, the normal hermeneutic activity in disease, and Pynchon's great subject.

She has contact with many sects: in advanced societies, such as Southern California, "socially segregated subuniverses of meaning," as Berger and Luckmann observe,[1] tend to multiply. When she sees a way of linking them together Oedipa is conscious of other terrors than paranoia. She dreads the anomic, the world collapsed into filth and randomness; but she also dreads an evil order. Pynchon invents the Scurvhamite sect, who abandoned a very mechanical double predestinarianism ("nothing ever happens by accident") for the consolations of single predestination to damnation. Yet even on her wild San Francisco night Oedipa doesn't unambiguously believe in the patterns to which the evidence is apparently pointing. For instance, she dismisses the evidence of the children's rhymes. The entire structure is *á la fois posé et déçu.* We do not learn whether the dove, harmonizer of tongues, which would make all these meaning-systems mutually intelligible, descended with the auctioneer's hammer; *au fond,* the plot remains suspended.

What concerns us is precisely the existence of what seem to be systems that could transmit meanings, as in the account of San Narciso, the town which looks like a printed circuit, "an intent to communicate. There'd seemed no limit to what the printed circuit could have told her (if she had tried to find out); so, in her first minute of San Narciso, a revelation trembled, just past the threshold of meaning." The revelation would be of the kind that explains the whole of history, the present condition of America, Inverarity, Wharfinger's play, and so on; it would explain how waste has meaning, just as, couched as an acronym, WASTE forms a sentence ("We await silent Tristero's empire"). But Oedipa is poised on the slash between meaning and unmeaning, as she is between smog and sun; interminably confronted with meaningless binary choices—artificial light in sunlight, the statue of the hooker/nymph, which is both still and windblown—and by repetitions of the San Narciso situation: windows and bottles emptily reflecting the sun, messageless. The need of a revelation, the sense that such systems exist to transmit sense, drives us to find meaning in them, for we feel "as if, on some other frequency ...words were being spoken." This is the sense in which Professor Mendelson is right in emphasizing the pentecostal themes in the book [see p. 134]; fifty may follow forty-nine, and if it were

[1]Peter L. Berger and Thomas Luckmann, *The Social Construction of Reality* (New York, 1967), p. 85.

called we should all become competently polyglot, able to hear the words we think are being spoken but cannot quite hear.

This is why Oedipa continues her game of strip-Botticelli with the world. Her trial run with Metzger—merely on the plot of an old movie—sensitized her for a revelation; just as the flight of the rogue aerosol foreshadows a world which, though unpredictable, is determinate. And so she continues to spot the clues, though never sure where they are, in her head or out there. The text only says it is "as if...there were a revelation in progress all around her." Options remain naggingly open, as when the naval action of Peter Pinguid, that ancestor of Inverarity, is described: "off the coast of what is now Carmel-by-the-Sea, or what is now Pismo Beach, around noon or possibly towards dusk, the two ships sighted each other. One of them may have fired; if it did the other responded." This niggling dubiety is Oedipa's, and the text's.

The messages sent by the illicit system are normally without content; this could be true of the novel. The clues pile up. *The Courier's Tragedy* (played in a theater located between a traffic-analysis firm and a wildcat transistor outfit, circulation and communication) relates not only to the supposed history of Tristero but to incest, tongueless attempts to pray, an anti-Paraclete. The bones of the dead are turned into ink, a means of empty communication (or into wine and cigarettes, which belong to other systems). Ralph Driblette has heard a message in the system of the play; so could Oedipa, if she gave herself to it. Everything can be legitimated, systematized. But there are only clues, "never," we are told, "the central truth itself, for if that should blaze out it would destroy its own message irreversibly." If the systems are to work, and the book to work as a system, it will be because the reader can do what Oedipa could not when confronted with Maxwell's demon: make the piston move, reverse the entropy of communication as that device reverses physical entropy. But if you make the eyes of this novel move, or if you believe in the original plot on which it depends, you risk a kind of madness, which is the ultimate human cost of holding everything together in a single design. The systems are there to be filled: children's rhymes, the "coded years of uselessness" in the mattresses of the poor, the societies of queers and failed suicides, all to be handled if you want a central truth, a word to reconcile your time with eternity. Nobody helps; Oedipa's friends drop away. The more she en-

codes the trash of America the more critical her isolation becomes. She is like the poor of whom she has heard, camping among
telephone wires; she walks as if inside a digital computer, among
either-ors, waiting for the systems to contain a message. Either
there is a Tristero, or she is "orbiting in the ecstasy of a true
paranoia."

We can't, of course, be told which, and we question the novel as
Oedipa does the Tristero plot. That plot is pointed to as the object of some possible annunciation; but the power is in the pointing, not in any guarantee. One could talk for hours about this
remarkable work, but at the bottom of all one said would be the
truth that it imitates the texts of the world, and also imitates their
problematical quality. If one coded *Lot 49*, its radical equivoca-
tions would be instantly evident—the cultural code, for example,
is as little the inert congeries proposed by Barthes as the hermeneutic code is a progress to *dévoilement*. Its separation from
its exterior and its totality are precisely what it is *about*. It is an
invitation to the speaking animal to consider what he makes of
the world into which he introduces his communication systems;
and it asks him to read a text, to reread it, to produce it if that is
a better word. In its totality it poses the choice: *plein/vide,* as
it so often does in its texture. To seek an answer is to be disappointed, *déçu*. Deception is the discovery of the novel, not of its
critics. ...

Gravity's Rainbow: Three Reviews

Richard Poirier: Rocket Power

The fantastically variegated and multi structured *V.*, which made Thomas Pynchon famous in 1963 and the wonder ever since of anyone who has tried to meet or photograph or interview him, is the most masterful first novel in the history of literature, the only one of its decade with the proportions and stylistic resources of a classic. Three years later came *The Crying of Lot 49,* more accessible only because very much shorter than the first, and like some particularly dazzling section left over from it. And now *Gravity's Rainbow.* More ambitious than *V.,* more topical (in that its central mystery is not a cryptogram but a supersonic rocket), and more nuanced, *Gravity's Rainbow* is even less easy to assimilate into those interpretive schematizations of "apocalypse" and "entropy" by which Pynchon's work has, up to now, been rigidified by his admirers.

At thirty-six, Pynchon has established himself as a novelist of major historical importance. More than any other living writer, including Norman Mailer, he has caught the inward movements of our time in outward manifestations of art and technology so that in being historical he must also be marvelously exorbitant. It is probable that he would not like being called "historical." In *Gravity's Rainbow,* even more than in his previous work, history—as Norman O. Brown proposed in *Life Against Death*—is seen as a form of neurosis, a record of the progressive attempt to impose the human will upon the movements of time. Even the very recording of history is such an effort. History-making man is Faustian man. But while this book offers such Faustian types as a rocket genius named Captain Blicero and a Pavlovian be-

"Rocket Power," by Richard Poirier. From *Saturday Review of the Arts,* 1 (March 3, 1973), 59-64. Reprinted by permission of *Saturday Review* and the author.

haviorist named Edward Pointsman, it is evident that they are slaves to the systems they think they master.

For Pynchon, the additional comic horror of the Faustianism peculiar to this century is that it can no longer be located in the mad heroics of individuals. It is instead part of the bureaucratic enterprise, of the technological systems that have set history on a course which, like the final descent of the book's rocket, is "irreversible." Any depersonalization of history may therefore be imagined as perverse, with the technological system being turned back upon ourselves in a corporate exercise of masochism like that of one character in the book; she turns her ass to the whip not in surrender but in despair, in order to discover whether she is still human and can cry in pain. The ultimate whip in *Gravity's Rainbow,* the end product of the system, is the supersonic rocket, the German V-2 of the Second World War. It is Moby Dick and the *Pequod* all in one, both the Virgin and the Dynamo of Pynchon's magnificent book.

If in the structure of his books Pynchon duplicates the intricate networking of contemporary technological, political, and cultural systems, then in the style and its rapid transitions he tries to match the dizzying tempos, the accelerated shifts from one mode of experience to another, which characterize contemporary media and movement. As the recurrent metaphors of the book would have it, we are being delivered beyond the human "margin," beyond "gravity," and the natural beauties created by its pressures. Our exhilarations are at the expense of any safe "return," any re-entry, except a self-destructive one, into the atmosphere that has made the earth a congenial and precarious "home" for our vulnerable, time-ridden natures.

In Pynchon we "return" to ourselves, come back to the remembered earth of our primal being, reified by the objects to which we have joined our passions, our energies, and our needs. We have become like the young Gottfried, a soldier who allows himself to be placed inside a specially assembled V-2, number 00000, then to be fired beyond the speed of sound, over scenes he thinks he would remember fondly were he able to see them, and down to fiery annihilation.

It is impossible to summarize a book of some 400,000 words in which every item enriches every other and in which the persistent paranoia of all the important characters invests any chance detail with the power of an omen, a clue, to which, momentarily, all other details might adhere. The novel clarifies itself only to create further mysteries, as one such pattern modifies or displaces another. This is a cumulative process with no predictable direction so that any summary is pretty much the product of whatever creative paranoia the book induces in a reader. To complicate matters further, characters are not introduced as they customarily are in fiction, with some brief account of identity and function. Instead, any one of the chapters—which are separated not by numbers but by little squares apparently meant to simulate the sprocket holes in a film—suddenly immerses us in a scene, a mass of persons and furnishings, much as if it were flashed before us on a screen.

In *Gravity's Rainbow* there are some 400 characters all bearing Pynchonesque names (Old Bloody Chiclitz is back, by the way, from *V.* and *The Crying of Lot 49*), along with a fair number of people who, if you bother, can be found in reference books (e.g., such pioneers in organic chemistry as Kekulé, von Liebig, and Clerk Maxwell). There are scores of submerged references, including one to "The Kenosha Kid." I'd guess this is Orson Welles, born in Kenosha, Wisconsin. A most apt allusion, if one thinks of the hero of *Citizen Kane* and of how his last word, "Rosebud," is taken as some clue to the lavish assemblage of his wealth and power, when it is instead the name of a little sled, at the end consigned to junk and fire, that he loved as a boy. Any reference or detail in the book can redeem itself this way. But no one of them should ever be regarded as a central clue, and the reader need not fret unduly at what he might miss.

No one, for example, will want to keep track of the hundreds of alphabetical agencies from World War II and the international cartels that are mentioned in the book, nor is anyone expected to. The confusion is the point, and CIA is not what you think it is, but Chemical Instrumentality for the Abnormal. The book is full of disguises, of changes and fusions of identity. The principal character in the main plot is Lt. Tyrone Slothrop, whose ancestry goes back to Puritan stock in colonial New England, but he is sometimes also known as Ian Cuffing, a British correspondent, and sometimes as Der Racketmensch, a title he picks up in Berlin when he sports a cape and helmet looted from a Wagnerian opera company (*"Fickt nicht mit dem Raketemensch,"* the poor bastard cries, using a veronica to elude two would-be muggers). He picks up yet another title and another costume in a small German town where, at the behest of some little kids, for whom he will always do anything, he plays the role of Plechazunga, or the Pig Hero, in the yearly pageant to celebrate a tenth-century liberator who appeared in a flash of lightning. He continues to wear his pig costume through a whole series of subsequent adventures.

Aside from the main plot, which deals with a competitive effort to see who can first put together a facsimile of Rocket 00000, there are at least four other major plots, one of which would alone make or enhance the reputation of anyone now writing fiction. There is the story of Lieutenant, later Major, Weissmann, better known by his aforementioned ss code name of Captain Blicero, his love for the Herero tribesman Enzian, both in South-West Africa and in Germany, and his later relationships with Gottfried and with Katje, a double agent who also has an affair with Slothrop. There is the story of Franz Pökler, who has worked on the rocket for Weismann-Blicero, partly out of fascination but also with the hope thereby of recovering his wife and his daughter Ilse from the concentration camps. There is the story of Tchitcherine, a Soviet intelligence officer, of his exile in central Asia just before the war, his search for his half brother, Enzian, in what Pynchon calls simply "the Zone" after the war, his Koestler-like dialogues with Comrade Ripov, who might have him exterminated, and the subsequent, successful search for him by his German girl, the adoring Geli. And then there is the story of the half brother, Enzian himself, a leader of the *Schwarzkommando* (they are Hereros exiled in Germany for two generations from South-West Africa) and the organizer of their effort to locate all the parts necessary to put together and fire Rocket Number 00001. In all these is a species of travel writing about Berlin before Hitler, London during the Blitz, the Zone after the war, central Asia in the 1930s, German Southwest Africa early in the century—all of it apparently staggeringly authentic not only in researched detail but in tone, in creating the spirit of times and places Pynchon has never seen.

There are also dozens of wondrous ancillary plots featuring characters whose motives and activities are essential to the movement of all the major ones. Probably the most important of these is an elusive Doctor Laszlo Jamf, whose early career as a behaviorist brought him from Darmstadt for a year at Harvard. While there, by agreement between Infant Slothrop's father and I. G.

Farben, who will later subsidize Slothrop's education at the same university, Jamf conditioned Infant Tyrone's sexual reflexes. Unfortunately, Jamf's later deconditioning process is ineptly managed so that in London in 1944 Slothrop finds himself getting a hard-on at times and places where the V-2 rocket is to fall.

This phenomenon has not gone unnoticed by Slothrop's superiors, especially Edward Pointsman, in an experimental group called The White Visitation. What mystifies them is that, because V-2 is supersonic, the sound of approach follows rather than precedes the sound of impact. The conceivable stimulus for Slothrop's conditioned response therefore follows the explosion it should warn him about so that, given his repeated proximity to spots where the rocket is to fall, he should be dead. It has to be assumed, therefore, that his conditioning has given him special powers of responding not to the rocket sound but to mysterious precursors of its arrival; to some configuration of sights and circumstances. As it turns out, his map of the location of various girls around London perfectly synchronizes with another map kept by the authorities marking V-2 hits. (The reader is free, without any prodding from Pynchon, to play with the joke that perhaps Slothrop's capacity to read signs about the intent of the heavens is part of his Puritan inheritance; he is one of the Elect, one of the Saved.) In any case, Jamf can be said to have programmed the score and bangs for both Slothrop and the rocket, since one of his accomplishments when he later phased himself from behaviorism into organic chemistry was the development of Imipolex G, a plastic essential to the mysterious Rocket 00000.

The central character is the Rocket itself, and all the other characters, for one reason or another, are involved in a quest for it, especially for a secret component, the so-called *Schwarzgerät*, which was wrapped in Imipolex G. Because the multiple search gradually exposes the interlocking relationships among the cultural, economic, and scientific aspects of contemporary life and its historical antecedents, Pynchon can properly refer to it as "the terrible politics of the Grail." Slothrop is compelled because rockets turn him on and because Pointsman contrives to have him observed in his obsession before removing his testicles for analysis. (The designated guinea pig gets away when the wrong man is picked up wearing Slothrop's Pig Hero costume.) Enzian wants to reassemble the Rocket as a final Revelation to his people: the white races who practiced genocide upon them have devised now an instrument of their own annihilation, which is figuratively and, as their firing of the Rocket will show, literally "irreversible." Tchitcherine's pursuit of the rocket is a pretext for finding and destroying Enzian, thus removing the humiliation of having a black half brother. The real powers on the Anglo-American side, whom Pynchon calls "They," indulge Pointsman and Slothrop for the same reason that their Soviet counterparts indulge Tchitcherine—so that They might come into possession of the rocket assembly but, more importantly, so that They might destroy at last the *Schwarzkommando*. "They" want the world to be bleached, as the name Blicero suggests, after Blicker, a folklorish German nickname for Death, for blankness.

What only a few of the various searchers suspect, and what none of Them knows, is the lesson made obvious by the compulsion of the search: the Rocket has taken possession of everyone, and Gottfried is only a physical manifestation of their collective ultimate destiny. Gottfried *is* the *Schwarzgerät,* and Rocket 00000 was assembled in such a way as to make room for his body, covered with an aromatic shroud of Imipolex G. The "secret" is that sex, love, life, death have all been fused into the Rocket's assembly and into its final trajectory.

It can and will be said that such a book as this would have no audience except one prepared by the kind of analytic study of literature that has been in vogue for some thirty years. It's been said already of *V.* and of the works of other related contemporary novelists like William Burroughs, who shares, by the way, Pynchon's marvelous sensitivity to the metaphysical implications of technology, especially film technology, and the way the mind can schizophrenically work like a film projector. But the argument that writers like Pynchon and Burroughs are a by-product of contemporary literary criticism is trivial, since, for one reason, the two books—*Moby Dick* and *Ulysses*—that come to mind most often as one reads *Gravity's Rainbow* indulged in the same kind of complexity, not because criticism had made it fashionable to do so, but because the internal nature of culture made it necessary. And it is further beside the point because *Gravity's Rainbow* marks an advance beyond either book in its treatment of cultural inheritances, an advance that a merely literary education and taste will either distort or find uncongenial.

However outwardly similar, these three works do not conceive of the world in the same way. For historical reasons alone, including a radically changed idea about the structure of human personality, they would have to be vastly different from one another. Where they are alike is in the obligation, assumed without condescension, to shape the world occasionally in compliance with techniques developed outside literature or high culture. All three books take enormous, burdensome responsibility for the forces at work in the world around them, for those "assemblies" of life, like movies, comics, and behavioristic psychology, that go on outside the novel and make of reality a fiction even before a novelist can get to it. That is why all three books are full of renditions of styles and forms other than those derived from literature itself. The rhetoric in *Moby Dick* often owes as much to the political oratory of Melville's own time as to the works of Shakespeare. *Ulysses* has as much of the newspaper and the music hall as of Homer. Film is everywhere in *Gravity's Rainbow*. So is musical comedy — any given scene might break into a lyric. So are comic books, and although Plastic Man and Sundial are directly mentioned, Superman, Batman, and Captain Marvel, the superheroes of the World War II comics, determine the tone and the conduct of many of the characters.

This kind of thing is now familiar enough, but what distinguishes Pynchon in *Gravity's Rainbow*, especially from such writers as John Barth and Borges, is that he does not, like them, make use of technology or popular culture or literary convention in an essentially parodistic spirit, though he tended to do so in *V.* He is not so literary as to think it odd, an in joke, that literary techniques are perhaps less powerfully revealing about human nature and history than are scientific ones.

Pynchon, who was a student of engineering at Cornell, knows and respects the imagination embedded in the instrumentalities of science. If he is a scholar of film and super-comics, he is, even more, a scholar of mathematics. There are learned disquisitions on, among other things, organic chemistry and the theory of pauses in classical music, the possibilities of "dodecaphonic democracy" where all the notes in a work get equal hearing, something Pynchon might have gotten from Glenn Gould. Whether or not there is "dodecaphonic democracy" in Beethoven, there is most surely a kind of cultural democracy in Pynchon, and it is different from that in Melville or Joyce, the latter of whom shows a high-cultural nostalgia that is absent from Pynchon. Pynchon is apt to wax nostalgic about lost moments of Ameri-

can adolescence, especially moviegoing, and his idea of character derives more from cinematic media, post-Freudian psychology, and drugs than from other fiction.

Pynchon is willing and able, that is, to work from a range of
perspectives infinitely wider, more difficult to manage, more
learned than any to be found elsewhere in contemporary literature. His genius resides in his capacity to see, to see feelingly,
how these various perspectives, apparently so diverse and chaotic,
are begotten of the same technology, the same supportive structures that have foundations in the theology of the seventeenth
century and the science of the nineteenth. A good example is his
exploration into what are called "frames" in photography, the relation of "frames" to acceleration in moving pictures and in
rocketry, and the consequence of this relationship to the human
image. About Pökler's work on the rocket, we are told that, in
pre-war experiments, models of the rocket were dropped by
Heinkel airplanes from 20,000 feet and that "the fall was photographed by Askania Cinetheodolite rigs on the ground. In the
daily rushes you would watch the frames around 3,000 feet, where
the model broke through the speed of sound. There has been this
strange connection between the German mind and the rapid
flashing of successive stills to counterfeit movement, for at least
two centuries—since Leibniz, in the process of inventing calculus,
used the same approach to break up the trajectories of cannon
balls through the air. And now Pökler was about to be given proof
that these techniques had been extended past images on film, to
human lives."

This kind of speculative writing abounds in the book, brilliantly bringing together technological and much earlier analytical methods that combine to the eventual distortion of lives.
Such passages indicate a dimension of mind and of meditative
interest that combines the talents of Henry Adams with the talents
of Henry James. One thinks of similar excursions in Mailer, but
it is precisely Mailer's limitation that he hasn't shown the courage
to admit, as Pynchon continually does, that there are forms of
inquiry into the nature of life that are beyond the reach of the
Novelist's imagination (Mailer's self-enhancing capitalization),
that the Novelist's imagination is often less inclusive or daring
than the imagination of mathematics or organic chemistry.

It is not enough to say that Pynchon records the effects of technology on human lives or adapts the methods of technology to

the investigation and dramatization of them. Any number of writers have done and are doing that. What he is doing is of far more historical and literary significance. He is locating the kinds of human consciousness that have been implanted *in* the instruments of technology and contemporary methods of analysis; not content with recording the historical effect of these, he is anxious to find our history *in* them. Kekulé's dream, in which he discovered the shape of the benzine ring, the basis of aromatic chemistry, is as beautiful to Pynchon, as humanly revealing, as mythological as in any dream in *Finnegans Wake*. In the case of Pökler and his daughter, Pynchon is showing how the poor man comes to recognize the insidious aptness, for someone of his predilections, of the bait and punishment meted out to him by his superiors. He is allowed to see his long-missing daughter once a year—he cannot even be sure whether it is the same girl one year to the next—in a children's town called Zwölfkinder:

"So it has gone for the six years since. A daughter a year, each one about a year older, each time taking up nearly from scratch. The only continuity has been her name, and Zwölfkinder, and Pökler's love—love something like the persistence of vision, for They have used it to create for him the moving image of a daughter, flashing him only these summertime frames of her, leaving it to him to build the illusion of a single child—what would the time scale matter, a 24th of a second or a year (no more, the engineer thought, than in a wind tunnel, or an oscillograph whose turning drum you could speed or slow at will…)?"

She is what Pökler calls his "movie child," the more so since he remembers that on the night of her conception he had been aroused to sex with her mother by a porno film of the 1930s starring one Margherita Erdman, later to be a sometime bed mate of Slothrop. The loved child was in that sense begotten of a film and has since become as if "framed" by film, just as Gottfried is at last "framed" by the Rocket that Pökler helped develop. And both film and Rocket derive from the same analytical and technological legacies.

Everybody in the novel is to some extent similarly "framed," and in the various senses imagined in the wistfully recurrent references to John Dillinger coming out of the Biograph moviehouse, the movie images not yet faded from Dillinger's eyeballs (they are images of Clark Gable going manfully to the chair), Dillinger walking into the ambush prepared for him. At the end of *Gravity's Rainbow* Slothrop, the most "framed" of all, is given a piece of cloth by his buddy, the brawling sailor Bodine, who claims he dipped it in Dillinger's blood that night in Chicago. Dillinger got out of the "frame" only by dying, Gottfried by annihilation, Slothrop finally by some gradual dispersal of self, once the "framed" need to find the Rocket has expended itself. He more or less simply gets lost in the novel, begins to "thin, to scatter," until it's doubtful that he can ever be "found" again in the conventional sense of "positively identified and detained."

The only good way out of the "frame" would have been a saving surrender to peripheral vision. Apparently, it is only there that love is possible, especially love for Pynchon with his extraordinary affection for adolescent girls. As Slothrop sits with Bianca, Margherita's sweet little daughter, herself the offspring of film—conceived while her mother participated in the orgy that would later excite Pökler and lead to the conception of Ilse, the other "movie child"—he senses the timid and frightened desires in her. She wants to escape being "framed." He remembers similar glimpses of possibility when, as a kid, he wheeled around the roads of his hometown in New England, on the lookout for girls:

"Her look now—this deepening arrest—has already broken Slothrop's seeing heart: has broken and broken, that same look swung as he drove by, thrust away into twilights of moths and crumbling colony, of skinny clouded-cylinder gas pumps, of tin Moxie signs gentian and bitter sweet as the taste they were there to hustle on the weathered sides of barns, looked for how many Last Times up in the rear view mirror, all of them too far inside metal and combustion, allowing the days' targets more reality than anything that might come up by surprise, by Murphy's Law, where the salvation could be."

Even while being unpretentiously exact, these images of an American adolescence seem, in their very substantiality, to belong to the images of "framing," which in turn belong to the whole historical vision of the book. The vision confirms itself, not by generalization or by abstraction, but as a natural emanation from a mind in which ideas are saturated in the color, texture, and minuteness of daily experience. There are of course any number of other, equally reverberating structurings or assemblies, but a good many of them are designedly without this kind of human poignancy. One obvious example is the sign of double integrals, resembling two elongated S's. It is at once a mathematical principle behind the velocity rate of the Rocket, the insignia of the ss, the shape of the tunnels at Nordhausen, the shape of lovers side by side in bed; in physics, the symbol of entropy is S. This kind of patterning has become a tiresome game, and in Pynchon it is, when blatant, usually the object of high spoofing, a symptom of mechanical paranoia.

Readers who get impatient with this book will most likely be too exclusively literary in their responses rather than not literary enough. They'll stare at designs without listening to voices, wonder about characters when they should be laughing at grotesques, and generally miss the experience in a search for the meaning. Above all, they'll be discomfited by a novelist who posits a world in which experience is often most meaningfully assembled in ways considered alternative, often antithetical to literature, like science, or inferior to literature, like film and comic books. It is not possible dogmatically to feel this way about literature and enjoy *Gravity's Rainbow,* or, I would suppose, read the times with much comprehension.

If literature *is* superior to any of these things, then it takes a book as stylistically wide-ranging as *Gravity's Rainbow* to prove it. To know what the book is up to, one must also know the nonliterary genres, so to speak, in which life has been expressing itself. These include not only science and pop culture but the messages sent out by those who usually escape the notice of either, the lost ones, those not "framed," not in the design of things. The signs of their existence are to be found in the waste along the highway, the litter in the trunks of cars, the stuff in the bureau drawer. In his cataloguing of such wastes Pynchon here and in *The Crying of Lot 49* is the most poignant and heartbreaking "realist" since Dreiser.

This is a terribly haunted book. It is written by a man who has totally isolated himself from the literary world of New York or anywhere else. This remoteness is what has freed him from the provincial self-importance about literary modes and manners that is the besetting limitation of writers like Philip Roth—there are some twenty sequences here superior in kind to *The Breast,* accomplished as it is, and at least ten superior to Saul Bellow's *Mr. Sammler's Planet.* Pynchon is almost unbearably vulnerable to every aspect of contemporary experience, open to every form of sight and sound, democratically receptive to the most common and the most recondite signatures of things. "I resist anything better than my own diversity": what Whitman said of himself could be said of Pynchon and of the inexhaustible and elastic powers of synthesis that make his book a kind of assembly of so many other kinds of contemporary assembly, including that of the Rocket.

Pynchon is far too historically intelligent to suggest, however, that the schizophrenic paranoia of his own time is unique to it or that its causes are attributable to that bugaboo Technology. Slothrop can trace his ancestry to a member of Governor Winthrop's crew on the *Arbella*, the flagship of the great Puritan flotilla of 1630, and to a William Slothrop who wrote a nearly heretical book on the relations between the Elect and the Preterite, those who have been passed over, those not elected to salvation. Puritanism is evoked as an early version of the paranoia conditioning us to look for signs of Election and rendering the rest of mankind and its evidences invisible, merely so much waste. The book is therefore a profound (and profoundly funny) historical meditation on the humanity sacrificed to a grotesque delusion—the Faustian illusion of the inequality of lives and the inequality of the nature of signs.

George Levine: V-2

Several months after the publication of *Gravity's Rainbow*, the book having disappeared quickly from its unnatural position on the best seller list, and the renewed excitement about the mystery of Pynchon having subsided, it is still difficult to talk rationally about Pynchon's work. A measure of intellectual machismo these days is the number of pages of *Gravity's Rainbow* one has been able to read, the number of puns and literary games one has been able to detect. The book is, as almost everyone knows by now, an exceptionally difficult one. It makes *V.*, Pynchon's massive and brilliant first novel, look like a two-finger exercise, a model of simplicity and clarity. Still giddy from three months of reading through it, I want to confess at the outset to remaining awestruck, to being convinced that Pynchon has become the most important American novelist now writing.

But it's not comforting committing oneself to Pynchon's writing,

"V-2," by George Levine. From *Partisan Review*, 40 (1973), 517-29. Copyright © 1973 by Partisan Review, Inc. Reprinted by permission of the author.

and his critics and reviewers are bound to have a hard time. The discomfort comes not because he knows so much about technology, popular culture, history, and the street, nor because he creates long sequences of perverse and nauseating intensity, but because his writing challenges fundamental, usually unspoken literary and cultural assumptions. The assumption, for example, that order and unity are intrinsically valuable, that characters and objects are unequivocally distinguishable, that vulgarity and obscenity and what are conventionally called "cheap jokes" may be used but not taken on their own terms, that there are clear demarcations between fantasy and reality, between the physical and the metaphysical, that man's fate is in man's hands, and, perhaps, that there is such a thing as freedom. Perhaps most disturbing, these challenges are playful, implied frequently with the kind of deliberate banality or comedy that makes such solemn formulations as mine seem inappropriate.

No writer I know of is more resistant for form, nor more sensitive to it. *The Crying of Lot 49* finds a shape for the chaotic energies Pynchon first released in *V.* It gives us a central character, Oedipa Maas, a central plot, a single paranoia, and a predominant paranoid question: is Oedipa paranoid or is the plot she discovers real? But chaos is a constant presence, both as a threat to Oedipa and to the form of the book, and as the conspiracy closes in through the last pages, chaos beckons almost as a consolation. In *Gravity's Rainbow* chaos is (if it's imaginable) the center, not the periphery. Perhaps there is a central character—Slothrop, the conditioned paranoid New Englander whose sexuality is attuned to the rocket for which everybody is searching. But Slothrop literally dissolves as a character in a world of hundreds of characters, thousand of objects, each with its own story, its own paranoia. Even a bulb named Byron has his story, his plot. The plot, too, has an apparent center, the quest for the mysterious rocket 00000 and for the Schwarz-gerät which allows it to defy gravity. But nobody, including the inventors of its parts, seems to know how it is put together, and the stories that appear to circle around it pull out of its gravitational attraction.

Paranoia allows plot—is plot. But to carry the pun that far is to turn narrative into madness. This was part of the game in *V.*, but here the parody of the plotted novel is already old hat and rather too comforting, since parody gives us the old form to hang on to. The choice between paranoia and chaos, between Herbert

Stencil and Benny Profane of *V.*, is further complicated here. Slothrop, the novel's rough equivalent to Profane, shares without understanding it an obsession like Stencil's. But his paranoia is justified by the facts—or almost. He struggles with the Stencil-Profane qualities in himself, and as he simultaneously recognizes and resists paranoia, he becomes less and less a self to be contended with. The primary focus of the reader's narrative concern through the center of the book, Slothrop attracts to his rescue several of the other major characters—particularly Katje Borgesius (a cross between Lucrecia and Borges) and Pirate Prentice (the psychic who takes over other people's perceptions); and he is the focus of a plot by Ned Pointsman (the master Pavlovian) which ends in the mistaken castration of Major Marvy. Yet the Slothrop plot is not resolved, or even unresolved. Like Slothrop, it simply dissolves in the antiparanoid condition of chaos. At one point, the rather obscure multivoiced narrator alludes to the two aspects of Slothrop: "If there is something comforting—religious, if you want—about paranoia, there is still also antiparanoia, where nothing is connected to anything, a condition not many of us can bear for long. Well right now Slothrop feels himself sliding into the anti-paranoid part of his cycle, feels the whole city around him going back roofless, vulnerable, uncentered as he is, and only pasteboard images now of the listening Enemy left between him and the wet sky. Either they have put him here for a reason, or he's just here. He isn't sure that he wouldn't, actually, rather have that *reason.*"

I'd prefer a reason, too. Somebody, somewhere, must have a reason for something. Or, in the tradition of naturalistic fiction in which nature brooded indifferently over the fates of heroes and heroines, at least the strength and the suffering of the protagonist could imply values brought by man into the indifferent world. But here people become objects, aspects of that very indifferent world they fear. Moreover, the indifferent world may not, after all, be indifferent, though it is surely unintelligible or translatable only into the formulas of mechanics. Yet it is impossible not to follow the clues Pynchon plants as he leads us on with symbols, allusions, suggestive images, repetitions. But the patterns are almost impossible to decode, or can be decoded as Weissman decoded the spherics in *V.*: "The world is everything that is the case." The curious pleasure that comes with recognition of such clues as that *Gravity's Rainbow* is about V-2 or that an orgy takes the shape of a snake with its tail in its mouth or that images of black and white pervade the action doesn't get one very far.

Form teases rather than satisfies. The book begins, for instance, with a line implicitly picked up at the end: "A screaming comes across the sky." On the last pages, a Los Angeles theater manager named Zhlubb hears a terrifying noise: "'I don't think that's a police siren.' Your guts in a spasm, you reach for the AM radio. *'I don't think...'."* The noise, we have to assume, is the noise of a rocket (as it was on page one), except that you can't hear this kind of rocket until *after* it hits. And this is probably the rocket for which most of the major characters in the novel have been searching or living. Inside it is the lover (screaming?) of the rocket master—our old friend Weissman, by the way, code name Blicero. The rocket is about to hit a movie theater where we are apparently sitting watching a film which might well be called *Gravity's Rainbow.* We have, in good old literary style, come full circle, the narrative resolved, except that we are now participating in an ultimate, shaping paranoid vision into which Pynchon has been inducing us—destroyed if we accept it, dissolved if we don't. The shape seems to be there, but the more seriously we look for it, the less convincing it is.

As with *V.,* critics will be busy organizing this book's extraordinary incoherence for a long time. But the felt experience of the book for me runs counter to my passion to organize it. It is a book of moments wonderfully, satisfyingly realized by Pynchon. The connections are mine. As we move to the last chapters and the characters seem to be approaching their objects, the prose and the narrative fragment even more violently, more recklessly. If some things are pulled together, more fall apart. Zhlubb, for instance, is an entirely new character, appearing only on the last six pages. The last chapters are broken into titled fragments, and each of the fragments seems itself to fall apart. Insofar as we demand order here, we become either *"We,"* the preterite, the passed over, the victims of the destructive human systems which have led to the dominance of technology, the dehumanization of human beings and their relations, and mass slaughters (Indians, Khirgis, Dodos, dogs, Jews, and Hereros are among the mass-slaughtered here), or *"They,"* the dehumanizers. The scenario is is that of a horror movie, and Dracula is a presiding figure. As Father Rapier says to the damned double agents gathered in a museum which seems an early hell: "We have to carry on under the possibility that we die *only* because They want us to: because They need our terror for their Survival. We are their harvests."

To play the critic's game with Pynchon is not only to read but to participate in his scenario. That is, we become either the manipulated We to his uncannily ingenious They (which, I think, is part of his fun as it might be part of ours), or, more solemnly, play They to the We of multifarious and discontinuous experience. Obviously, there's no way to escape participation in the game. We should play it carefully.

The book describes a world of unintelligible and unintelligent energies, a world in which the primary fact is not thought or feeling or belief but energy itself. The energy is so potent (manifest in the imagined world and Pynchon's own prose) that it crosses the barrier between matter and spirit (and that barrier, that "interface," as Pynchon calls it, is a presiding preoccupation of the book): naturalism becomes spiritualism, and seances, emanations and mystical visions become as commonplace as technology and orgies. As the energy builds, sweeping cartels, people, light bulbs, rockets, sex, races, films, dope, technology in its path, it moves beyond the control of any elements that participate in it. A critical mass develops, a mass to be celebrated because it can't be contravened: "Critical mass cannot be ignored. Once the technical means of control have reached a certain size, a certain degree of *being connected* one to another, the chances for freedom are over for good." The world, this book, are beyond return, beyond freedom. Technology is assimilated to theology, and the mass to be celebrated is connected with both Catholic and Calvinist ritual, though it may be a black mass.

Energy creates the same kind of mystique of objects that we find in *V.*, though here it is carried even further. Although humans may be transformed into objects (as V. herself came apart like a bad joke), objects themselves are alive, full of a significance we can't quite comprehend but we can feel. Pynchon's language is itself full of this kind of energy, and through it he assimilates the world of science fiction and horror movies to the texture of our own culture. In both worlds, objects have assumed an importance larger than human, have, like Dracula, made slaves and automatons of people who do not believe in his power or believe too late. Their human energy is transformed into inhuman energy in an act which simulates love. And of course our society is driven (it would seem now uncontrollably) by a passion for production and possession, driven in a way which finally wrests power from humans and invests it in things. A consumer culture loves its possessions, lives for them, is ultimately transformed by them.

Partly as a consequence of this sense of the power of objects, one of the important aspects of Pynchon's style is the catalogue: the reverent, uncannily precise notation of things. Echoing and parodying the traditions of naturalism, Pynchon describes objects not with the planned banality of the writer determined to capture the "real," but with a vision that the real is really a kind of science fiction, that the ordinary is electric, alive, threatening, in process. To take a minor but characteristic example, here is a description of Slothrop's desk, which

> hasn't been cleaned down to the original wood since 1942. Things have fallen roughly into layers, over a base of bureaucratic smegma that sifts steadily to the bottom, made up of millions of tiny red and brown curls of rubber eraser, pencil shavings, dried tea or coffee stains, traces of sugar and Household Milk, much cigarette ash, very fine black debris picked and flung from typewriter ribbons, decomposing library paste, broken aspirins ground to powder. Then comes a scatter of paperclips, Zippo flints, rubber bands, staples, cigarette butts and crumpled packs, stray matches, pins, nubs of pens, stubs of pencils of all colors including the hard to get heliotrope and raw umber, wooden coffee spoons, Thayer's Slippery Elm Throat Lozenges sent by Slothrop's mother, Naline, all the way from Massachusetts, bits of tape, string, chalk...above that a layer of memoranda, empty buff ration books, phone numbers, unanswered letters, tattered sheets of carbon paper, the scribbled ukulele chords to a dozen songs including "Johnny Doughboy Found a Rose in Ireland"..., an empty Kreml hair tonic bottle, lost pieces to different jigsaw puzzles showing parts of the amber left eye of a Weimaraner, the green velvet folds of a gown, slate blue vèining in a distant cloud, the orange nimbus of an explosion (perhaps a sunset), rivets in the skin of a Flying Fortress, the pink inner thigh of a pouting pin-up girl...a few old weekly Intelligence Summaries from G-2, a busted corkscrewing ukulele string, boxes of gummed paper stars in many colors, pieces of a flashlight, top to a Nugget shoe polish can in which Slothrop now and then studies his blurry brass reflection, any number of reference books out of ACHTUNG library back down the hall—a dictionary of technical German, an F.D. *Special Handbook* or *Town Plan*—and usually, unless it's been pinched or thrown away, a *News of the World* somewhere too—Slothrop's a faithful reader.

Obviously, this goes on longer than it has to, except that it is
fun and, like so many other catalogues throughout the novel, it is
not "background." Although it implies enough connections so
that we are obliged to bring to bear some of our conventional
sense of how descriptions like this work in conventional novels—
after all, isn't this really about Slothrop—in fact the passage is
about itself.

The catalogue describes objects alive and in motion, no deader
than the earth in its large geological movements, nor than consuming and waste-producing organisms. It implies a whole world
and culture and *is* a world and a culture, pointlessly alive, described
with the uncanny precision of a mad scientist. The products that
constitute the world have been transformed into semisexual
waste. Almost everything is empty or used: shoe polish tins, hair
tonic bottles, cigarette packs, ukulele strings, eraser rubbings,
ration books. Sexuality, waste, bureaucracy smudge together in
the various strata, while humans turn to brass, machines have
skin, clouds have veins, and sunsets and explosions have become
indistinguishable.

And, since this is Pynchon, one looks for the implicit connections. Sure enough, there are plenty of them: not only the stars
Slothrop uses to pinpoint his sexual exploits (which also mark the
hits of the German V-2), the "orange nimbus of an explosion,"
the piece of a dog calling to mind the dog hunts that Pointsman
and his Pavlovians conduct, the dictionary of technical German
whose language permeates the rocket sections. And then, inescapably, there is the puzzle, the pieces of incoherent experience
making no sense but implying larger worlds, equivalent to the
passage itself in its fragmentariness, its suggestion of a whole
Slothrop (whom we never quite put together before he blurs away
and dissolves). But all of this goes on in a world historically
authentic. The products are of their time. Note that the spoons
are wooden, not plastic, the flints and the hair tonic are rightly
named, the pinups perfectly characterized, and so on.

The surfaces which occupy so much space in *Gravity's Rainbow*
accumulate, puzzlingly, discontinuously, as here, sometimes
comically, sometimes grotesquely, sometimes with a technically
dispassionate precision which can be terrifying. Nothing disappears from this world, but everything is transformed, like the
cigarette in ashes, the eraser in curls, the ribbon in flecks. The
presiding power is energy itself, gradually leveling human expe-

rience and feeling into geological strata. We're warned that physics will become metaphysics in the epigraph to the first book, which would be unequivocally serious if it weren't from a real rocket master, Wernher von Braun. "Nature does not know extinction; all it knows is transformation. Everything science has taught me and continues to teach me, strengthens my belief in the continuity of our spiritual existence after death." But how, in the midst of these wonderfully recorded objects undergoing their inexplicable transformation can one be, as one of Pynchon's characters explicitly wishes, "simply here, simply alive."

The energies of transformation affect everyone, even the apparently evil spirits whose capacity to feel anything but the need to feel has died and has led them to drain the life from all around them. Katje Borgesius, the witch, shares the pain of her victims; Weissman-Blicero loses all of his last three lovers; Pointsman is disgraced and cannot even catch his most interesting experiment, Slothrop. Webley Silvernail—a "guest star"—wandering among the Pavlovian cages, speculates: "All the animals, the plants, the minerals, even other kinds of men, are being broken and reassembled every day, to preserve an elite few, who are the loudest to theorize on freedom, but the least free of all." Here is the Dracula metaphor again, though with the new consciousness that Dracula, too, is a slave. What is there left to worship, or fear? Father Rapier has noted that the "critical mass" is too great, and Franz Pokler finally speaks, "In the name of the cathode, the anode, and the holy grid." The objects, the released energy, are out of control. Once the zero point is crossed, there is no return, and the rocket submits to gravity: "All the rest will happen according to the laws of ballistics. The rocket is helpless in it. Something else has taken over. Something beyond what has been designed in." And that is true of Pynchon's book, as Pynchon knows. We cannot redeem it for order or assimilate it to our conventional modes of control.

The analogue to this in Pynchon's style is its refusal of outrage, its dispassion in the face of the perversions, monstrosities, dehumanizations it chronicles. As narrator, he almost finds a way to be "simply here," and not to flinch. But not to flinch in such a context is almost intolerable, and to make bad jokes along the way is to encourage the kind of protests about inhumanity that Pynchon regularly gets. The wonderful bad pun on Hobbes in the law firm of Salitieri, Poore, Nash, De Brutus, and Short, is borderline.

But the terrible limericks, the awful pop songs—authentic in their awfulness—the accumulated obscenities, the grotesque post-Dickensian names (e.g., General Pudding, Osbie Feel, Rollo Groast, Teddy Bloat, Blodgett Waxwing, Micro Graham, Geli Tripping, "Merciful" Evans, Jessica Swanlake) must be taken entirely on their own gross terms before we even begin to try to redeem them with literary critical cunning. Pynchon knows we laugh at this sort of stuff when we're not being literary, and when we do here we begin to feel some of the respect for the nonliterary which makes Pynchon so hard to swallow and so special.

As he has assimilated and transmuted so much in American culture, so he has assimilated American literature as well. He pushes the Whitmanesque dream of total acceptance and total democracy so that we can begin to feel some of its potential non-Whitmanesque terrors. Yet he also participates, perhaps perversely, in that dream. Pynchon has been accused of lack of feeling (one thinks of Esther's nose job in *V.*, or Major Marvy's castration here), but his prose is implicitly full of respect for what is, and of awe, and of love. It is not merely, here, in the treatment of Roger Mexico's love of Jessica, which has some of the quality of sentimental romance. But in Slothrop's (and Pynchon's) affection for the preadolescent Bianca, Pökler's for his daughter Ilse, though both relationships are consummated in what would seem to be very unsentimental fucking. Worse—or better—it is even in the gold droplets of urine on Katje's pubic hairs which General Pudding passionately licks. It is in the perversions, the sodomies, the orgies, the rockets, the Dodo birds, and banana sandwiches. Only a writer who cares can see with Pynchon's intensity and range, can remember with such vividness, can juxtapose so recklessly and creatively.

Pynchon makes everything, even monstrosity, imaginable, and in doing so he has forced his art to catch up with the possibilities of feeling and action in our own times, to register them, to transcend them. He understands, especially, the peculiarly modern experience of being victimized into victimizing, of being forced to submit to anonymous energies in bureaucracies and computers and machines while becoming oneself an element in that energy. But even in simple conventional terms of realistic correspondence to the actual present, *Gravity's Rainbow* is a remarkable achievement. Pynchon, surely, invented Watergate and named its characters: Haldeman (dead-heap man), Ehrlichman (noble-man),

Kalmbach (quiet stream—still waters run deep, you know). It was his idea to give them German names. And who else would have provided a secretary named Harmony, a group called "the Plumbers" with its star Egil Krogh (Eagle Crow) and its comically bewigged spy named Hunt. Pynchon planted the sense of conspiracy and the actual discontinuities, irrationalities, incoherences, as well as the passionate faith of the doomed young subordinates. *Gravity's Rainbow* is full, too, of plots of big businesses larger than nations—Shell, I. G. Farben, for example. He knows that it's not Nixon but I.T.T. or Vesco's oil companies which are the real source of energy and power. And he knows that a man like Vesco can buy a country like Costa Rica. The fantasies, the parodies of science fiction movies, are part of the feeling texture of our present moment.

In making his own the central motifs of American literature and by subjecting them to the questions that our nonliterary culture forcibly implies, Pynchon has created a great historical novel, a great fantasy, a great parody. But more than that, he has found a potentially liberating literary mode. By making us wallow in our fantasies, our products, our bad jokes that we use to help redeem us from our numbness, he severs our connection with any of the mythologies which have contributed to our dehumanization, our transformation of people into objects. In *V.,* we watched how our myths, when acted out, not only removed us from the particularities of our own lives, but helped us to reduce those who didn't fit the myths to objects. Mass slaughter (we call it genocide these days) was one of the consequences.

Pynchon takes the post-Romantic exhaustion of feeling for granted and deals with the quest for new feeling. Death and sexual perversion (in which the lover becomes object) are other consequences. In *Gravity's Rainbow,* the Hereros of *V.* reappear as the Schwarzkommandos, participating like their white master in the pursuit of the ultimate energy—where sex and death come together—in the V-2. But the Hereros are now "The Empty Ones," deracinated, homeless, whose fulfillment can come only with death, and whose true object is suicide. Colonialism comes back to haunt the white masters, and the fantasy of Black violence (King Kong, along with Dracula, may well be the star of the show) pervades the book. The potentiality for annihilation now is total, and the Blacks and whites, colonials and colonists, are brothers, as the star Black, Enzian, is the brother of one of the star whites,

Tchitcherine, a Russian rocket man and paranoid, whose body is full of metal plates and who seeks to destroy his brother.

Literary and myth detectives will, clearly, have a picnic. Faulkner, Melville, Conrad, Lawrence, Borges, Whitman, Emily Dickinson, Malcolm X (not to mention Cole Porter, Superman, Frankenstein, Dracula, King Kong, "Have Gun Will Travel," Mickey Rooney, Clerk Maxwell, President Truman) are all presences here. Ahab sought the whale, McCaslin sought the bear, Slothrop seeks the rocket. Women are mysterious and untrustworthy and all-absorbing. Blacks are the occasion for guilt, violence, hatred, sexual fear. We have the conjunction of sex and death, the Puritan doctrine of the elect and the preterite, the reverence for power, the mutual love of men (both homosexual and straight), the attempted murder of the brother and the son, the American innocent in a duplicitous and morally exhausted Europe—except that America is morally exhausted, too. This catalogue can go on, and each item in it is both parodied and developed seriously.

But all of these myths appear in the context of popular and nonliterary culture, and as many critics have already noted, the predominant art influence is that of the film. All these myths appear in the frames of motion pictures so that we are at once entertained, engaged, and conscious of the potential artificiality. Films are collections of still photographs which create the illusion of movement and continuity. But they are rather like the coins in the Borges parable in his story "Tlön, Uqbar, and Orbis Tertius." That is, the coins lost yesterday and found today need not be the same. The picture in frame one is not the picture in frame two. Their connection is an illusion created by motion and electric energy. Thus the film creates in popular form the great American myths. Pynchon takes them as he finds them and pushes them at least one step beyond. Everywhere he takes enormous risks of banality or vulgarity (on the model of the motion picture) because he is unafraid to act out the fantasies of fear, of racial madness, of power, which are the staple of our popular media. He makes them both fantastic and felt reality.

The only American myth that survives is the anti-myth of Henry Adams. Adams is a presence in *V.* In *Gravity's Rainbow*, Pynchon has found a way to embody his anarchic vision. *The Education of Henry Adams* can, in fact, provide much of that gloss on the book that desperate literary seekers after coherence will be looking for, but the gloss cannot be comforting since it is an affirmation of incoherence. Here, for example, is Adams, not Pynchon:

> The sum of forces attracts; the feeble atom or molecule called man is attracted; he suffers education or growth; he is the sum of the forces that attract him; his body and his thought are alike the product; the movement of the forces controls the progress of the mind, since he can know nothing but the motions which impinge on his senses, whose sum makes education.

The technology, the preoccupation with Pavlovian conditioning, the persistent reduction of people to natural forces—all of these in Pynchon echo Adams's way of thinking. So too does the sense that the energy being produced by the world is being doubled every ten years (as Adams says), or is moving out of control (as Pynchon implies). In any case, Adams shares the view that the energy moves man into "a super-sensual world, in which he could measure nothing except by chance collisions of movements imperceptible to his sense, perhaps even imperceptible to his instruments, but perceptible to each other and so to some known ray at the end of the scale... —physics stark mad in metaphysics." The old myth of unity is dissolved. What remains for Adams as for Pynchon is energy, the irrational, unintelligible experience, particulars.

The "anti-paranoid" myth is the greatest risk Pynchon runs as a writer because formally it means Slothrop's fate, that is, dissolution. Parody can protect him from formlessness but not from the energies released by the destruction of old forms, by the accumulation of incoherent particulars which might relate in any of a thousand ways—and might not. Pynchon leaves it all open, disturbingly. And in the process he plays games with relationships. Metaphor is the key here. In *V.*, Fausto Maijstral, the Maltese poet, talks about how metaphor "is a device, an artifice. So that while others may look on the laws of physics as legislation and God as a human form with beard [the poet is alone] living a universe of things which simply are." Yet no one is more convincing than Pynchon in the invention of metaphors which force us to the equation of meaning with paranoia. As in *V.*, for example, *Gravity's Rainbow* gives us a letter—*s*—to worry over. Each *s* brings to mind the Schwarz-gerät which allows the V-2 rocket to defy gravity; Slothrop; the German SS; the shape of two lovers lying together; the shape of the tunnels in the rocket center at Nordhausen, which is based on the double lightning stroke and the sign of the double integral, and the "double integrating circuit in the guidance system of the rocket." U.S.W., until the snake's tail is in his mouth, and the violent energy expended doubles back on itself entropically reducing and homogenizing all elements. *S* is, of course, a double parabola, and the parabola, marking the flight of the rocket, is the shape of gravity's rainbow itself. Moreover, the upper arch of the parabola marks the interface between control and submission, the point where the energy and control of the Schwarz-gerät surrenders to "ballistics." But Pynchon can assimilate all this to the action of his characters, to the movement of his plots, and to his sense of the shape of Western culture. The arch of that parabola came, in this mythology, in the First World War:

> an English class was being decimated, the ones who'd volunteered were dying for those who'd known something and hadn't, and despite all, despite knowing, some of them, of the betrayal, while Europe died meanly in its own wastes, man loved. But the life-cry of that love has long since hissed away into no more than this idle and bitchy faggotry. In this latest War, death was no enemy, but a collaborator. Homosexuality in high places is just a carnal afterthought now, and the real and only fucking is done on paper.

One way to think of Pynchon's style in the context of this meaningless, dehumanized universe, is suggested in the book itself. Pynchon may seem to be describing, even celebrating, the death of a culture. But his style and language are the signs of life, not death. In a passage which might be taken as a metaphor for his own writing, Pynchon gives us a characteristically vulgar and authentic boogie-woogie song called "Sold on Suicide." Like the poetry of the Whole Sick Crew in *V.*, it is full of proper nouns. "In its complete version," the narrator says,

> it represents a pretty fair renunciation of the things of the world. The trouble with it is that by Gödel's theorem there is bound to be some item that one has omitted from the list, and such an item is not easy to think of off the top of one's head, so that what one does most likely is go back over the whole thing, meantime correcting mistakes and inevitable repetitions, and putting in new items that will surely have occurred to one, and—well, it's easy to see that the "suicide" of the title might have to be postponed indefinitely.

Gravity's Rainbow is a defense against suicide, not a celebration of it. Nobody in it really dies. Nobody exhausts reality or even the possibilities of myths of unity. Tchitcherine, employed to find a universal alphabet, fails in a kind of Tower of Babel. Though the world is driven by an anonymous energy which has seemed to deprive its inhabitants of the power of love, even the power of authentic life, that life is everywhere, "A face on ev'ry mountainside/ And a Soul in ev'ry stone." Even Pynchon's style, as he knows, cannot exhaust everything in the suicidal catalogue, but the catalogue itself is a vital achievement. The style, denying and asserting connection, creating metaphors, being "simply here," becomes the real possibility of freedom. It challenges us to take the risk of letting ourselves loose from the destructive myths which support us, and to face, with Pynchonian confidence and authority, an irrational world of objects.

Philip Morrison: [Review for *Scientific American*]

A V-2 missile links the two ends of the ballistic parabola that is gravity's rainbow. At one end is London, dogged and ingenious; the other end is by extension Germany itself. This bulky, intimate, particular and detached novel, a work of the first magnitude, is a tale of V-2.

There is a protagonist at each root of the parabola: in London, Slothrop, the young New England intelligence lieutenant, with a hidden childhood under psychological experiment; on the Continent, a mad and perverse S.S. officer, Captain Weissmann, commander of a V-2 battery. Slothrop leaves London to spend the year in fugue across shattered nations, in a search for the unique rocket, serial number 00/000, that Weissmann once requisitioned and launched with the S-Gerät, strangest of all the payloads of the Wehrmacht. The prose is intricate, turbulent, streaming without rest in a spate of idea, event and allusion.

Here we merely note that this is a novel of a new sort. James Joyce grounded his flowing work on the ledges of epic, myth and folklore. *Gravity's Rainbow* instead founds its intricacies and expertise of allusion on science and technology, adjusted to the

Review of *Gravity's Rainbow* by Philip Morrison. From *Scientific American*, 229 (October 1973), 131. Reprinted with permission. Copyright © 1973 by Scientific American, Inc. All rights reserved.

wartime *ambiance*. There are a number of remarkable set-piece
essays, one on organic chemistry and its origins, one on operant
conditioning, another on rocket dynamics. Ackeret and Leibniz,
the Poisson distribution and double integrals are references as
natural to Pynchon as limericks and vintages are to other novelists.
To sketch one example, an apt connection is made between the
serial wood engravings of late medieval German art, the calculus
of Leibniz, the successive frames of an Ufa film and the unfolding
time trajectory of the rocket, striking unheard a theater in London. Not all readers will persist up the wordstream past the bizarre and explicit sexual couplings, diverse as molecules, into the
analytic heart of the novel; those who do will gain a richness of
thought and motive, for which they must pay in spiritual coin.
The literary reviewers have treated the novel as seriously as it
deserves; it is a brilliant book, but be warned, that glow is icy
cold.

The Satiric Plots of *Gravity's Rainbow*

by Michael Seidel

Gravity's Rainbow is in large part a narrative satire. By narrative satire, in this context, I mean a process of modal plot-deformation; and by mode, I mean the dominant literary tendencies (or what Northrop Frye calls "the powers of action") that manifest themselves in controlled generic structures like tragedy, comedy, and romance. Mode is more a process than a prescription, and the satiric mode is that power of action which debases the ground of narrative plots. The essential subverting strategy in *Gravity's Rainbow* effectively hatches plots against the book's own characters. Pynchon deliberately confuses the literary meaning of *plot*—that is, a connected progress of events—with its psychological meaning—that is, the paranoid's schema of a world conspiring around him. Satiric plots envelop and depersonalize. They impede narrative action in an orgy of contingencies where individuals are inseparable from the "plots" that control them. Late in *Gravity's Rainbow,* the hopelessly confused Tyrone Slothrop asks, "This is some kind of plot, right?", and Seaman Bodine responds: "*Everything* is some kind of plot, man" (p. 603). Paranoia here is, by its nature, proliferating. Diverse accounts of Slothrop—deformed versions of him—are all that remain of Pynchon's hero as he is spread thin over the Allied Zone at the end of the book. And the many narrative styles in which the actions of *Gravity's Rainbow* are represented—from Kabbalistic revelation, to formulaic romance, to folk-myth, to cinematic parody, to comic book classic, to technological manual, to sewer fantasy, to rocket graffiti—assist the narrative in its satiric deformations or subversions.

It is the nature of satire not only to unsettle narrative ground, but to produce sets of satiric counterfeits for virtually every action

imprinted in the plot, almost as if too much of anything insures
its devaluation. In one of the interpolated tales delivered aboard
the *Anubis,* Pynchon has a woman passenger speak of stories that
mimic a master-plot; that is, she speaks of divine forgeries. She
warns that each "plot carries its signature. Some are God's, some
masquerade as God's. This is a very advanced kind of forgery"
(p. 464). Advanced forgery, of course, is one of Pynchon's ob-
sessive techniques in *Gravity's Rainbow,* a book which in its
larger forms depicts and mocks providential patterns of history
in the rise and fall of a V-2 rocket. The V-2 is an advance over the
more primitive model, Pynchon's first narrative, *V.* Forgery is
always the artist's craft, and, like the word *plot,* the verb *to forge*
has both generative and subversive connotations. For Pynchon,
the expansive mold of narrative allows for the shaping of material
from sources as variously rich as the forged sacred texts and slag
heaps of a civilization.

Even the title of *Gravity's Rainbow* encodes a series of counterfeit plots. Gravity's rainbow is the arc of the parabola, the gravita-
tionally plotted path of the V-2 whose trajectory determines the
book's action, an action initiated by the continental launchings of
the German V-2s toward London at the end of World War II and
realized by the re-assembly and belated launching of the fictional
A4 in the Zone after the war. Pynchon himself provides something
of a commentary on the plots and counterfeit plots of *Gravity's
Rainbow.* At one point late in the narrative he speaks of the
gradual course of human events, events that might be represented,
say, in a naturalistic, historical novel. He compares the course
of life to the parabolic arc inscribed in his title: "Most people's
lives have ups and downs that are relatively gradual, a sinuous
curve with first derivatives at every point." These are people
who participate in normative plots and never in satiric ones, who,
as Pynchon notes, "never get struck by lightning" (p. 664). To
get struck by lightning marks a "discontinuity in the curve of
life," a disruption of a personal and narrative curve. The satiric
plot is sudden and excessive. To be *hit by lightning* is a narrative
pun of sorts—to be enlightened and destroyed simultaneously,
exactly the choices presented at the conclusion of *Gravity's Rainbow.* The narrative's derivatives touch the gradual curve of life
only at "minus infinity across the cusp." From the point of inversion, the only direction is down: "from infinite miles per hour
changing to the same speed *in reverse,* all in the gnat's ass or red

cunt hair of the △ t across the point. That's getting hit by light-ning folks" (p. 664). For Pynchon, ascent contains descent, iden-tities become discontinuities.

Satiric narrative, then, demands at least two plots—the one that projects a course and the one that disrupts it. The two V-2 rockets at the end of *Gravity's Rainbow,* the 00000 and the 00001, are sa-tiric counterfeits of the rocket that opens the book. The German mythic voyager Blicero's rocket anticipates the projected goal of romance-epic quest, the transcendent mission to new lands, new Zones. Meanwhile, Oberst Enzian's suicide rocket prepares for the last descent, the entropic mission to no man's land, the light-ning bolt that will strike an entire persecuted and paranoid civilization. Each rocket marks a different plot and each sustains Pynchon's story-book parody of Manichaean mythologies, "one good Rocket to voyage to the stars and an evil one for the world's suicide" (p. 724).

These rockets, of course, are not as different as they seem. The two rockets, and the two rocket endings, confirm a pattern de-scribed earlier in Pointsman's White Visitation, a pattern of conditioned paranoia or madness: "the confusion of the ideas of the opposite" (p. 90). Such confusion is part of a satiric pathology. Blicero, the German whiteman (alias Weissmann) seeks the stars, while Enzian, the African blackman, seeks the realm of death; but as the sacrificial Gottfried suspects, the destinations may be the same, the "new Edge" may be the "new Deathkingdom" (p. 723). The plot of Blicero's mission contains a reverse potential at the parabolic cusp. As Gottfried remarks, "Gravity runs all the way out to the cold sphere, there is always the danger of falling" (p. 723). Such a danger is the very essence of satiric potential.

Early in *Gravity's Rainbow,* Pointsman analyzes all life's pro-cesses in a way that anticipates the satiric significance of the numbered rockets at the end. Pointsman exists "in the domain of zero to one, not something to something...[he] can only possess the zero and the one" (p. 55). Pointsman the behaviorist bureaucrat, the debaser of human choice, plots against figures like Slothrop and Mexico, figures who, in effect, struggle to get out of the world of satiric opposites and into the world of the gradual curve, the world of human potential, the world of the traditional novel. The statistician Roger Mexico thinks different-ly: "But to Mexico belongs the domain *between* zero and one— the middle Pointsman has excluded from his persuasion—the

probabilities" (p. 55). Pynchon, of course, reserves for Slothrop
and Mexico the most traditional of *Gravity's Rainbow's* plots—
novelistic love stories—but it is no accident that both Slothrop
and Mexico find themselves removed from the scene at the end
of the narrative. Traditional characters in traditional plots re-
quire the movement from "something to something"—they cannot easily negotiate the satiric realm of the excluded middle.
Pointsman and the numbered rockets plot only the satiric "persuasion" of Pynchon's narrative. And the end comes for *Gravity's
Rainbow* when the potential for "probable" or novelistic action is
literally "opposed" by the final descent of the rocket.

Pynchon's endings are informed by the paradox, perhaps present in literature from its epic beginnings, that where there is
gain there is invariably loss, where there are new civilizations
there are invariably destroyed ones. But whereas the epic emphasizes the reconstructed human spirit in reconstructable civilizations, satire emphasizes resettlements in nowhere lands, kingdoms
of nothing. For Pynchon, epic territory becomes, like the burnt-
out Berlin of *Gravity's Rainbow,* an "inverse mapping" of what it
once was and might be. If the final missions of epic-narratives
encourage the idea of continuation, those who undertake these
missions are the signatories to their civilization's projected worth.
But when heroic figures of counterfeit value launch themselves
into oblivion, the epic mission is stymied, it becomes entropic—
the measures of unavailable energy, random, inert. Rather tell-
ingly, the final launch of *Gravity's Rainbow,* the mission of
Blicero and Gottfried, counterfeits the first epic of mission in the
western tradition. Pynchon describes Blicero's scheme as a "German Odyssey." But such an odyssey has only a random destination;
there is no one place to go. Of destinations, the new Odysseus can
only ask of the planets in outer space, "which one would be the
last home island?" In satire there are no homecomings.

Blicero's counter-epic question charts a directional confusion,
a bathetic journey. At every stage in the book life turns towards
death, continuation towards destruction, creation towards annihilation. London is "Death's Antechamber" at the beginning of
Gravity's Rainbow, and in the doomed theater at the end of the
book Pynchon returns, symbolically, to where he began. The
epigraph to Part I of *Gravity's Rainbow* quotes the words of
Wernher von Braun on death. As one of the developers of the
German V-2 and as one of the fathers of the nuclear age, von

Braun also symbolically links the beginning and the ending of the book. The epigraph is profoundly ironic: "Nature does not know extinction; all it knows is transformation. Everything science has taught me, and continues to teach me, strengthens my belief in the continuity of our spiritual existence after death." Von Braun's words receive their only considered response in the one-word epigraph to the fourth, and last, part of *Gravity's Rainbow,* significantly titled *The Counterforce.* Pynchon quotes one of Richard Nixon's shorter speeches: "What?" In Part IV the rocket falls again. What, indeed? What of von Braun's strengthened belief? Those who would design systems for the destruction of the race are only satirically equipped to speak on the primacy of creation over extinction. When the rocket falls, the book ends with its own destructive tail in its mouth; it uses up all available energy.

The entropic line of descent in satiric plots inevitably takes its toll on those caught up in the narrative design. But in satire descent is more than an end; it is also the line of individual and racial inheritance. The fate of character in satire is a fate marked not only by the lightning bolt of destruction but by the preterite birth, the human accident. Pynchon establishes a law of inheritance for *Gravity's Rainbow* that holds for the shape of the book as well as for the characters in it: "So, when laws of heredity are laid down, mutants will be born" (p. 275). The very phrase takes the shape of the process it describes, a shape and a process that can be extrapolated for the larger plot of the narrative. Pynchon's almost consoling "So" invites a more settling conclusion than he delivers. Laws are presumably laid down, if laid down at all, for healthy births, not for mutants. Yet mutants will be born. Such a disruption of organic inheritance is as old as the account of the degenerate citizen and city in the interior books of Plato's *Republic* where in all cycles of growth there are inevitable accidents of generic transmission. Plants, as Plato writes, produce fruits hopelessly out of season. Proliferate or mutational inheritances are metaphorical misbegettings. In narrative satire, what is metaphoric is made literal. Mutants will be born. We learn from *Gravity's Rainbow* that its hero is a Plasticman, a rocket-mutant. Slothrop's inherited destiny helps determine the shape of the narrative he is in: "Whatever we may find, there can be no doubt that he is, physiologically, historically, a monster" (p. 144).

Similarly, the generic laws of literary inheritance assume healthy births, sound transmissions; but satiric forms produce the monstrous—hence satire's penchant for generic deformation. Having de-formed, satire takes as its subject the very deformity it has produced, something like the giant Adenoid Pynchon lets loose in the opening pages of *Gravity's Rainbow*. Rabelaisian monstrosities—misbirths—move through narrative worlds whose paths distort what were once recognizable as paradigmatic wanderings, quests, trials, threshholds, penetrations, resolutions, and revelations. Through such paradigmatic experiences, heroes are initiated, tried, and perhaps encultured. But satiric narratives perform the opposite—they dehumanize heroes and debase heroic inheritances. Part Two of *Gravity's Rainbow* opens with an epigraph honoring the cinematic monster-hero, King Kong, as "the tallest, darkest leading man in Hollywood." Kong's giganticism in the movie allows the mutant ape enough power to take over, temporarily, the society in which he appears, but the giant ape's very size creates for him an impasse of desire. He cannot love his captured heroine decorously, therefore he rages monstrously through the metropolis. In *Gravity's Rainbow* King Kong is a prototype not only for Slothrop, the leading man who cannot love decorously, but also for the African Herero on a suicide mission, Enzian. Kong is a black "scapeape" fallen from an "erection," the Empire State Building, just as the Herero Enzian prepares to mount the "steel erection" or A4 rocket for his final plunge. The plight of Kong, Slothrop, Enzian, and all of *Gravity's Rainbow*'s modern "hereros" is the plight of all mutants—they are born fruits out of season, they carry the seeds of their own destruction.

The prominent satiric hero of *Gravity's Rainbow*, Tyrone Slothrop, is a "truly classical case of some pathology, a perfect mechanism." Occasionally he is able to "disengage" the clutch of the "iron-cased engine" that drives him (p. 207), but only occasionally. More often he is prey to the disturbed course of the narrative—he loses personality in the complexities of the Zone. His character is satiric in that what is most human about Slothrop is also most vulnerable to narrative deformation. He is the victim of someone else's circumstances. After the rights to his body were sold in the early 1920s by his father to the Pavlovian, Laszlo Jamf, Slothrop experienced a bizarre human loss. An aberrant process—a molecularly conditioned mutation—takes choice away from him.

Somehow Slothrop carries encoded within him the ability to mark the impact of V-2 rockets. His conditioning by Jamf in the 1920s bears a relation to Jamf's later work on the Imipolex G plastic (Kryptosam, with its chemical convertible to melanin or skin pigment) which Blicero uses in his last V-2. Therefore Slothrop's organic disturbance in a way predicts the death technology of the War and of the post-War periods. His penis leaps to attention prior to rocket impact. Even the human impulse to love is here degeneratively programmed. As Katje Borgesius remarks early in the book, the trigonometic "plot" of the V-2 parallels Slothrop's impulses but charts only a destructive path from conception to annihilation. Between its two points, in its five minutes of flight, it "lives an entire life," patterned in a strange "act of love" that is essentially at odds with the more human desire for continuance. In Pynchon's parodic rocket life of masculine line and feminine target, the arc of flight counterfeits erection, ejaculation, and detumescence. But the thrust before *Brenschluss,* the turn at the cusp, and the downward acceleration to impact is at best onanistic —a subversion of the course that allows for the organic promise of renewal.

Slothrop's sexual stimuli are part of the satirically inverted structure of *Gravity's Rainbow:* the confusion of the organic and the mechanistic, the opposition of the procreative and the destructive, the parody, in every sense, of modernity's Second Coming. Slothrop is virtually brother to the V-2 rockets, and Pynchon fulfills a satiric pattern in the narrative when Slothrop, the human being, is taken apart at the same time the two A4 rockets are assembled in the Zone. Pynchon calls the rocket assembly a "Diaspora running backwards," and as the rockets come together, Slothrop falls apart—only variants of his story exist, he takes proliferative form. The Diaspora reversed, of course, is another satirically inverted sacred plot, much like the secular rocket's reverse speed at minus infinity across the cusp. And what happens to Slothrop in the Zone is equivalent to Pynchon's narrative subversion of the gradual curve of character. As he is enlightened, he is destroyed.

The tracings of the variable lines of personality and plot in *Gravity's Rainbow* are not unlike those in a much earlier satiric narrative in which a character, marked from birth, is confused by the systems that determine him. In Laurence Sterne's *Tristram Shandy,* the titular hero is born unlucky, and he ends his time on earth, like Slothrop, distributed over the European continent. The comparison of these narratives is not an idle one: the problems experienced by characters in both are modally similar. Late in *Tristram Shandy,* Sterne's hero, like Pynchon's, tries to pattern his life in a series of lines, to recreate his linear history. But for each of the previous volumes of his *Life and Opinions* he can produce only a sorry squiggle. As a character and as a recorder of character, Tristram is abashed by his efforts. His life is all fits and starts, and the lines that he plots resemble none familiar to novelists or their readers. If he lives through his seventh volume, Tristram promises to reform, to produce a "tolerably straight" line. But he goes immediately off course again, and before proceeding with his chaotic life on the continent he digresses for a chapter on lines. What has happened is clear enough. In satire the literal and metaphoric impediments to narrative resolution become themselves the subjects of narrative obsession. Tristram considers the straight line, the *"right line,"* the *"best line,"* the weighty line, but resists following it: "by what mistake—who told them so—or how it has come to pass, that your men of wit and genius have all along confounded this line, with the line of GRAVITATION?" (Vol. 6, Ch. 40).

A modern victim of gravitational descent, Tyrone Slothrop, finds that he, too, is incapable of following straight lines. Tristram Shandy grows desperate as a character in seemingly random motion; Slothrop merely gives in to paranoia. He loses the desire to choose his course. And as he loses the desire to choose, he literally loses form. His preterite inheritance makes him over-ready to play the role of satiric victim. Whether as Rocketman or, later, as Pigman, Slothrop only rarely tries to separate himself from the proliferate courses he follows. It is only in isolated instances— usually during moments of affection with Katje or Bianca or Geli —that Slothrop makes gestures toward a more integrated gathering in of his various selves. Those who care about Slothrop, like Sir Stephen Dodson-Truck from the White Visitation, are taken "off his case." In the Zone Slothrop is rarely a fictional character who genuinely chooses and desires; he is instead a comics hero, a paranoid Plasticman—whom he must resemble, given his curious connection to the Imipolex G polymer in which Blicero encases Gottfried at last.

The action of Pynchon's narrative is so arranged to delimit and subvert Slothrop's desires, to debase his mission, to unsettle his ground. This happens so often that Slothrop eventually begins to catch on. He says to himself, in a moment of wonderful reflexivity, after he thinks of his pursuit of the A4 as the pursuit of the Holy Grail: "The Schwarzgerät is no Grail, Ace, that's not what the G in Imipolex G stands for. And you are no knightly hero. The best you can compare with is Tannhauser, the Singing Nincompoop" (p. 364). Slothrop, in self-mockery, grasps the ways in which the narrative mocks him, and the more he understands the less he tries to remain Slothrop. He moves through the Zone, only intermittently processing information about the conditions that condition him; finally "bridges that might have led back are down now for good." Slothrop grows "less anxious about betraying those who trust him. He feels obligations less immediately. There is, in fact, a general loss of emotion..." (pp. 490-91). The elaborate surface motion at the end of *Gravity's Rainbow,* the many movements through the Zone, run counter to the depth of "emotion" in the narrative's primary character. This, too, is an essentially satiric condition.

As characters, satiric heroes are victims; they are disallowed the luxury of human choice or even self-determined motive because the promiscuous contingencies of the narratives in which they appear are so oppressive to the shapes of humanity, so enervating, that the only relief is in the loss of will, the loss of distinction. Characters in satire are rendered inhuman, less than integral, driven mad like Swift's horse-deluded Gulliver, or simply exhausted like Pynchon's Slothrop.

As the action in *Gravity's Rainbow* develops, Slothrop learns, even from his necessarily limited perspective, that basically two courses govern his life: his past personal history—that is, his conditioning as the Infant Tyrone—and his present quest—that is, his investigation of his own prescience, his relation to the future. Whether he has control of what he does or whether he *is* the control of what is done to him by the likes of Pointsman is largely a question of modal emphasis. Slothrop is both the "seeker and sought," also the "baited and bait." His movements resemble the mini-journey, described by Pynchon, of each individual's skin cells as they migrate on the great epidermal quest. If all cells could talk—and Pynchon's satire has them talking—they would debunk the notion that surface wanderings mean something. The human body produces a set of cryptic Kabalistic pro-

gram notes for "an old and clandestine drama" (p. 147): "It's
been a prevalent notion. Fallen sparks. Fragments of vessels
broken at the Creation. And someday, somehow, before the end,
a gathering back to home. A messenger from the Kingdom, arriving at the last moment. But I tell you there is no such message, no such home—only the millions of last moments...no
more. Our history is an aggregate of last moments" (pp. 148-49).

When Slothrop loses his character in the multiple plots of
Gravity's Rainbow, he, as an aggregate of cells, is made into an
aggregate of last moments. After an especially intense episode in
Part Two consisting of a Mediterranean night of love and a morning sunrise with Katje, Slothrop's clothes are stolen from his front
room. A first fragment of him is gone. Stark naked, he pursues
the thieves, covering himself with a purple satin sheet as he descends the stairs. From the floor below he leaps out of a terrace
window, falling into a fortunately placed thickly branched tree.
Slothrop descendent is Slothrop regressive, a naked ape in regal
robes. He plunges into the midst of a croquet game, a satiric hero,
in effect, having interrupted a novel of manners. And there he
stands: disturbed at love, displaced, naked under a royal toga,
the king-beast Kong of the epigraph to this section of the book.
Slothrop's fall from the treetop is a satiric fall, a speeded up
version of the descent of man. Slothrop's losses are always satire's
gains. As Pynchon takes the ground from beneath his hero's feet,
Slothrop finds himself pulled away from Katje, from himself,
from love. Finally, at the end of the narrative, he has and is
nothing.

The descent or degeneration of character is a defining feature
of satiric narrative. But degeneration is based, for Pynchon at
least, on a more generally conceived model that treats of the
demise of the specially gifted and specially fated individual. This
is a potentially tragic, as well as satiric model, a potentially
Oedipal model. Plot as paranoia is at the heart of the Oedipus
story, a situation in which an individual life is plagued by desires that mock choice. The difference between a tragic and a
satiric rendering of circumstance has more to do with the attitude
taken toward the victim than with the essential nature of victimi-
zation. In the Oedipus story, Oedipus is the sickness of his plague-
ridden city. A human life *becomes* a human institution. Oedipus,
honored among men for his greatness, is, in a horrifying way,
greater than he knows, greater than he fears. He is more than one

man. In *Gravity's Rainbow* Pynchon provides a satiric version of the story, not only in Slothrop, but in the strange man at the White Visitation who actually thinks he *is* the Second World War—he plans to die on V.E. Day. He, too, is greater than one man. But the absurdity of the situation makes him satiric, someone who has lost his senses in a senseless situation.

In *The Crying of Lot 49,* Pynchon had named his heroine Oedipa Maas—something more than Oedipus. The Oedipal dilemma, the unravelling of a series of knots only to tie other, larger, knots tighter, is a pattern that continues to inform *Gravity's Rainbow.* Like Oedipus, Slothrop is born into a condition that determines him. He tries to know, to choose, to change, but he succeeds only in revealing things essentially uncanny, things, according to Freud, once known but forgotten. When characters are stone-determined, monstrously deformed, swollen, or, as Pynchon says of his Oedipal Slothrop, "genetically predisposed," their quests for information reveal a strange personal course. Attempts to understand their "plots" are analytic nightmares— as characters, they break down, digress, swerve, and, finally, submit. In Oedipally tragic plots, those fated would of needs be reborn to escape the course determined for them. In Oedipally satiric plots, those fated never even gain the energy to resist their destiny.

"Is this the way out?", someone asks on the first page of *Gravity's Rainbow,* only to have the narrator explain the tragic-satiric dilemma. Rocket paranoia "is not a disentanglement from, but a progressive *knotting into,* " an allusion to the tragic denouement that in satire becomes an entropic unravelling. In the Oedipus story, the presumed historical and rational accomplishments of the hero are implicitly connected to a mythic system conceived before the hero was conceived. Oedipus is a descendant of the Theban *spartoi,* earth-born men, earth monsters whose wants are primal and whose characters contentious. He circulates in an antithetical world where paranoia, an interface of personality and plot, makes all action pathological. Oedipus' search leads to the womb where he has sown his own seed. In *Gravity's Rainbow,* Slothrop's search leads him to a satirically inflated version of his own penis, the A4 rocket. In both cases, an unfortunate destiny is the only available choice. As the behaviorist Pointsman knows, "in the stone determinacy of everything, of every soul" there "will be precious little room for any hope at all" (p. 86).

Hope for Pynchon is not simply a matter of personal destiny, but a larger issue in history itself. *Gravity's Rainbow* is a historical novel; one of its obsessions is with historical potential and historical timing. Like Ford Madox Ford in *Parade's End* or Günter Grass in *The Tin Drum,* Pynchon records the pageant of human and bureaucratic orders between the century's two great wars, an interface he sees as crucial.

Pynchon's hero, Tyrone Slothrop, grows up in the 1920s and 1930s. He is the human interface between wars. The historical "timing" of *Gravity's Rainbow* is itself an interface that contributes to the modal shift in Pynchon's narrative from an essentially novelistic to an essentially satiric presentation of orders. The first sensate experience in the narrative—the V-2 screaming across the sky—sounds the difference between World War I and World War II. The drawn-out pain in the trenches of the First World War is temporally radicalized by the immediate, impersonal, and random shock of the V-2 warheads as they fall on London. Europe's recollections of World War I, as Paul Fussell has recently recorded [see p. 213 below], are its homage to its own fading dignity. Afterwards, in the 1920s, civilization spawns a new order that conspires to annihilate permanently what remains of humanity in the race. For Pynchon, the First War plays out the collective dying gasp of individuals and individually distinct cultures. The postwar system represents the burgeoning power of a dehumanized, technological, internationally corporate elite, the huge chemical cartels and energy conglomerates that determine and control events. The historical conspiracy that leads to and through World War II touches, for Pynchon, in some way or another on the development of the V-2 rocket in Germany. Pynchon defines the modern order by drawing a hand with a pointing finger (a middle finger, "giving the finger") in the body of his text: "*A Rocket-cartel. A structure cutting across every agency human and paper that ever touched it*" (p. 566). The pointing finger tells as much about the strategy of the book as it does about its satirically focused subject. The rocket-system is the emblem in *Gravity's Rainbow* of a radical shift in historical sensibility and a corresponding shift in the radicals of narration. With the Rocket-cartel the human agency in fiction—the novel—is replaced by the proliferate fiction of satire, a fiction of bureaucracies and degenerate systems. In the IG Farben cartel, systems technology becomes a violation of a natural cycle: "Taking and not giving back, demanding that 'productivity' and 'earnings' keep on increasing with time, the System removing from the rest of the World these vast quantities of energy to keep its own tiny desperate fraction showing a profit: and not only most of humanity—most of the World, animal, vegetable and mineral, is laid waste in the process" (p. 412).

In one of his last lectures, Laszlo Jamf, the conditioner of the Infant Slothrop, explains the nature of the work undertaken between the wars. Jamf says to his students, among them those who will design the V-2 guidance system, there is a "lion in each one of you. He is either tamed—by too much mathematics, by details of design, by corporate procedures—or he stays wild, an eternal predator" (p. 577). Jamf, of course, prefers the routine, the perfectly German system. In the very last lecture of the year in Pökler's class, he makes his strongest plea for the "wave of the future," for the ultimate routine in which life is denied by the "move beyond life, toward the inorganic." Denaturing is a subversive act. The Laszlo Jamfs of the century certify Pynchon's satiric vision: "'Here is no frailty, no mortality—here is Strength, and the Timeless.' Then his [Jamf's] well-known finale, as he wiped away the scrawled C—H on his chalkboard and wrote, in enormous letters, Si—N" (p. 580). Jamf's Si—N stands for the inorganic bond, Silicon and Nitrogen, the basis of the "plastic" state, a transformation from the organic bond, Carbon and Hydrogen. But, needless to say, the discovery and the process is the negation of life. Jamf's bond is an original SIN that leads to a lifeless order, a satiric descent, the "dark and silent frame" at the end of *Gravity's Rainbow*. Modern analysis finally bites through the apple.

In the represented narrative action of *Gravity's Rainbow*, the most vulnerable characters are those, like Slothrop, most literally worked over by the inter-war period or those, like Brigadier Ernest Pudding, who effectively lose influence in the modern world after World War I. Pudding is a fascinating case. He is an old war horse whose personal glory came at Ypres during one vicious day of fighting. At the White Visitation in the 1940s, the aging commander's nerves, his will, his desires and his mind, are, as his surname suggests, softening. And his "e(a)rnest" Christian name is more a slightly fey remnant of the Wildean pre-war drawing room than the sadomasochistic, coprophilic regimen of the back chambers at the White Visitation. Brigadier Pudding's first reaction to the attempt by Pointsman to track down the curious link between Slothrop and the V-2's is the reaction of an old-fashioned Britisher in an old-fashioned novel of manners: "Isn't it beastly?"

Pudding is one of the characters in the narrative who works— and is worked by Pointsman—backwards. He becomes part of an obscenely contrived parodic elegy for World War I. The retired and reactivated Brigadier was not ready for the Second World War. He had tried, in his limited way, to hold the contours of Europe in hand after the First War by writing a book, an unfinished and unfinishable history of the shifting balance of power in Europe, *Things That Can Happen in European Politics.* Precisely because too many things can happen, and too many do, the controlled older world of European life and politics gives way to the proliferate satiric system.

Pudding's difficulty with his chosen subject indicates the ways in which World War I and World War II differ for Pynchon. The older order of men, those defined by a European class structure, by property, by rank, by family, those represented in traditional novels, find themselves victims in a conspiratorial, bureaucratic world where individuals count for nothing. Earlier, in the 1914-1918 War, men who endured the degradation of living for weeks on end in the trenches "came to love one another decently" (p. 616). Love is not a word that occurs frequently in the post-World War II Zone of *Gravity's Rainbow,* and for Pynchon to use it in reference to World War I is to sing his elegy for a race of young men who found "in the faces of other young men evidence of otherworldly visits." Human love, for Pynchon, is a kind of salvation, "some poor hope that may have helped redeem even mud, shit, the decaying pieces of human meat" (p. 616). About love, even homosexual love, and about redemption, a novelist can write books of limited human transcendence.

In *Gravity's Rainbow,* the elegy for the human losses of World War I releases Pynchon's satiric narrative scheme for the new "time" of the corporate order. He marks the transformation of the "life-cry of that love" in the trenches to a kind of "bitchy faggotry" in a world that knows only bureaucratic penetration. The passing from those "elegant rooms of history," as Pynchon refers to pre-World War I Europe, to the chambers of the White Visitation or the rubble heaps of the World War II Zone makes civilization itself seem random or entropic, "nothing but events" (p. 56).

Unlike the First World War, the Second is in no sense elegiac. All human dimension dwindles: "the true war is a celebration of markets." The technocrats, bureaucrats, behavioral scientists, industrial scientists, are the "new ruling elite...with no right at all to be where they are" (p. 521). The mention of "elite" recalls the older European class elite, those who enjoyed their rights from a time well before the Industrial Revolution and Techno-logical Revolution, before the Virgin and the Dynamo, before the *V.* of Pynchon's first large narrative and the V-2 of his third. Pynchon's "new elite" makes no attempt whatever to adjust human institutions to human desires; it merely engineers the "conspiracy between human beings and techniques" (p. 521) which determines an historical routine that becomes a satiric subject.

Gravity's Rainbow in part tells the story of scattered individuals who unsuccessfully try to resist the advance of the new bureau-cratic modern order. In trying to understand what is happening in Europe, a character like Brigadier Pudding, the World War I hero, cannot understand the nature of the Second World War, the significant thing that *did* happen in European politics. Pud-ding is only nominally in command at the White Visitation; in reality his command is pure torture for him. Pudding's World War I history becomes pornographic as World War II poisons the memory of Ypres. At the White Visitation, Pointsman controls the destruction of Pudding's world—he lets the Brigadier plot his own demise. In the chambers prepared for him, Pudding enacts a series of ritual tortures, all grotesque parodies of heroism and human love. The recreation of the First World War within the confines of the White Visitation, the symbol of the new war, is thematically and structurally subversive in *Gravity's Rainbow.* Pointsman produces a set of debased counterfeits: "not malignant puns against an intended sufferer so much as a sympathetic magic, a repetition high and low of some prevailing form" (p. 232). What Pointsman does to Pudding is, in effect, what Pynchon does to the prevailing form of fiction, the novel. To control Pudding, Pointsman abruptly alters the derivatives on the sinuous curve of his life; to control the means of narrative presentation in *Grav-ity's Rainbow,* Pynchon creates a set of repetitions low, high, and "somewhere over" the traditional and expected fictional parabola of gravity's rainbow.

Pointsman, the new elitist torturer, needs the Second World War to maintain his behaviorist bureaucracy. Like all systems of the new order, and like all systems in satire, Pointsman's usurps the individual's will. Near the rat cages, what Pynchon calls the "rationalized forms of death," at the White Visitation, one of Pointsman's men, Webley Silvernail, pauses and wishes he could set the rats free—and not only the rats, but all the animals, all the men who "are being broken and reassembled every day, to preserve an elite few, who are the loudest to theorize on freedom" (p. 230). The series of rooms at the White Visitation control the process of segmentation that makes Pudding, and those like him, less whole. Control is a word with several meanings. In science, *control* determines the means for verification. But in a narrative sense control implies who (or what) dominates the action. Characters who lose control are paranoid, they also lose control of what happens to them, of how they "act." Pointsman pursues a character like Slothrop because he knows what has to be done to *control* him as a subject in his scientific domain. Of Slothrop, Pointsman insists that *"We must never lose control."* He means that he must never lose Slothrop in the Zone and he must never lose the scientific *control* of his effort to determine the landings of the V-2. In another sense, never to lose control is to deny basic human impulses, and, of course, this is exactly what happens in Pynchon's satiric narrative. When Pointsman loses Slothrop in the Zone, he loses the White Visitation's control of its own fate because the bureaucracy has all its hopes pinned on Slothrop. But it is part of *Gravity's Rainbow*'s deeper modal irony that when Slothrop loses control of himself, he becomes the product of the century, conditioned by its original sin, determined by its inhumanity. Slothrop's paranoia is the pathology of the modern individual who suffers from a satiric fate stronger than desire, from a negating belief stronger than faith.

In depicting the movement beyond the earliest decades of this century as an elegiac loss of human character, a passing from an old to a new Europe, Pynchon is not alone. The titles or works about this period embody the elegiac note: Proust's *A la Recherche du Temps Perdu*, Aldington's *Death of a Hero*, Hemingway's *A Farewell to Arms*, Remarque's *All Quiet on the Western Front*, Woolf's "Time Passes" section of *To the Lighthouse*, Ford's *Parade's End*, even Jean Renoir's film *La Grande Illusion*. And novels like *Tender Is the Night*, Hemingway's *The Sun Also Rises*, Dos Passos' *U.S.A.*, and Günter Grass's *The Tin*

Drum, novels that pass beyond the war into the 1920s and later, record the frustrations of character and plot in the new order, an order more frenzied, more possessed, more pathological than that before 1914. F. Scott Fitzgerald's *Tender Is the Night* actually contains a funeral oration in which Dick Diver looks out upon the tragic hill of Thiepval and, in the carnival twenties, mourns the world that died, twenty lives per foot, in the surrounding trenches.

Pynchon is not alone either in his treatment of World War II as the great "systems" conspiracy. Empires and civilizations had already fallen, only the destruction of human monuments remained: London, Berlin, Dresden, Tokyo, Hiroshima. Gunter Grass sees the Second World War as the prolonged scream of a lunatic; Joseph Heller sees it as a huge market conspiracy with a "catch" in it everywhere; Kurt Vonnegut sees the impersonal slaughter at high altitude; Pynchon sees it as the paranoid culmination of the century's history. Most of the memorable—and memory-ridden—characters in all these works hold to lost worlds, to worlds that measure values by more humanly accountable actions. In so doing, they resist the direction in which the war takes them, they resist dehumanization. But in *Gravity's Rainbow,* characters like Brigadier Pudding, Slothrop, Mexico, Katje, and even some minor characters like Sir Stephen Dodson-Truck, can resist only up to a point. Willy-nilly, the forces of history determining the movements in the narrative carry the action to the Zone's Nordhausen, to death's country. Like the African Hereros, whose saga spans the narrative as it does the twentieth century, all characters move, if move they must, to forms of racial suicide. The Hereros journey to Nordhausen to seek extinction—and extinction is the satiric end that subverts continuance: "North? What searcher has ever been directed *north?*" (p. 706). "But what's north?" asks Pynchon: "The Herero country of death" (p. 706).

To hold to life in *Gravity's Rainbow* is to run counter to the satiric, preterite end of an entire paranoid civilization. The modern man or modern hero is a death hero, a paranoid, as Pynchon tells it, whose supreme wish is simply to "perfect methods of immobility" (p. 572). At the beginning of the book the inhabitants of London fear for their lives as the falling V-2 rockets threaten "to bring events to Absolute Zero" (p. 3). The lights that go out as the V-2 descends on the metropolis go out again at the end of *Gravity's Rainbow;* when the rocket comes, the darkness comes. Pynchon's vision for the century is a final vision because after the rocket launching in the post-War Zone the narrative is thrust ahead in time to the age of nuclear warheads. In the last paragraphs of the book, as the missile descends over Los Angeles, the light that burns out in the film projector freezes the frames of history. The end of *Gravity's Rainbow* readies the ground for a final burial, this time not only for the older orders of Europe, but for all humanity. Anticipated by the rocket falling on London in 1944 at the beginning of the book, fictionally realized by the launching of the V-2 from Nordhausen at the end of the book, and historically "collapsed" with the eschatological coming of the nuclear missile, the final page of *Gravity's Rainbow* reveals the satirically entropic order. There is no holy grail, no pot of gold at the end of the rainbow, only a parodic transcendence, a direct hit, and the strains of William Slothrop's seventeenth-century hymn for the preterite. The concluding dirge of *Gravity's Rainbow* is the "crying" of everyone's "lot."

In a limited way, but surely in an important way, the sections of *Gravity's Rainbow* that reveal the true nature of human loss in the book are the short, almost abortive, love episodes scattered through the narrative. These are episodes that defy the progress of technological death, that run counter to satire. Slothrop's love for Katje Borgesius makes him legitimate as a character in the older sense of one who is capable of feeling desire and loss. Mexico's love for Jessica establishes him as the central antagonist to the dehumanizing nature of the Second World War. Katje's love for Weissmann is perhaps the most haunting sequence in the narrative, "the saddest story of all" (p. 661). Katje, like Slothrop in a way, is the subject for the perversions of others; she loses will. All she has left her are memories, and what was once love turns to sadomasochism. Sadomasochism becomes the only means available to her for the simple expression of human emotion. Katje is one of Pynchon's last human beings in a world no longer fit for the living. Her fate is to suffer; she is the debased female, the tortured object of love. But in suffering, she is at least reassured that "she can still be hurt, that she is human and can cry at pain" (p. 662). In Pynchon's satiric Zone, such humanity is often the largest measure of an enduring spirit.

The carefully timed and narratively measured love interludes in *Gravity's Rainbow* are vestiges from forgotten novelistic worlds. Nowhere is this clearer than in what must be seen as a intrusion into the satire of World War II—the Christmas Vespers episode at Kent. Roger Mexico and the elegiacally named Jessica Swanlake escape from the war's action to a church in the country. Literally, they move away from the war. That movement for Pynchon represents a movement away from destruction and "back to" a central ritual in the history of the race. Pynchon calls his scene of Christmas Vespers the war's evensong. The ritual, witnessed by Roger and Jessica, celebrates the human scale of worship and love. The birth of Christ is a charismatic event, repeated and represented as a cyclic event. The representation is whole, and Pynchon contrasts it with a war that is, by its nature, fragmentary, that "wants a machine of many separate parts, not oneness, but a complexity" (p. 131). Roger and Jessica effectively "cause" the Christmas Vespers scene in the narrative—they go to it, in all senses, as lovers. After the interlude in Kent the intensity of their love is diminished. The paranoia-producing war intervenes. Mexico is the only figure in *Gravity's Rainbow* fully to recognize the "great swamp of paranoia" that exercises an almost permanent control during the war. And he also recognizes that despite his desires, he is somehow part of a system he detests; he, as much as Slothrop, is defined genetically by the events of the twentieth century. "The War is my mother," says Mexico, and he is part of its "intelligence."

In the Christmas Vespers, with Jessica, Mexico manages a moment of peace in the midst of chaos. The nature of Advent and the context in which it becomes celebratory makes the new historical order of World War II in *Gravity's Rainbow* seem almost a violation of human privacy and human spirit. The war transforms and debases all that touches it. At one point, Thanatz alludes to the symbol of the war, the V-2, as a "baby Jesus, with endless committees of Herods out to destroy it in infancy" (p. 464). The analogy is unsettling. If the rocket escapes, like the infant Christ, is its subsequent launch its crucifixion? In the satiric configuration of the narrative, the test stands of the V-2 are compared to "the stations of the cross" (p. 502). Later, after launch, the rocket's projected impact is a version of ritual sacrifice, a typological crucifixion. The lingering narrative question is whether history holds out any but parodic hope for a second coming, for salvation.

The only hint of an answer Pynchon offers is revealed in the Christmas Vespers. There *is* hope for some, even in the war's dead winter. When the magi arrive bearing gifts, the Christ child in the church scene smiles. Pynchon offers alternatives: "Is the baby smiling, or is it just gas? Which do you want it to be?" (p. 131). The choice looks backward and forward, to past and future worlds. A smile belongs to the human spirit; "gas" belongs to the counterfeit world of satiric narrative, to the final satiric vision, the entropic "yawn" of destruction to which the word gas, a coinage from the Greek *chaos,* is related. In the Christmas Vespers Pynchon gives his characters and his readers back, momentarily, to the world of the novel; he gives them a small choice.

The Brigadier Remembers

by Paul Fussell

...The quality and dimensions of this lunacy of voluntary torment [in remembering the Great War] have never been more acutely explored and dramatized than by Thomas Pynchon in *Gravity's Rainbow*. Here for almost the first time the ritual of military memory is freed from all puritan lexical constraint and allowed to take place with a full appropriate obscenity. Memory haunts Pynchon's novel. Its shape is determined by a "memory" of the Second War, specifically the end of it and its immediate aftermath, when it is beginning to modulate into the Third. Just as Harris, Marshall, Robinson, and Burgess have worked up the Great War entirely from documents and written fictions, so Pynchon, who was only eight years old in 1945, has recovered the Second War not from his own memory but from films and from letterpress—especially, one suspects, the memoirs and official histories recalling that interesting British institution of the Second War, the Special Operations Executive (SOE). Like its American counterpart, the Office of Strategic Services, the SOE performed two functions, espionage and sabotage. The unmilitary informality of the SOE's personnel has become proverbial: like an eccentric club it enrolled dons, bankers, lawyers, cinema people, artists, journalists, and pedants. Of its executive personnel the *TLS* observed, "A few could only charitably be described as nutcases." Its research departments especially enjoyed a wide reputation for sophomoric bright ideas and general eccentricity. From the laboratories of its "inventors" issued a stream of cufflink compasses, counterfeit identity documents, plastic explosives, and exploding pencils and thermos bottles and loaves of bread and nuts and bolts and cigarettes. Among booby traps its masterpieces were the exploding firewood logs and coal-lumps designed to be introduced into German headquarters fireplaces, as well as the explosive animal droppings (horse, mule, camel, and elephant) for placement on roads traveled by German military traffic. One department did nothing but contrive "sibs"—bizarre and hair-raising rumors to be spread over the Continent. It was said that even more outré departments staffed by necromancers, astrologers, and ESP enthusiasts worked at casting spells on the German civil and military hierarchy. Euphemized as "The Firm" or "The Racket" by those who worked for it, the SOE had its main offices at 62-64 Baker Street, and established its departments and training centers in numerous country houses all over Britain.

It is an organization something like the SOE, wildly and com- ically refracted, to which the American Lieutenant Tyrone Sloth- rop is assigned in *Gravity's Rainbow*. His initial duties, in September, 1944, are to interpret and if possible to predict the dispersal pattern of the V-2 missiles falling on London, a task for which, it is thought, he has a curious physiological talent. This work brings him into contact with numerous colleagues pursuing lunatic researches in aid of Victory: behaviorist psychologists experimenting on (abducted) dogs; parapsychologists persuaded that the application of Schrödinger's *psi* function will win the war; spirit mediums; statistical analysts; clairvoyants; and other modern experts on quantification, technology, and prediction. Their place of work is The White Visitation, an ancient country house and former mental hospital on the southeast coast. The commander of the motley unit at The White Visitation is Brig- adier Ernest Pudding, a likable but senile veteran of the Great War called back to preside over this fancy enterprise in the Second War. (In choosing his name Pynchon may be echoing the name of the onetime Director of Operations of the actual SOE, Brigadier Colin Gubbins [born 1896], a badly wounded winner of the Mili- tary Cross in the Great War.)

The presence of Brigadier Pudding in the novel proposes the Great War as the ultimate origin of the insane contemporary scene. It is where the irony and the absurdity began. Pudding's "greatest triumph on the battlefield," we are told, "came in 1917, in the gassy, Armageddonite filth of the Ypres salient, where he conquered a bight of no man's land some 40 yards at its deepest, with a wastage of only 70% of his unit." After this satire of cir- cumstance he remained in the army until he retired in the thirties to the Devon countryside, where "it occurred to him to focus his

hobby on the European balance of power, because of whose long
pathology he had once labored, deeply, all hope of waking lost,
in the nightmare of Flanders." In his retirement he pursued the
hopeless hobby of writing a massive "book" titled *Things That
Can Happen in European Politics.* But events defeated him and
his resolution dissolved: "'Never make it,' he found himself
muttering at the beginning of each day's work—'it's changing out
from under me. Oh, dodgy—very dodgy.'" At the beginning of
the Second War he volunteered and was further disappointed:

> Had he known at the time it would mean "The White Visitation"…
> not that he'd expected a combat assignment you know, but wasn't
> there something mentioned about intelligence work? Instead he
> found a disused hospital for the mad, a few token lunatics, an
> enormous pack of stolen dogs, cliques of spiritualists, vaudeville
> entertainers, wireless technicians, Couéists, Ouspenskians, Skin-
> nerites, lobotomy enthusiasts, Dale Carnegie zealots…   (77)

His present situation is especially disappointing because the quality of the personnel seems to have fallen off between wars. The
nutty dog experimenter at The White Visitation, Ned Pointsman, happens to be the son of an able medical officer Pudding
knew at Ypres. Ned is "not as tall as his father, certainly not as
wholesome looking. Father was M.O. in Thunder Prodd's regi-
ment, caught a bit of shrapnel in the thigh at Polygon Wood, lay
silent for seven hours before they"—but the scene clouds over in
Pudding's memory and begins to fade: "without a word before,
in that mud, that terrible smell, in, yes Polygon Wood…or was
that—who *was* the ginger-haired chap who slept with his hat on?
ahhh, come back. Now Polygon Wood…but it's fluttering away."
No use: Pudding is losing the image he has been soliciting, and
only detached, incoherent details remain: "Fallen trees, dead,
smooth gray, swirlinggrainoftreelikefrozensmoke…ginger…
thunder…no use, no bleeding use, it's gone, another gone, another, oh dear…" (76).
   Sometimes Pudding's memories surface publicly during his
prolonged and rambling weekly briefings of the staff, occasions
designated by Pynchon as "a bit of ritual with the doddering
Brigadier." Mingled with "a most amazing volley of senile observations, office paranoia, gossip about the war," as well as with
such detritus as "recipes for preparing beets a hundred tasty
ways," are detached, incoherent "reminiscences of Flanders,"

little sensual spots of time and images engraved on the failing
memory:

> ...the coal boxes in the sky coming straight down on you with a
> roar...the drumfire so milky and luminous on his birthday night
> ...the wet surfaces in the shell craters for miles giving back one
> bleak autumn sky...what Haig, in the richness of his wit, once said
> at mess about Lieutenant Sassoon's refusal to fight...roadsides of
> poor rotting horses just before apricot sunrise...the twelve spokes
> of a standard artillery piece—a mud clock, a mud zodiac, clogged
> and crusted as it stood in the sun in its many shades of brown.

Brown triggers in Pudding a little lyric on human excrement as
the dominant material of Passchendaele: "The mud of Flanders
gathered into the curd-crumped, mildly jellied textures of human
shit, piled, duck-boarded, trenches and shell-pocked leagues of
shit in all directions, not even the poor blackened stump of a
tree..." (79-80).

Such discrete images take on coherence and something like
narrative relationships only during Pudding's secret fortnightly
"rituals," his surreal nocturnal visits to the "Mistress of the
Night," played by Katje Borgesius, a Dutch girl who has somehow
become attached to this mock-SOE. The passage in which Pynchon presents one of these ritual visits is one of the most shocking
in the novel: it assumes the style of classic English pornographic
fiction of the grossly masochistic type, the only style, Pynchon
implies, adequate to memories of the Great War, with its "filth"
and "terrible smell." The language and the details may turn our
stomachs, but, Pynchon suggests, they are only the remotest
correlatives of the actuality. Compared with the actual sights and
smells of the front, the word *shit* is practically genteel.

It is not easy to specify exactly the "allegorical" meaning of this
"Mistress of the Night" to whom the aging brigadier repairs so
regularly and punctually: she is at once Death, Fear, Ruined
Youth, and the memory of all these. She is what one must revisit
ritually for the sake of the perverse pleasant pain she administers.
She is like the Muse of Pudding's war-memory. She waits to receive
him in a setting combining bawdy-house with theater, and indeed
the scene of Pudding's visit constitutes the climax of the tradition
that the Great War makes a sort of sense if seen as a mode of
theater.

It is a cold night. Pudding slips out of his quarters "by a route

only he knows," quietly singing, to keep his courage up, the soldiers' song he recalls from the Great War:

> Wash me in the water
> That you wash your dirty daughter,
> And I shall be whiter than the whitewash on the wall.

He tiptoes along the sleeping hallways and through a half-dozen
rooms, the passage of which, like the traditional approach to the
Grail Chapel, constitutes a "ritual": each contains "a test he must
pass." In the third room, for example, "a file drawer is left ajar,
a stack of case histories partly visible, and an open copy of Krafft-
Ebing." The fourth room contains a skull. The fifth, a Malacca
cane, which apparently reminds him of the one he carried in 1917
and sets him thinking: "I've been in more wars for England than
I can remember...haven't I paid enough? Risked it all for them,
time after time...Why must they torment an old man?" In the
sixth and last room the memory of the war becomes more vivid:

> In the sixth chamber, hanging from the overhead, is a tattered
> tommy up on White Sheet Ridge, field uniform burned in Maxim
> holes black-rimmed..., his own left eye shot away, the corpse be-
> ginning to stink...no...no! an overcoat, someone's old coat that's
> all, left on a hook in the wall...but couldn't he *smell* it? Now mustard
> gas comes washing in, into his brain with a fatal buzz as dreams will
> when we don't want them, or when we are suffocating. A machine-
> gun on the German side sings *dum diddy da da,* an English weapon
> answers *dum dum,* and the night tightens coiling around his body,
> just before H-hour. ...

It is H-hour now, for he has arrived at the seventh room, where
the Mistress of the Night waits for him. He knocks, the door un-
locks "electrically," and he enters a room lighted only by "a scented
candle." Katje Borgesius sits in a throne-like chair, wearing
nothing but the black cape and tall black boots of the traditional
female "disciplinarian" in British pornography. She is made up
to resemble "photographs of the reigning beauties of thirty and
forty years ago," and the only jewelry she wears is "a single ring
with an artificial ruby not cut to facets" but resembling a convex
bloody wound. She extends it, and Pudding kneels to kiss it before undressing.

> She watches him undress, medals faintly jingling, starch shirt
> rattling. She wants a cigarette desperately, but her instructions are

not to smoke. She tries to keep her hands still. "What are you thinking, Pudding?"

"Of the night we first met." The mud stank. The Archies were
chugging in the darkness. His men, his poor sheep, had taken gas
that morning. He was alone. Through the periscope, underneath a
star shell that hung in the sky, he saw her...and though he was
hidden, she saw Pudding. Her face was pale, she was dressed all in
black, she stood in No-man's Land, the machine guns raked their
patterns all around her, but she needed no protection. "They knew
you, Mistress. They were your own."

"And so were you."

"You called to me, you said, 'I shall never leave you. You belong
to me. We shall be together, again and again, though it may be years
between. And you will always be at my service.'"

Pudding now undergoes his ritual of humiliation. He creeps
forward to kiss her boots. He excites her by reminding her of an
incident in the Spanish Civil War when a unit of Franco's soldiers
was slaughtered. She is pleased to remember. "I took their brown
Spanish bodies to mine," she says. "They were the color of the
dust, and the twilight, and of meats roasted to a perfect texture...
most of them were so very young. A summer day, a day of love:
one of the most poignant I ever knew." "Thank you," she says to
Pudding. "You shall have your pain tonight." And she gives him
a dozen blows with the cane, six across the buttocks, six across the
nipples. "His need for pain" is gratified; he feels momentarily
rescued from the phony paper war he's now engaged in, reinstall-
ed in his familiar original world of "vertigo, nausea, and pain."
The whipping over, she obliges him to drink her urine. And then
the climax of the ritual: he eats her excrement. It is an act reminiscent of their first encounter at Passchendaele: "The stink of
shit floods his nose, gathering him, surrounding him. It is the
smell of Passchendaele, of the Salient. Mixed with the mud, and
the putrefaction of corpses, it was the sovereign smell of their
first meeting, and her emblem." As he eats, "spasms in his throat
continue. The pain is terrible." But he enjoys it. Finally she com-
mands him to masturbate before her. He does so and departs
regretfully, realizing anew, when he reaches his own room again,
that "his real home is with the Mistress of the Night..." (231-36).

It is a fantastic scene, disgusting, ennobling, and touching, all
at once. And amazingly rich in the way it manages to fuse literal
with figurative. The woman is both Katje and the Mistress of the

Night, credible for the moment in either identity; she is both a literal filthy slut in 1945 and the incarnation of the spirit of military memory in all times and places. As allegory the action succeeds brilliantly, while its literal level is consistent and, within the conventions, credible: Pudding, we are told later, died in June, 1945, "of a massive *E. coli* infection" (533) brought about by these ritual coprophagic sessions. And yet what he was "tasting" and "devouring" all the time was his memories of the Great War. Pynchon is not the only contemporary novelist to conceive a close relation between perverse sexual desire, memories of war, and human excrement. In *An American Dream* Mailer offers a scene analogous to that of Pudding and Katje, only here the memories are of the Second War. It is after recalling the sadistic, bloody details of his shooting of four Germans in Italy that Stephen Rojack proceeds to sodomize the "Kraut" Ruta. It is this scene that Alfred Kazin has in mind when he observes, "As always in reading Mailer's descriptions of intercourse, one is impressed by how much of a war novelist he has remained." As we perceive in the work of Mailer and Pynchon and James Jones, it is the virtual disappearance during the sixties and seventies of the concept of prohibitive obscenity, a concept which has acted as a censor on earlier memories of "war," that has given the ritual of military memory a new dimension. And that new dimension is capable of revealing for the first time the full obscenity of the Great War. The greatest irony is that it is only now, when those who remember the events are almost all dead, that the literary means for adequate remembering and interpreting are finally publicly accessible.

Chronology of Important Dates

1937   Thomas Pynchon born on Long Island, New York.

1959   Graduation from Cornell University.

1963   Publication of *V.*

1966   Publication of *The Crying of Lot 49.*

1973   Publication of *Gravity's Rainbow.*

Notes on the Editor and Contributors

EDWARD MENDELSON, editor of this volume, is Associate Professor of English at Yale University. He has written on various aspects of modern literature, and is literary executor of the Estate of W. H. Auden.

PAUL FUSSELL, John De Witt Professor of English Literature, Rutgers University, has written *Samuel Johnson and the Life of Writing, The Rhetorical World of Augustan Humanism*, and other books.

ROGER B. HENKLE, Associate Professor of English at Brown University, is an editor of *Novel*, and is completing a study of comedy and middle-class culture in nineteenth-century England.

FRANK KERMODE is King Edward VII Professor of English at Cambridge University. Among his books are *Romantic Image, The Sense of an Ending*, and *The Classic*.

GEORGE LEVINE, Professor of English at Rutgers University, is the author of *The Boundaries of Fiction* and co-editor with David Leverenz of *Mindful Pleasures: Essays on Thomas Pynchon*.

PHILIP MORRISON is book editor of *Scientific American*.

JAMES NOHRNBERG, Professor of English at the University of Virginia, recently published *The Analogy of "The Faerie Queene."*

RICHARD POIRIER, Professor of English at Rutgers University, has written *A World Elsewhere, The Performing Self*, and other books.

JONATHAN ROSENBAUM is on the staff of the *Monthly Film Bulletin*.

F. S. SCHWARZBACH taught at University College, London, and is presently at Washington University, St. Louis.

MICHAEL SEIDEL, author of *Epic Geography: James Joyce's Ulysses* and co-editor of *Homer to Brecht: The European Epic and Dramatic Traditions*, is Associate Professor of English at Columbia University.

ROBERT SKLAR, for many years a professor at the University of Michigan, is author of *F. Scott Fitzgerald: The Last Laocoön* and *Movie-Made America.*

JOSEPH W. SLADE, author of the first book about Pynchon, teaches at Long Island University and is editor of *The Markham Review.*

TONY TANNER is Professor in the Writing Seminars at the Johns Hopkins University. He is the author of *City of Words* and *The Reign of Wonder.*

Selected Bibliography

Books and Periodical Contributions by Pynchon

"The Small Rain," *Cornell Writer*, 6:2 (March 1959), 14-32.

"Mortality and Mercy in Vienna," *Epoch*, 9:4 (Spring 1959), 195-213.

"Low-Lands," *New World Writing*, 16 (1960), 85-108.

"Entropy," *Kenyon Review*, 22:2 (Spring 1960), 277-92.

"Togetherness," *Aerospace Safety*, 16:12 (December 1960), 6-18. Article on safety procedures for the Bomarc guided missile.

"Under the Rose" *Noble Savage*, 3 (May 1961), 113-51. Rewritten as Chapter 3 of *V.*

V. Philadelphia: J. B. Lippincott, 1963.

"The Secret Integration," *Saturday Evening Post*, 237:45 (December 19-26, 1964), 36, 39, 42-44, 46-49, 51.

"A Gift of Books" [comments by eight writers on neglected books], *Holiday*, 38:6 (December 1965), 164-65, Pynchon's comment is on *Warlock* by Oakley Hall.

The Crying of Lot 49, Philadelphia: J. B. Lippincott, 1966. Excerpts appeared as "The World (This One), the Flesh (Mrs. Oedipa Maas), and the Testament of Pierce Inverarity," *Esquire*, 44:6 (December 1965), 164-65; and "The Shrink Flips," *Cavalier*, 16:153 (March 1966), 32-33, 88-92.

"A Journey into the Mind of Watts," *New York Times Magazine*, June 12, 1966, pp. 34-35, 78, 80-82, 84.

"Pros and Cohns" [letter to the editor], *New York Times Book Review*, July 17, 1966, pp. 22, 24. On the origin of the name Genghis Cohen.

Gravity's Rainbow. New York: Viking Press, 1973.

Selected Critical Studies

Bergonzi, Bernard. *The Situation of the Novel.* London: Macmillan, 1970. "America: The Incredible Reality," pp. 80-103.

Davis, Robert Murray. "Parody, Paranoia, and the Dead End of Language," *Genre,* 5 (1972), 367-77.

Friedman, Alan J., and Manfred Puetz. "Science as Metaphor: Thomas Pynchon's *Gravity's Rainbow,*" *Contemporary Literature,* 15 (1974), 345-59.

Hausdorff, Don. "Thomas Pynchon's Multiple Absurdities," *Wisconsin Studies in Contemporary Literature,* 7 (1966), 158-69.

Henderson, Harry B., III. *Versions of the Past.* New York: Oxford University Press, 1974. pp. 277-85.

Hunt, John W. "Comic Escape and Anti-Vision: the Novels of Joseph Heller and Thomas Pynchon," in *Adversity and Grace,* ed. Nathan A. Scott, Jr. Chicago University of Chicago Press, 1968. pp. 87-112.

Kazin, Alfred. *Bright Book of Life.* Boston: Little, Brown, 1973. pp. 275-80.

Kirby, David K. "Two Modern Versions of the Quest," *Southern Humanities Review,* 5 (1971), 387-95.

Lewis, R. W. B. *Trials of the Word.* New Haven: Yale University Press, 1965. pp. 223-24.

McConnell, Frank D. "Thomas Pynchon," in *Contemporary Novelists,* ed. James Vinson. London: St. James Press, 1972. pp. 1033-36.

Mangel, Anne. "Maxwell's Demon, Entropy, Information: *The Crying of Lot 49,*" *Tri-Quarterly,* 20 (1971), 194-208. Reprinted in *Mindful Pleasures* (see below).

Olderman, Raymond W. *Beyond the Waste Land.* New Haven: Yale University Press, 1972. "The Illusion and the Possibility of Conspiracy," pp. 123-49.

Puetz, Manfred. "Thomas Pynchon's *The Crying of Lot 49:* the World is a Trystero System," *Mosaic,* 7:4 (1974), 125-37.

Richardson, Robert O. "The Absurd Animate in Thomas Pynchon's *V.: a Novel,"Studies in the Twentieth Century,* 9 (1972), 35-58.

Richter, David. *Fable's End.* Chicago: University of Chicago Press, 1974. "The Failure of Completeness: Pynchon's *V.,*" pp. 101-35.

Schmitz, Neil. "Describing the Demon: the Appeal of Thomas Pynchon," *Partisan Review,* 42 (1975), 112-25.

Schaub, Thomas Hill. "Open Letter in Response to Edward Mendelson's 'The Sacred, the Profane, and *The Crying of Lot 49,*'" *Boundary 2,* 5 (Fall 1976), 93-101. Response to an essay reprinted in the present collection.

Slade, Joseph W. *Thomas Pynchon.* New York: Warner Paperback Library, 1974.

Wagner, Linda W. "A Note on Oedipa the Roadrunner," *Journal of Narrative Technique,* 4 (1974), 155-61.

Young, James Dean. "The Enigma Variations of Thomas Pynchon," *Critique,* 10 (1968), 69-77.

Collections of Essays

Critique, 16:2 (1974). Essays by John P. Leland, Lance W. Ozier, Richard Patteson, and Scott Simmon.

Twentieth Century Literature 21:2 (1975). Essays by Richard Poirier, W. T. Lhamon, Jr., Scott Sanders, Lance W. Ozier, and William Vesterman.

Mindful Pleasures: Essays on Thomas Pynchon, ed. George Levine and David Leverenz. Boston: Little, Brown, 1976. Essays reprinted from the Pynchon number of *Twentieth Century Literature* by Poirier, Lhamon, Sanders, and Vesterman; and new essays by Catharine R. Stimpson, George Levine, Edward Mendelson, Marjorie Kaufman, David Leverenz, and Matthew Winston.